ON COALITION COURSE

ON COALITION COURSE

Arun Kumar

PRESS TRUST OF INDIA
in association with

GYAN

GYAN PUBLISHING HOUSE
NEW DELHI - 110002

ON COALITION COURSE
(Politics)

ISBN : 81-212-0609-X

Published in 1998 in India by
Gyan Publishing House
5, Ansari Road
New Delhi 110 002
Laser Typesetting : Grow Computers, Delhi.
Printed at Mehra Offset Press, New Delhi.

CONTENTS

List of Illustrations

1. **BACK IN THE HOT SEAT :** Atal Bihari Vajpayee comes to his South Block office after the swearing in on March 19.

2. **OPEN GOVERNMENT** : In a break with tradition, Vajpayee's coalition government was sworn in in the forecourt of Rashtrapati Bhavan.

3. **AIMING HIGH** : BJP President, L.K. Advani, at an election meeting in Godhra, Gujarat.

4. **CATCH'EM YOUNG :** A babe in arms attends Sonia Gandhi's election rally in Rohtak.

5. **FIRST VOTE :** First Citizen, K.R. Narayanan, in another break with convention, casts his vote at a polling station in Rashtrapati Bhavan.

6. **PARADISE REGAINED :** Voters in Anantnag, Kashmir, **queue up to** vote despite militant threats

7. **PROPAGANDA ON WHEELS : A Congress 'Rath' in Delhi** seeking to expose alleged misdeeds of BJP.

8. **PARTY TIME :** A vender selling Congress Party posters and badges at AICC headquarters.

Preface

One more election, another hung house and yet another coalition. And the same inevitable questions—How long would it last? Would political stability elude India? So what was different about the fractured verdict of 1998? For one, the players had changed. Instead of a large group (Congress) backing a rag-tag group of small parties from outside, the largest single party was leading the coalition with all but one of the supporting smaller parties represented in the government. Again a process of polarisation seemed to be underway with Congress and the left retaining their support bases and JD losing its lead position in the front. The verdict of 1998 also changed political equations with TDP's dramatic switch over from UF to BJP bandwagon bringing the process of political flux into sharp focus.

Granted that alliances were more in the nature of seat adjustments rather than partnerships, yet three broad formations were in place before the elections. This was unlike 1996 when the alliances took shape after the elections and somehow held despite internal squabbles. Also barring an unforeseen event that could tilt the balance completely, days of single party dominance seemed to be over for a long time to come. The nation appeared to be truly on coalition course this time. Constitutional pundits again offered advice on what the President should do or not do in the event of a hung house, and came forth with suggestions for alternative system models. Faced with the pulls and pressures from its allies, BJP itself suggested a constitutional review making known its preference for a Presidential system. But there was also talk of evolving a 'coalition culture'— a new set of rules for a whole new ball game.

This book tells it all. While 'The Turning Point' in 1996 took a long look back at the shifting voting patterns since the first General Elections, this one essentially focuses on the verdict of

1998. It also profiles the major contenders to power, their strategies and the issues they raised to woo the voters in the elections that nobody wanted.

Besides a comprehensive computer analysis of the results, it seeks to provide an in-depth view of the unfolding political scene in various states and regions. The accompanying graphics make the picture complete.

This is the fifth of a series of books on elections brought out by PTI since 1989. It may sound like a cliche, but the fact is that it would not have been possible to bring out the publication so fast without all round cooperation. Editiors, correspondents, photographers across the country, besides transmission and engineering staff all deserve a big thanks for what they did. The work of Uday Shankar and Shivendra Singh Rautela in turning cold statistics into meaningful graphics needs to be specially acknowledged. So does that of Bhaskar Patil who generated a whole series of computer reports. I am particularly thankful to M.K. Razdan, our General Manager, for his constant support to the project.

PARTY POSITION

Abbreviation	Party	Seats
BJP	Bharatiya Janata Party	182
INC	Indian National Congress	141
CPM	Communist Party of India (Marxist)	32
SP	Samajwadi Party	20
ADMK	All India Anna Dravida Munnetra Kazhagam	18
RJD	Rashtriya Janata Dal	17
SAP	Samata Party	12
TDP	Telugu Desam Party	12
CPI	Communist Party of India	9
BJD	Biju Janata Dal	9
SAD	Shiromani Akali Dal	8
TC	West Bengal Trinamul Congress	7
JD	Janata Dal	6
DMK	Dravida Munnetra Kazhagam	6
SHS	Shivsena	6
BSP	Bahujan Samaj Party	5
RSP	Revolutionary Socialist Party	5
HLDR	Haryana Lok Dal (Rashtriya)	4
PMK	Pattali Makkal Katchi	4
RPI	Republican Party of India	4
TMC	Tamil Maanila Congress	3
LS	Lok Shakti	3
MDMK	Marumalarchi Dravida Munnetra Kazhagam	3
NC	Jammu & Kashmir National Conference	3
ANC	Arunachal Congress	2
FBL	All India Forward Bloc	2
MUL	Muslim League	2
AIICS	All India Indira Congress (Secular)	1
ASDC	Autonomous State Demand Committee	1
HVP	Haryana Vikas Party	1
JP	Janata Party	1
KCM	Kerala Congress (M)	1
MIM	All India Majlis-e-Ittehadul Muslimeen	1
MSC	Manipur State Congress Party	1
PWP	Peasants and Workers Party	1
RJP	All India Rashtriya Janata Party	1
SDF	Sikkim Democratic Front	1
SJPR	Samajwadi Janata Party (Rashtriya)	1
TRC	Tamil Rajiv Congress	1
UMF	United Minorities Front, Assam	1
Ind.	Independents	5
	Total:	543

Other Parties

AGP	: Asom Gana Parishad
AIICT	: All India Indira Congress (Tiwari)
AMB	: Amra Bangalee
CPIMLL	: Communist Party of India (Marxist-Leninist-Liberation)
FPM	: Federal Party of Manipur
GNC	: Garo National Council
HPDP	: Hill State People's Democratic Party
HVC	: Himachal Vikas Congress
ICS	: Indian Congress (Socialist)
JKAL	: Jammu & Kashmir Awami League
JMM	: Jharkhand Mukti Morcha
JMMM	: Jharkhand Mukti Morcha (Mardi)
KEC	: Kerala Congress
KCP	: Karnataka Congress Party
KVP	: Karnataka Vikas Party
MGP	: Maharashtrawadi Gomantak Party
MNF	: Mizo National Front
MPP	: Manipur People' s Party
MPVC	: Madhya Pradesh Vikas Party
NTRTDP	: NTR Telugu Desam Party (Lakshmi Parvathi)
PDP	: People's Democratic Party
PP	: National Panthers Party
SADM	: Shiromani Akali Dal (Simranjit Singh Mann)
UDP	: United Democratic Party
UGDP	: United Goans Democratic Party
URMCA	: United Reservation Movement Council of Assam

The Equation in New Parliament

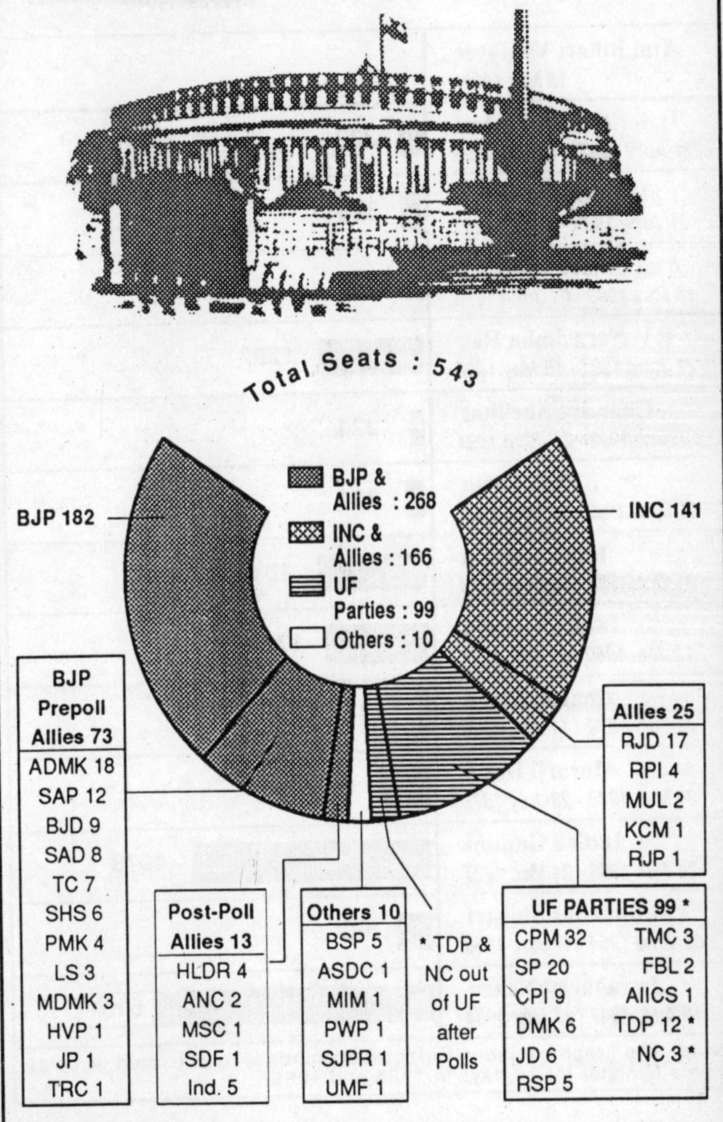

Prime Ministers

Tenure in Number of Days

Atal Bihari Vajpayee *19 Mar 1998 -*	
Inder Kumar Gujral *21 April 1997 - 19 Mar 1998*	333
H.D. Deve Gowda *01 June 1996 - 21 Apr 1997*	325
Atal Bihari Vajpayee *16 May 1996 - 01 June 1996*	17
P.V. Narasimha Rao *21 June 1991 - 16 May 1996*	1792
Chandra Shekhar *10 Nov. 1990 - 21 June 1991*	224
V.P. Singh *02 Dec. 1989 - 10 Nov. 1990*	344
Rajiv Gandhi *31 Oct. 1984 - 02 Dec. 1989*	1859
Indira Gandhi *14 Jan. 1980 - 31 Oct. 1984*	1753
Charan Singh *28 July 1979 - 14 Jan. 1980*	171
Morarji Desai *24 Mar. 1977 - 28 July 1979*	857
Indira Gandhi *24 Jan. 1966 - 24 Mar. 1977*	4078
Lal Bahadur Shastri *09 June 1964 - 11 Jan. 1966*	582
Jawaharlal Nehru *15 Aug. 1947 - 27 May 1964*	6131

Note: The graph excludes Gulzari Lal Nanda who officiated twice as Prime Minister for 28 days in 1964 and 1966.

1
A Balancing Act

Exactly 656 days after he left, Atal Bihari Vajpayee was back in the Prime Minister's chair in South Block atop Raisina Hill overlooking Lutyens' New Delhi. As he surveyed the office once occupied by his hero Jawaharlal Nehru, "the man India awaits", as BJP publicists hailed him or the soft "mask" of the hardline saffron brigade as critics would have it, Vajpayee must have wondered how long would it last this time. Would his government be able to give the nation a stable polity or would it crumble again under the weight of its own contradictions as coalitions in the past have? Like him, these questions have been assailing the minds of people, politicians and constitutional experts alike ever since the electorate gave a fractured verdict for the fourth time in nine years to set India on coalition course again.

The pulls and pressures that Vajpayee faces became all too evident even before his government took office on March 19 when *Puratchi Thalaivi*—or "revolutionary leader" as AIADMK chief J. Jayalalitha is called by her supporters first went into a sulk declining to hand over the letter of support sought by the President K.R. Narayanan from BJP's all pre-poll allies. Then two days later when she relented after a visit by Vajpayee's trouble shooter Jaswant Singh, Jayalalitha laced her "unconditional support" with a heap of abuse for the BJP leadership. BJP's other allies may have been less strident in public, but apparently there was a lot of haggling and hard bargaining over who got how many berths in the ministry and which coveted portfolio.

Thanks to the compulsions of the numbers game, former home minister Buta Singh, who returned to the House as an independent after being expelled from the Congress, got the communications portfolio in the cabinet rank. But his luck did not last beyond a month as Jayalalitha got him sacked when one of her own ministers, R. Muthiah was asked to resign after he was chargesheeted in a Chennai court. Janata Party's sole survivor Subramanian Swamy failed to get in despite pressure from foe-turned-friend Jayalalitha, but his threat to vote according to conscience apparently deprived bête noire R.K. Hegde of the finance or defence portfolios he cherished. George Fernandes first insisted that he would stay out and his Samata Party would be represented by Nitish Kumar. But he changed his mind at the last minute "under pressure" to get two berths—defence for himself and railways for Nitish. Later taking a cue from Jayalalitha, Samata kept up the pressure for dismissal of Rabri Devi government in Bihar, but in a more "decent manner" in the words of a party spokesman.

Vajpayee kept external affairs to himself to avoid the kind of heartburn witnessed during his previous 13-day reign in 1996 when the party's lone Muslim minister Sikander Bakht sulked at home for a week on being given urban affairs. This time he got industry. Vajpayee wanted to give finance to Jaswant Singh, but the party leadership cited his Chittorgarh defeat in the Lok Sabha poll to keep him out. But the Prime Minister got him in anyway as deputy chairman of the Planning Commission as also vanquished BJP spokesman Pramod Mahajan as his political adviser.

Besides Vajpayee, the council of ministers included 24 members of BJP, 11 of cabinet rank and 13 ministers of state, four from AIADMK, two cabinet and two junior, and one cabinet and a junior minister each from Akali Dal, Lok Shakti and Biju Janata Dal. Samata Party got away with two cabinet berths, but Mamata Banerjee's Trinamul Congress insisted on extending support from only outside. There was a minister each from Shiv Sena, Pattali Makkal Katchi (PMK), Tamil Rajiv Congress and Arunachal Congress besides three independents, Buta Singh, Ram Jethmalani and Maneka Gandhi.

Union Council of Ministers

as constituted on March 19, 1998

Cabinet Ministers

BJP : A B Vajpayee (PM)
: L K Advani
: Ananth Kumar
: Sikandar Bakht
: Satyanarayan Jatiya
: M M Joshi
: M L Khurana
: P R Kumaramangalam
: Kashi Ram Rana
: Yashwant Sinha
: Sushma Swaraj
SAP : George Fernandes
: Nitish Kumar
ADMK : M Thambi Durai
: R Muthiah
IND : Ram Jethmalani
: Buta Singh
SAD : S S Barnala
LS : R K Hegde
SHS : Suresh P. Prabhu
BJD : Naveen Patnaik
TRC : K Ramamurthy

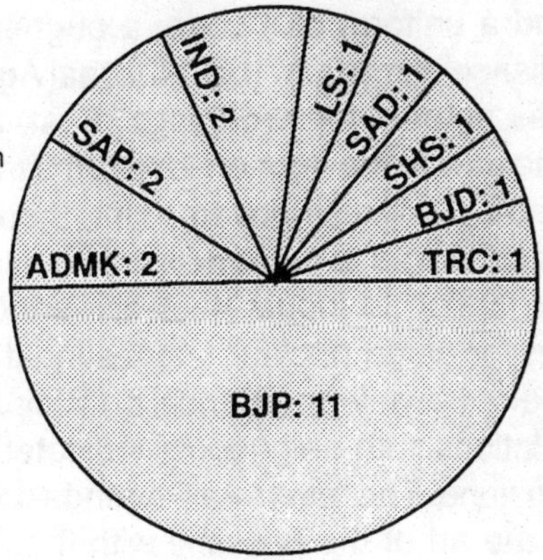

Total: 22

Ministers of State

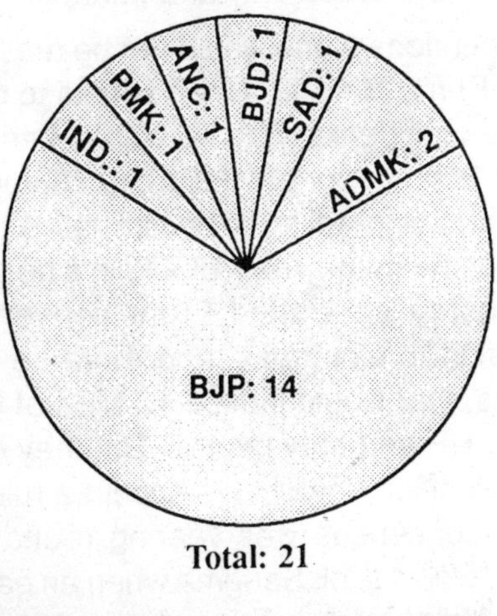

Total: 21

BJP : Bandaru Dattatreya
: Ramesh Bais
: Uma Bharati
: Santosh K Gangwar
: Babulal Marandi
: Mukhtar Abbas Naqvi
: Ram Naik
: A K Patel
: Babagouda R Patil
: Debendra Pradhan
: Kabindra Purkayastha
: Vasundhara Raje
: Sompal
: Satyapal Singh
ADMK : R K Kumar
: R Janarthanan
SAD : Sukhbir Singh Badal
BJD : Dilip Ray
PMK : Dalit Ezhilmalai
ANC : Omak Apang
IND. : Maneka Gandhi

With little apparent ideological affinity among the various constituents, forging a common programme should have been a more difficult task than cobbling together a cabinet. Yet it turned out to be a lesser headache. Steering clear of ideological issues like the temple at Ayodhya, abrogation of Article 370 of the Constitution conferring a special status on Jammu and Kashmir and a uniform civil code, a bugbear for the Muslims, the BJP alliance came up with a "National Agenda for Governance", which was notable for two things. First, a declaration of intent to go ahead with the economic reforms initiated in 1991 by Narasimha Rao's Congress government, though with a '*Swadeshi*' touch. Second was a more dramatic declaration that it would exercise the option to induct nuclear weapons. But no time-frame was set for going nuclear suggesting it might have been more of a rhetoric, while insistence on reciprocity in promoting peaceful relations with neighbours indicated a rolling back of the Gujral Doctrine. The "please all" agenda confirmed yet again that politics is the art of the possible with the compulsions of the numbers game bringing out the virtues of the "consensual approach". Suggesting that the opposition and ruling parties should not behave like permanent enemies, it declared: "... a nation of nearly 100 crore people, representing a sixth of humanity, cannot be governed on the arithmetics alone of majority and minority."

But knowing that good intentions alone would not be able to save his government, all the Prime Minister's men set out to get the numbers right before the confidence vote he was asked to secure within ten days. With 264 supporters including 253 pre-poll allies and eleven who had agreed to back him later, the coalition was still eight short of the magic mark of 272 in a house of 543. Their only hope rested on United Front convenor Chandrababu Naidu's aversion to Congress, and more so on compulsions of home politics, that would induce 12 MPs of his TDP to break ranks with the UF and stay neutral. But they did better than that. With the opposition unwilling to accept a ruling party nominee as speaker, consensus was veering round to former Lok Sabha speaker Purno Agitok Sangma when an early morning call from Advani to Naidu totally changed the situation hours before the noon deadline for filing nominations on March

23. Taking umbrage at UF's "unprincipled, unilateral" decision to back the Congress nominee, Naidu "disassociated" himself from the front and asked a little-known young lawyer Ganti Mohan Chandra Balayogi, 46, to contest the post. He almost could not make it thanks to a delay in his flight from Hyderabad. Racing down from the airport to Parliament, Balayogi filed his papers with only minutes to spare even as a miffed Sangma felt betrayed. Sangma gamely stayed on in the contest though Balayogi's election next day was a foregone conclusion. Congress and UF did not challenge the voice vote then, but demanded a division on the confidence vote four days later on March 28. Vajpayee won by 13 votes with 274 "ayes" and 261 "noes". Except Balayogi, all the 12 TDP members backed Vajpayee, but the National Conference of Farooq Abdullah abstained breaking ranks with UF. Maverick Subramanian Swamy left before the vote to catch a flight and a sulking Prem Singh Lalpura of the Akali Dal refused to take his oath unless he was made a minister as promised. He lost his membership of the Lok Sabha for not taking his oath in time and was expelled from his party for indiscipline.

The President did his own bit to ensure a modicum of stability for the new dispensation that had replaced the 13-party "united dalliance", as a wag described the outgoing UF government that did not last even two years under two Prime Ministers. Unlike his predecessor Dr. Shanker Dayal Sharma, who, following convention had invited Vajpayee to form the government in 1996 as the leader of the largest single party, K.R. Narayanan merely asked if he was "able and willing" to do so. And when Vajpayee asserted that he was indeed willing, the President insisted on documentary proof that he was able too with the necessary numbers. Then as Jayalalitha started acting hard to get, forcing Vajpayee to return to him with only a list of 240 instead of the promised 264, Narayanan started consultations with the Congress, the Left Front and some of the smaller parties down to an independent like Buta Singh. He even took it upon himself to call Naidu in Hyderabad to confirm that his TDP would stay neutral during the trial of strength as he had publicly declared. And after Jayalalitha changed her mind and sent the letter of support to Vajpayee to the President directly, he sent her a fax to inquire whether her nominees would also participate in the government. Then shortly after, Sonia Gandhi, who had by then taken over as Congress president, told the media outside Rashtrapati Bhavan that her party had not staked claim to form the government as the numbers were not with them, he finally called Vajpayee late in the night of Sunday, March 15, to make him the Prime Minister.

The presidential communique set out the constitutional position that it was the head of state's prerogative to choose the Prime Minister and then went on to give the rationale of his choice. While he did call Vajpayee first as the leader of the largest single party and pre-poll alliance, Narayanan suggested that it did not give him an inherent right to form the government. For in the final analysis it's the numbers which determine the fate of a government and Vajpayee got the call only after the President was convinced that he had the numbers with him—264 in a House with an effective strength of 527 not counting the 12 TDP MPs who would stay neutral. The transparent procedure followed by Narayanan not only spared him the type of criticism faced by Dr. Sharma, but also helped to pin down politicians to their public positions—so that the fear of adverse public opinion may induce them to think twice before shifting their stands at the drop of a hat. Narayanan also let it be known that no single formula would work for all times to come as India grapples with the problems of a hung House and coalition politics.

Long before the contours of a fractured verdict began to emerge, constitutional experts started offering the President advice on what he should do in the event of a hung House. Who has the mandate to govern, the largest single party (BJP—179), the largest pre-poll alliance (BJP—252), or a larger collective (Congress plus United Front—264) in opposition to such an alliance. Predictably the answers generally went along party lines. A former secretary general of the Lok Sabha, Dr. Subhash Kashyap suggested another alternative: The President could ask the Lok Sabha itself to choose its leader by sending a message under Article 86(2) of the Constitution. But jurist Soli Sorabji, who was to later take over as the Vajpayee government's attorney general, found the suggestion impracticable. While Sorabjee had also supported Dr. Sharma's 1996 invitation to Vajpayee, others like former Delhi High Court Chief Justice Rajender Sachar had found his decision untenable. There is no constitutional convention of necessarily calling the single largest party when it is in minority, he said. And the much cited Sarkaria Commission's recommendations also relate to "the largest support of others including independents." At best, critics said, Dr. Sharma should have given the first chance to demonstrate majority support—as Dr. Narayanan was to do in 1998—to the largest single party or pre-poll alliance. But he actually chose to install a government admittedly in a hopeless minority. In not inviting the United Front in the first instance, Dr. Sharma was apparently dissuaded by the past experience of short lived coalitions. But this logic, experts said, could not be used to deny a combination of parties with majority support to form a government. Fresh elections should be considered only as the last resort. Former President, R. Venkataraman, who faced similar posers in 1989 and 1991, still thinks Dr. Sharma did the right thing in 1996 as he says, "if you follow this rule, the President shall not be charged with partisanship and all that." Luckily for RV, Rajiv Gandhi had declined his invitation to form the government in 1989 though his Congress was the largest single party, and made way for V.P. Singh. And Rajiv Gandhi's assassination on May 21, 1991 so altered the voting pattern in the second phase of the poll that there was no serious challenge to P.V. Narasimha Rao's minority government. RV, who fancied himself as a 'copybook' President did the same thing when the V.P. Singh government fell in 1990. He called the Congress, the BJP and the left front turn by turn, and finally settled for Chandra Shekhar, backed by no more than 54 MPs of his own, but armed with a promise from Rajiv Gandhi that he would be supported from outside for at least a year. But two Haryana cops posted outside Gandhi's 10 Janpath residence spoiled the fun in just forty days. But that's another story. Constitutional pundits, as is their wont, disagree. But some do question a mechanical application of the single largest party principle. In fact the Constitution, running into 395 Articles and 12 Schedules, makes no reference to political parties, except in the Tenth Schedule—

commonly known as the anti-defection law. This makes floor-crossing by less than a third of party's strength in a legislature illegal. The only insight that the Constitution offers is that the Prime Minister shall be appointed by the President, and the council of ministers "shall be collectively responsible to the House of the People (Lok Sabha)". The first offer to the single largest party convention is based on the presumption that it is more likely to command a majority in the House—as responsibility to the House implies. Thus constitutional expert Fali S. Nariman wanted Narayanan also to follow the conventiuon "if he wants to be above controversy". But, "there are no absolutes in this," said he, "...the overriding factor is who, in the mature judgement and opinion of the President, will be able to command a majority".

Later he described the emergence of coalition governments in India as the product of assertive federalism of the country's polity and a reflection of unity in diversity. Narayanan, who received the World Statesman Award '98 from the Appeal of Conscience Federation in New York on April 28, said it was this pervasive democratic system that had helped in maintaining the unity of India, a vast country of contrasts, diversities and differences. "Some Western political observers had described the system as a functional anarchy," he noted "but there is method, rhythm and meaning in this apparent chaos as there is a popular consensus behind the coalition governments that have emerged from our general elections." India, he observed, had elaborate parliamentary rules of procedure at a time when most countries suffered under despotism or anarchy. The choice of a constitutional democratic system in India, he said, was a "historical heritage combined with the passionate devotion of the Indian national movement to democracy and social justice". That's why it had survived in India, unlike many other countries which succumbed to military dictatorship of one kind or another.

Coalitions, experts say, are not incompatible with political stability going by the European experience with countries like Italy practically going without single party rule. India too has had its share of coalitions, successful ones at that, in Kerala and West Bengal, with the Jyoti Basu-led Left Front government starting its fifth successive term in 1996. At the Centre too,

Indira Gandhi ran a minority government for two years after the Congress split in 1969. The 1977 Janata government that overthrew her emergency regime too was essentially a grand coalition of four major opposition groups—Bhartiya Lok Dal, Congress(O), Jana Sangh and Socialist Party—which came apart due to their mutual contradictions within two years. Charan Singh's minority regime that followed was briefly backed by the Congress in 1979 in Indira Gandhi's quest for a return to power. Her son, Rajiv Gandhi, deployed the same tactic in backing Chandra Shekhar in 1991.

Later as the Vajpayee government embarked on the tight-rope walk of consensual politics with the likes of Jayalalitha, his home minister Lal Krishna Advani floated the idea of a presidential form of government. The proposal stirred a hornet's nest with strident reactions from the opposition particularly the Left dubbing it "undemocratic". An unfazed Advani stuck to his guns saying a fresh look at the Constitution was necessary in the light of its working in the last fifty years. Advani told the BJP national council session in Gandhinagar where he laid down the office of party president that what he proposed was equally democratic. Parliamentary democracy was not one of those basic features of the Constitution which could not be altered in terms of the Supreme Court ruling in the Keshavanand Bharati case, he asserted. Democracy did not mean only parliamentary system of government. It could be the presidential form also, though both have their plus and minus points, Advani said. Seeking to allay fears that there was a hidden BJP agenda behind his proposal, he said eminent jurists, parliamentarians and men of integrity would go into the merits and demerits of either system and there would be a public debate before their recommendations were placed before Parliament.

Those who favour a presidential system said this change could be one of the answers to the present scene of confusion and chaos in the wake of a hung Parliament and state legislatures. As the life of a government would no longer depend on the support of the majority of the members of the Lok Sabha at a given time, expensive mid-term polls could be averted. But critics see the biggest drawback of the presidential system in that the executive would not be answerable to the legislature and this would rob the Parliament of its supremacy. They also want the government to spell out first the changes it was contemplating and allay fears that a constitutional review may be used as a tool to carry out BJP's own hidden agenda which it had put on the backburner due to compulsions of coalition politics. There were other choices too. One could go in for the US model, where the president is the chief executive or opt for the French model where there is a Prime Minister too, but appointed by the President. Then there is the German model where the Chancellor, or the head of the government cannot be removed unless his successor has been selected.

On his part, Vajpayee expressed a determination to expand the BJP-led alliance to ensure its longevity. Running the coalition was a great experiment, he told the party forum, and the BJP would ensure its success. "People have put us on test. We have got this chance after 50 years of toil and sacrifice. We cannot afford failure on this score," he declared. Given the taste of things to come in the first few days in office, it would not be an easy task. Despite the Prime Minister's assurance to Parliament about not misusing Article 356, Jayalalitha wanted him to keep up the pressure on Karunanidhi's DMK government in Tamil Nadu. If Buta Singh was sacked to give a lie to her accusations of double standards, special secretary (home), Ashok Kumar found himself kicked upstairs to the Planning Commission after giving a clean chit to Chennai. And her war of words with two other Central ministers, Ramakrishna Hegde and Ram Jethmalani, threatened to paralyse the government. But though Jayalalitha's letter bombs hit the headlines, each constituent appeared to have its own agenda. If Jayalalitha wanted her pound of flesh for having brought 27 seats to the coalition, so did others. Only in states, where the allies have long-term stakes in sticking together are they likely to be more accommodating. Besides causing embarrassment to the government with his statements relating to his pet aversions — multi-nationals, Tibet and China—George Fernandes' Samata and BJP may be essentially fighting for the same turf in Bihar with the presumed decline of Laloo Prasad Yadav. Hegde would like to topple Janata Dal chief minister J.H.

Patel in Karnataka, while Naveen Patnaik and Orissa BJP want the Congress government of J.B. Patnaik sacked. Om Prakash Chautala who has promised "unconditional support" of his Haryana Lok Dal (Rashtriya) would like BJP to ditch Bansi Lal and join him in an alliance for the assembly poll. Mamata Banerjee hoping to dislodge Jyoti Basu in West Bengal is seeking action against his "corrupt, anti-people Marxist government." Like Bihar, West Bengal too may witness a clash of interests between the Trinamul Congress and BJP as both eye the rural areas. Despite losses in Maharashtra, Shiv Sena supremo Bal Thackeray not only has a certain clout, but also knows how to use it. Smaller parties within the alliance have seemingly forged a little front of their own to keep certain issues on which they don't share perceptions with BJP out of the "national agenda".

As Vajpayee embarked on a tight-rope walk of consensual politics and his home minister Advani sought a system's change to give stability to the Indian polity at this juncture, it became apparent that what was needed was for the Indian politicians to sit together and evolve a coalition culture as they draw up the rules of a whole new ball game.

[illegible] State.

2
The Contenders

The fractured verdict of 1998 had its fallout for all the big three—BJP, Congress and the United Front. The last one not only turned out to be the worst loser, but appeared to be on the verge of breaking up under its own contradictions. Unlike the last time there was little debate over who had the mandate. BJP, a whisker short of majority made no mad rush to the Rashtrapati Bhavan to stake a claim. The Congress, its gamble over Jain Commission Report having failed, did make a feeble attempt to join hands with the same UF it had pulled down only a few months back. And after initial hesitation, the UF prodded by the Left was veering round to backing the Congress, when their convenor Chandrababu Nadu put paid to their dreams of another shot at power.

BJP: Changing Colours

After waiting for 18 long years to set up a government of their own at the Centre, BJP found little to cheer when it actually found itself in power. For the first time polling almost as many votes as the Congress, BJP won 182 seats to retain its status as the largest single party in the 12th Lok Sabha. Yet the arithmetic of the House dictated that it would remain a virtual prisoner of its 18 disparate pre and post-poll allies. And in holding back the letter of support to the Vajpayee government, AIADMK leader Jayalalitha only gave a glimpse of the shape of things to come. Dictates of coalition politics called for restraint and the responsibility of power as also its promise of "governance with a difference" called for a new response.

No wonder, *Parivartan* or change was the new buzz-word in the party which was perceived to have set ideas of its own on everything. "A party that lets itself be overwhelmed by the trappings of power inevitably loses its direction and sense of purpose," warned party president Lal Krishna Advani before laying down office at the party's national council meeting in Gandhinagar on May 3 less than fifty days after BJP came to power. Elaborating on his earlier "New BJP" speech to the national executive in Delhi on April 11, Advani stressed that BJP was the most central idea of Indian polity today, but this "ideological movement" could be promoted only through political dexterity. The current situation demanded that the BJP "enrich its governance capabilities" and "deepen and widen its horizons of concerns". If Advani ended his speech with a reassuring, "we haven't forgotten anything," so did Vajpayee with "I remember everything". As low profile RSS full-timer Kushabhau Thakre,76, took over, Vajpayee suggested that "political work is not merely the quest for power" yet added that since "we haven't reached our objective, the *yatra* will continue, but its nature will change".

BJP worked out a new three-pronged strategy to navigate the course of this new journey through coalition land. First, to initiate a national debate on a new system of government— with Advani clearly rooting for the presidential system—that would give it stability and in turn allow them to pursue their goals unmindful of the compulsions of coalition politics. Second, try to "attract more and more educated, skilled professionals" and give them specific responsibilities to overcome its relative inexperience in handling power. Third, change its *chal, charitra aur chehra* (behaviour, character and persona) to shed its image of a party with upper-caste bias. Not only does it plan to woo dalits, adivasis and other backward castes, but also make concerted efforts to make a real dent in the east and the south.

Congress: Wait and Watch

The once mighty Congress which once held sway over the whole of India was left with a precarious hold on only four states —Madhya Pradesh, Orissa, Nagaland and Mizoram—with a total population of only a 100 million. The last of northern states, Himachal Pradesh, slipped out of its hands as did Meghalaya in the northeast. It had done well in Maharashtra and Rajasthan, to again finish with its 1996 tally of 141, but the outlook after the Lok Sabha poll didn't look too good in Madhya Pradesh and Orissa. The Congress appeared divided between those who wanted to rush into another "secular" experiment and those who wanted to wait it out to reap the anti-establishment vote in the next round.

The balance of power initially seemed to shift to Baramati, from where Maratha strongman Sharad Pawar had led the Congress to a spectacular victory in Maharashtra. He made an all-out effort to win UF support for a Congress-led government, but when that failed the party appeared ready to settle for a constructive role "in the process of formation of a stable, secular government". Others like veteran Congress leader Siddhartha Shankar Ray wanted the party to "sit in the opposition ... and fight BJP on principles and ideology." Finally, the Congress turned back to the Nehru-Gandhi family and an all too willing Sonia Gandhi was soon calling the shots. She had been pulling the strings in the party since the May 21, 1991 assassination of Rajiv Gandhi. The choice of P.V. Narasimha Rao as Prime Minister, his replacement by Sitaram Kesri as Congress president five years later and the decisions to pull the plug on H.D. Deve Gowda and I.K. Gujral all apparently had her nod. Once she decided to come out and campaign for the party, there was no going back. Yet the takeover when it came was a relatively easy affair thanks to intra-party rivalries. So much so that the octogenarian Kesri went without a fight after creating a little bit of fuss. Her confirmation as the party president by a specially convened AICC at Delhi's Siri Fort auditorium on April 6 was a mere formality. But more important was her election as chairperson of the Congress Parliamentary Party (CPP) without being a member of either House. First, the Congress Working Committee (CWC) asked her to "guide" the CPP in "electing" its leader. But the CPP changed the rules to choose her instead with none of the rival claimants—Sharad Pawar, the old warhorse from Kerala K. Karunakaran and Andhra Congress leader K. Vijaya Bhaskara Reddy—willing to pull back except for her. This put her just a step away from being the prime minister in the event of a fragile BJP government falling in a hung House. It was time for change in the Congress too. Planning a complete restructuring of the 112-year old party, Sonia Gandhi set up a task force headed by P.A. Sangma to prepare itself for a return to power. Like the shadow cabinets of Britain, 17 different committees were set up to keep tabs on the functioning of crucial ministries under BJP rule. Four other committees were set up to see why the Congress fared so badly in Bihar, UP, Orissa, West Bengal, Karnataka and Tamil Nadu. The party's top policy making body CWC too was reconstituted and the post of vice president held under Kesri by Jitendra Prasad, who had also served as political adviser to Narasimha Rao was abolished. But for now the Congress was clearly left with two options. First, try to buy peace with the United Front partners, whom it had rubbed the wrong way only a few months back, and win back some of BJP's discontented allies like Jayalalitha's AIADMK, and its own rebel Mamata Banerjee's Trinamul Congress. The second was to let the BJP coalition tie itself up in knots and pave way for the Congress comeback in the next round which may come sooner than later.

United Front: Picking up the Pieces

United Front found itself torn between those like the Left, who wanted to prevent a BJP-led government at all costs and those like the AGP and the TDP, for whom the Congress was the bigger enemy in their states. The dilemma it posed to the Front convenor Chandrababu Naidu was the toughest of them all. For close to two years that the UF was in power, Naidu had played a larger than life role in national politics. Backed by just 17 MPs of his TDP, the Andhra Pradesh chief minister held the balance of power and the UF acknowledged this role by annointing him as their convenor. With his tally coming down to 12 this time, he was again in a position to play the kingmaker. The results indicating that UF and Congress together could just make it posed a dilemma for Naidu, but the mood was clearly anti-Congress in the party. Naidu first toyed with the idea of neutrality, declining to do "anything that directly or indirectly helps the Congress" before parting ways with the UF and extending support to the Vajpayee government on the floor of the House.

Even after parting ways, Naidu left a chink open. The people in the UF had failed to understand his political compulsions, he said later. He was willing to go in for any adjustment except on going with the Congress. His fight was restricted to the Congress, said Naidu and his equation with the UF could change again.

With its strength down from 177 to 84 not counting the 12 TDP members, the contradictions within it started coming to the fore. Like the TDP, AGP which lost all its five seats, also views the Congress as its prime enemy. Farooq Abdullah's National Conference too was caught in a cleft. It didn't want to be seen siding with a "communal" BJP, yet could not afford not to have a friendly government at the Centre. But others, including the Left, the SP, JD and the DMK-TMC combine appeared ready to do business with the Congress.

For the Left Front too, Congress had been the prime enemy as its prime ministerial candidate Jyoti Basu was wont to point out to Naidu. And if the leftists had still retained their hold on West Bengal with 33 of the 42 seats it was largely thanks to the rebel Trinamul Congress taking away a bulk of the Congress vote. Yet in their anxiety to checkmate the BJP, both he and CPM general secretary, Harkishan Singh Surjeet were ready to either support a Congress-led government or be backed by that party. But there were differences over the issue within the Marxist camp. CPI, which was once the main opposition party in Lok Sabha in the 'fifties, now down to nine seats with a mere 1.75% of the national vote was left playing second fiddle to CPM. On the verge of losing its status as a national party, it favours a united left to take on the BJP.

Mulayam Singh Yadav's SP, which brought the second largest chunk of 20 seats to the UF, has few qualms about tying up with the Congress as it counts for little in its main UP base today. Though SP didn't win a seat in Maharashtra, its alliance with the Congress helped them to stop the BJP there. But to give BJP a real battle in UP, Yadav also needs to rope in BSP, a real uphill task given the state of relations between him and former BSP chief minister Mayawati.

Reduced to just six, the JD, which gave the UF its two Prime Ministers—H.D. Deve Gowda and I.K. Gujral, both of whom were brought down by a treacherous Congress—was understandably none too keen to back it nor could it plumb for BJP. The DMK-TMC combine faced a similar dilemma. It couldn't back Congress after the Jain Commission accusations, but keeping arch enemy AIADMK at bay in Tamil Nadu was its greater concern.

3
Into the Battle

As they went into the battle of 1998, fears of another hung Parliament appeared to have spawned several marriages of convenience sowing the seeds of another uneasy coalition. Like 1996, three major formations led by the Congress, BJP and the UF emerged to fight it out in the poll that attracted 4750 contestants including 1493 of the seven national parties, for the 555 seats. State parties put up 555, while unrecognised registered parties had 789 besides 1913 independents.

Placed as the forerunner by most opinion polls, BJP sought to make a dent in the south by forging alliances with Jayalalitha's AIADMK in Tamil Nadu, Rama Krishna Hegde's Lok Shakti in Karnataka and Lakshmi Parvathi's TDP (NTR) in Andhra. And to consolidate its foothold in the east, it continued its alliance with Nitish Kumar's Samata Party in Bihar, while forging new ties with rebel West Bengal Congress leader Mamata Banerjee's breakaway Trinamul and Naveen Patnaik's Biju Janata Dal in Orissa. Winning 87 of the 151 seats in the north and 76 of of the 118 seats in the west, BJP had made handsome gains in the two zones in 1996, but had failed to impress voters much in the south, or the east except Bihar. In the north, where the BJP and allies had gained 15 seats last time thanks to a tie-up with Bansi Lal's Haryana Vikas Party and a post-poll coming together with Parkash Singh Badal's Shiromani Akali Dal in Punjab, the arrangement held. So also in Maharashtra where an alliance with Bal Thackeray's Shiv Sena had helped the combine gain 24 seats with an eight per cent swing. But elsewhere in the west, BJP was essentially on its own with even Shiv Sena putting up nine candidates against it in Madhya Pradesh and one in Gujarat. The alliances were dictated by the fact that though in 1996 BJP had polled just about the same number of votes—a little over 20 per cent—its tie-ups in various states translated into a swing of about 3.5per cent and gained them 71 seats in a tally of 195 seats won with the support of only a quarter of voters. The strategy worked even better this time despite a few setbacks.

At 112, India's oldest party, the Congress too made a few tie-ups to stem the tide of '96 when an eight per cent swing across the nation handed it its worst ever poll debacle—a loss of 106 seats as its votes dropped even below the 34.5 per cent it had polled in 1977 after Indira Gandhi's thirty months of Emergency rule. In the north, where it dropped 17 last time, it made some adjustments in Punjab with the Bahujan Samaj Party, which was an ally of Akali Dal last time. In UP, it reached an understanding of sorts with Ajit Singh's Bhartiya Kisan Kamgar Party, but found Mulayam Singh Yadav unwilling to concede any seat there. His Samajwadi Party, however, joined the Congress in an alliance with RPI in Maharashtra. In Gujarat, where Congress had retrieved a good deal of lost ground in 1996, adjustment talks with the Rashtriya Janata Party (RJP) of Shankersinh Vaghela, whose government in Gujarat it had propped till the other day, could not make a headway. In the south too, where the Congress had lost 55 seats last time, its efforts to forge alliances with Hegde's Lok Shakti in Karnataka and Jayalalitha's AIADMK floundered with both opting for BJP. Only in Kerala the United Democratic Front comprising the Congress, Muslim League and the Kerala Congress (Mani) survived.

The 13-party United Front as it emerged after the 1996.poll, decided to stick together even as some of its constituents did not fight shy of contesting against each other in several places. In Uttar Pradesh, for instance, while Mulayam Singh Yadav's Samajwadi Party put up candidates in all but four of the 85 seats, Janata Dal and the two Left parties too together had 31 nominees of their own. Farooq Abdullah's National Conference did battle for the UF in Kashmir, but turned neutral during the crucial confidence vote. In the south, the DMK-TMC combine spearheaded UF campaign in Tamil Nadu, TDP in Andhra, Janata Dal in Karnataka and CPM in Kerala. In the east, Left Front made up of the CPM, CPI, Forward Bloc and Revolutionary Socialist Party (RSP) did battle in West Bengal, while CPM took the lead in Tripura and Prafulla Kumar Mohanta's Asom Gana Parishad in Assam. Janata Dal took up the challenge in Bihar and Orissa with the two communist parties pitching in in Bihar.

As the battle lines were drawn, in the north, Congress appeared to be engaged in a virtual straight contest with the BJP in Himachal, Rajasthan and Delhi and BJP-HVP and BJP-Akali combines in Haryana and Punjab. In UP, it looked like a four-way fight among the BJP, BSP, UF (SP) and the Congress. And in Kashmir both BJP and the Congress had to contend with the National Conference, which had boycotted the polls last time.

Down south, it was a virtual straight contest between the Congress and TDP in Andhra, and a triangular one among BJP-Lok Shakti, Congress and JD in Karnataka. In Tamil Nadu, it was essentially a straight contest between DMK-TMC and BJP-AIADMK combines, while Congress and CPM-led United Democratic and Left Democratic Fronts did battle in Kerala.

In the east, BJP-Trinamul adjustments made the Congress position untenable in West Bengal against the Left Front. But it still posed the main challenge to JD and BJP-BJD combine in Orissa. In Bihar, it was more of a triangular fight among JD, BJP-Samata and Congress-RJD. In the northeast, Assam was to witness a straight contest between the Congress and Asom Gana Parishad with CPM posing a formidable challenge in Tripura. Thanks to boycott calls by underground Naga factions, it was a virtual no-contest for the Congress in Nagaland, but it faced tough fights at the hands of local units in rest of the region. In the west, Maharashtra saw a fierce battle between BJP-Shiv Sena and Congress-SP-RPI combines. But in Madhya Pradesh and Gujarat both BJP and Congress chose to confront each other alone. Vaghela's RJD proved a damp squib in Gujarat.

Promises to Keep

The complex poll scenario offered few clear choices to the Indian voter and despite all permutations and combinations, it was difficult to see how any single party or combination would be able to reach the magic mark of 272. Yet all the three combinations led by the BJP, Congress and UF promised the all-elusive stability and a lot more though the bread and butter issues generally took a back seat in their election manifestos.

Banking on the charisma of Atal Bihari Vajpayee, BJP went into battle on the twin planks of a stable government with an able Prime Minister. Promising to provide a "dynamic, pro-people, pro-development, anti-status quoist stability," the BJP manifesto claimed they would do in ten years what others could not do in fifty.

Congress chose not to project a Prime Minister even as Sonia Gandhi emerged as its star campaigner, but cited its "knowledge of and experience in running a government" to back its claim. Asserting that non-Congress governments had never been stable, the party manifesto suggested that "stability is not a cover for maintaining the status quo or justifying a policy of caution," and declared: "it means change that improves the living conditions of all".

The 13-party United Front too promised stability even as its various constituents continued to be at loggerheads with several leaders nursing Prime Ministerial ambitions. They yet managed to formulate a common programme and a Joint Policy Declaration though most of the allies issued their own separate manifestoes too. Promising "stability and security for the Indian people" through "good governance and a clean administration", it declared, "Stability of the government to last a full term is only the necessary but not the sufficient condition to ensure stability for the people in their lives."

Economic Reforms

Another common theme running through the agenda of the three was economic reforms with each promising to continue the liberalisation process though with varying emphasis. BJP, for one, said it would restrict foreign direct investment to non-priority areas and encourage it to promote exports rather than target domestic market. FDI, it said, was welcome in a non-predatory role in joint ventures rather than in 100 per cent subsidiaries. Its economic policy, said the BJP, would ensure 8-9 per cent annual growth, access long-term debt market in insurance and pension funds, cut non-productive expenditure, control and rationalise subsidies, simplify tax laws and reduce the size of government. To the industry, it offered to create a forum like Japan's MITI to promote a working relationship with it. The Industrial Development and Regulation Act would be replaced by a new Act to simplify industrial approvals. Indian private sector companies will be involved in the insurance sector to ensure a climate of competition. Specialisation in unit banking was planned through consolidation and mergers to create 'global-size' banks. It also promised one crore jobs a year.

On the other hand, the Congress, which initiated the economic reforms in 1991 under P.V. Narasimha Rao, said it would encourage foreign institutional investors and strive to restore their confidence. It promised to get the economy moving again, increase investment in agriculture, rural infrastructure, revive buoyancy in capital market, encourage disinvestment in public sector units and give greater autonomy to banks. To promote industrial growth, it promised to strengthen Tariff Commission, delicense all industries, other than defence and security related and work closely with the industry to cope with the World Trade Organisation. New laws relating to companies, foreign exchange management and sick industries were also suggested, while vowing to create around one crore jobs every year. Health insurance and pensions business would be opened to Indian companies, life insurance industry restructured, and joint ventures permitted with Indian companies having majority equity, it said.

Promising to carry forward its common minimum programme, the UF claimed that under its rule FDI was set to record a 50per cent increase from 2.1 billion dollars in 1995-96 to an expected 3 billion dollars in the fiscal year ending March 31, 1998. It vowed to continue to strive for "a higher standard of living and a better quality of life through faster economic growth and enhanced social justice" under its CMP. It also promised to protect domestic industry and provide greater employment.

Corruption

To deal with corruption in high places, all the three combinations were one in suggesting setting up of a Lok Pal with both the Congress and BJP promising to bring the Prime Minister in its purview. All elected representatives, BJP said would have to make yearly declarations of income and assets. To the Central Bureau of Investigation (CBI), the premier institution dealing with corruption, it promised "greater autonomy", while the Congress assured it of "functional autonomy" with all cases to be transparent and time bound. The UF did not say anything about CBI, but said it would amend the Official Secrets Act to ensure openness and transparency in governance.

National Security

To take care of the country's security concerns, BJP wanted to set up a National Security Council, which would undertake a strategic review. Seeking a re-evaluation of India's nuclear policy, BJP expressed itself in favour of induction of nuclear weapons. It would also take active steps to persuade Pakistan to abandon its present policy of hostile interference in India's internal affairs by supporting terrorist and insurgent groups, the BJP said.

The other two combinations, Congress and the UF, were for setting up high-powered commissions on defence reforms, but both kept silent on the nuclear issue. The Congress too vowed to fight Pak-supported terrorism, but said it would also build closer economic, trade, cultural, educational and political ties with it. The UF said it would continue its initiatives with Pakistan.

Centre-State Relations

On the contentious issue of imposition of President's rule in the states, both BJP and UF promised to take steps to prevent misuse of Article 356 of the Constitution in this regard. In addition, BJP said it would immediately implement the Sarkaria Commission recommendations on Centre-state relations. BJP also favoured formation of several smaller states like Uttaranchal, Vananchal, Vidarbha and Chhattisgarh besides full statehood for the national capital of Delhi.

To give a better deal to the states, the Congress called for setting up the 12th Finance Commission, suggesting introduction of a Value Added Tax (VAT) system by the turn of the century. It too favoured creation of new states where assemblies have passed resolutions for them. The UF was for transfer of Centrally sponsored welfare schemes to the states.

On Kashmir too, the three combinations differed. While BJP was forthright in demanding abrogation of Article 370 giving a special status to Jammu and Kashmir, UF was for giving maximum autonomy to the state by keeping the article. Congress was silent on the subject.

Minorities

On the issue of minorities too, BJP was equally forthright saying it would wind up the Minorities Commission and let the Human Rights Commission take up its responsibilities. Sticking again to its guns, it vowed to introduce a uniform civil code with 'progressive elements' of each tradition included.

Of the other two, the Congress expressed itself against a uniform civil code and said a new ministry for minorities would be created for coordination and integration, besides a commission for minority educational institutions. Promising a substantial increase in the corpus of Maulana Azad Education Foundation, it said Urdu would get its due status. It also promised recruitment of minorities in police and armed forces.

The UF promised to set up a Minority Development Authority and provide separate budgetary allocations for minority education. While the corpus of the Azad Foundation would be raised by Rs. 150 crore, more Urdu primary schools would be established. Additional reservations for Dalit Christians were also promised.

Ayodhya

Similarly, in line with its known stand on the Ayodhya issue, BJP promised construction of a temple at the site of the demolished Babri Masjid, but by exploring "consensual legal and constitutional means." But the Congress said it did not favour an out-of-court solution and would abide by the ruling of the Supreme Court. It also wanted a strict enforcement of the Protection of Places of Worship Act. So did the UF and wanted the issue to be resolved through either a reference to the Supreme Court or on the basis of consensus.

Media

BJP said it would make Prasar Bharati, set up recently to give functional autonomy to the state-owned broadcasting media, accountable to Parliament, permit TV uplinking from India and restrict foreign equity in media to 20per cent. While the UF said it would strengthen public sector broadcasting system and prevent growth of monopolies in media, the Congress did not come forward with a stated media policy.

Women

All the three combinations sought to woo the fair sex by promising one third reservation in all elected bodies. BJP, in addition, promised women free education up to graduation, including professional courses like medicine and engineering. Besides it promised a uniform civil code to bring about what it called "gender equality". The Congress, on the other hand was for a political campaign for ending discrimination against women and promised increased access of women to credit and anti-poverty schemes like the Integrated Rural Development Programme (IRDP). Besides one third reservation in Parliament and state assemblies, the UF offered equal rights in property and adequate facilities for working mothers.

4
The Campaign Carnival

From the traditional buttons, buntings and banners to the Internet, major contenders pulled all the plugs as the campaign carnival got rolling. Advertising agencies and image builders made a beeline to the party offices to tell politicians how to sell their election soaps. Sonia Gandhi's December-end decision to campaign for the Congress upset the spin doctors on either side forcing them to make course corrections to well-worked-out poll strategies. With several TV channels starting election specials, the Indian politician never had it so good with television bringing them home to voters in every nook and corner of the country. State-owned Doordarshan itself doled out 122 hours to various political parties for free. Politicians of all hues put on make-up, donned colourful clothes and many a time changed *kurtas* and jackets in their cars as they hopped from channel to channel to appear on the talk shows by the dozen. Top party leaders like Vajpayee, Advani, Sonia Gandhi, Sitaram Kesri, Mulayam Singh Yadav, Laloo Yadav and Bal Thackeray flew around in planes and helicopters that cost the earth—from Rs. 15,000 to one lakh an hour depending on the size. Stars were roped in with Bollywood action hero Vinod Khanna and southern screen sirens Vijayashanti and Gautami going saffron as Mulayam Singh Yadav found Muzaffar Ali, noted director of Umrao Jaan willing to take on Atal Bihari Vajpayee in Lucknow. But one time wrestler-actor Dara Singh only agreed to campaign for former deputy Prime Minister Devi Lal in Rohtak and BJP leader Madan Lal Khurana in Delhi Sadar. Tamil actors Sharat Kumar and Ramarajan contested for the DMK and AIADMK rivals, though super-star Rajnikanth who had last time backed the DMK-TMC combine chose to go on a holiday in Hong Kong, while the Congress brought in glamour girl Jayachitra. With Mohanbabu, TDP's star campaigner joining BJP this time, leading lady Jayaprada lent glitter to Naidu's crusade in Andhra. A former director general of police, P.K. Dutta took on would be home minister Lal Krishna Advani for the Congress and bandit queen Phoolan Devi fought a losing battle in Mirzapur for the SP. So did former Tisco boss Russi Modi beating his own drum in the steel town of Jamshedpur. But in the temple town of Khajuraho *Sanyasin* Uma Bharati won again.

BJP: Banking on Vajpayee

BJP banked on the Vajpayee charisma projecting him as a seasoned parliamentarian and the only viable candidate for the nation's top job to offer "A stable government and an able Prime Minister". Other slogans like *"Atal vade, Atal irade"*—firm promises, firm resolves — played on his name in asking people to "vote for a winner". And reflecting the exodus of Congressmen to BJP before Sonia Gandhi stemmed the tide was a ditty: *"Congress se aata hai, Bhajpa jaata hai... Congress ka dhanda jhootha hai"*-comes from the Congress goes to BJP... the Congress business is a sham—on the tune of a popular film song *"Chhithi aati hai"*. A 70-second film was shown in theatres across the country and released over local cable networks and satellite channels. Instead of promising Ram Rajya, BJP now asked "Can we afford a government of scams?" When Sonia Gandhi arrived on the scene, BJP first chose to ignore her, but soon changed tack after her frontal attack on Vajpayee. A war of words soon ensued with BJP attacking her foreign origin and raising the Bofors issue afresh. A BJP ad showed a khadi clad man pushing a fair little girl with a teddy bear in a stroller and thoughts of upcoming poll obviously on his mind. "My God, in this hour of crisis are we really going to hand over the country to someone with just two weeks political experience," the text had him wondering. BJP was the first to launch a website on the internet. But even before its message that BJP was above sectarian politics and devoted to India reached home, it ran into trouble. An article supposedly written by Vajpayee suggesting that the only solution to the country's ills was to cleanse the Muslims, caused a furore. Vajpayee quickly denied that he had penned it and claimed that it was a piece published in RSS organ, *Organiser*, in 1995, but as he had said even then he had no hand in it.

Allies AIADMK and Shiv Sena also went online with the AIADMK website in Tamil and English tracing the Dravidian movement and the careers of MGR and Jayalalitha. AIADMK also used Mallaya's Vijay TV to project the party. Launched on party supremo Bal Thackeray's birthday, the Shiv Sena site mainly carried his speeches and a few details about the party. Sena also distributed hundreds of lampooning audio cassettes and T-shirts in Maharashtra besides firing rockets that sent the party's bow and arrow symbol up into the sky.

Congress: Sonia to the Rescue

The Congress printed over 25 lakh posters featuring the Gandhis—Indira, Rajiv and Sonia—besides party president Sitaram Kesri, roped in singers like Kavita Krishnamoorthy and Udit Narayan to lend their voices to four short promotional films and issued a few ads with reports suggesting a modest budget of Rs. eight crore, about half of that of the rival BJP. Bringing glamour back to Congress devoid of a charismatic leader since the death of Rajiv Gandhi, his widow Sonia soon took centrestage emerging as the USP of India's oldest party. Ecstatic party workers danced to popular tunes parodying ditties like *"Ab to Sonia Gandhi aayi, jeet gayi ab Congress (I), Ho gayi teri balle balle, Ho jayegi balle balle"*—Sonia Gandhi has come now, the Congress will win now. Hitting the campaign trail on January 11 at Sriperumbudur, site of Rajiv Gandhi's May 21,1991 assassination, Sonia Gandhi quickly changed from a nervous political novice to an aggressive seasoned leader with mass appeal. Covering 134 constituencies in 34 days, travelling a total of 80,000 km. speaking in accented English and Hindi with greetings thrown in in the local lingo, she changed the very complexion of the campaign. Daughter Priyanka and son Rahul too pitched in with son-in-law Robert Vadara making an occasional appearance to keep the show going. The Congress campaign focused on the party's wide reach and its long experience: *"Poore Bharat se naata hai, sarkar chalana ata hai"* —the party belongs to the whole of India and knows how to run the government. Sample another one: *"Bharat ke jan-jan se lagav, Manavta ki seva swabhav"*-has an affinity with all the people of India, service to humanity is its creed. The Congress website with the party symbol embroidered on khadi on the home page sought to give the message of change within the ambit of tradition as it tried to cash in on its economic reforms programme.

In Bihar, Rashtriya Janata Dal leader Laloo Prasad Yadav, who had last time used talking parrots to woo the electorate for the parent JD, turned to pigeons and dancing girls sporting ear-rings shaped like his party symbol lantern. Its slogans: *"Laloo nahin yeh aandhi hai, Bihar ka doosra Gandhi hai"*—It's not Laloo, it's a hurricane; the second Gandhi of Bihar. And,*"Jiske haath mein hoga laalten, wohi jayega Parliament"*—One who has a lantern in his hand, only he will go to Parliament. A ditty to the tune of *"Mata ne bulaya hai"* went like this: *"Chalo election aya hai, Laloo ne bulaya hai, Rabri Devi ne yeh bigul bajaya hai."*-An election has come, Laloo has called and Rabri Devi has sounded a horn.

UF: Different Strokes

The United Front launched its campaign with a massive rally in Hyderabad with all the Front big-wigs from chief ministers Prafulla Mahanta, Jyoti Basu, M. Karunanidhi and Farooq Abdullah to Prime Minister Inder Kumar Gujral and his predecessor Deve Gowda holding hands aloft with convenor Chandrababu Naidu on the centrestage. Yet each leader seemed to have his eyes on the battle back home. Even Gowda with ambitions of staging a comeback some day was focused on Karnataka where the humble farmer would tell his listeners how he did them proud "sitting in Nehru's chair" in Delhi and then dose off in the car. Cash-strapped Janata Dal mainly relied on public meetings though it did release a few video films with old footage, Telugu Desam released films for the big screen besides launching a magazine praising Chandrababu Naidu's government in Andhra and M. Karunanidhi's DMK turned to nephew Maran's Sun TV to counter Jayalalitha in Tamil Nadu. With Akali Dal led by chief minister Parkash Singh Badal backing JD's Punjabi Prime Minister, Inder Kumar Gujral to the hilt, he had to keep telling his voters in Jalandhar, "Don't forget my election symbol is the wheel". The CPM, the only UF constituent on the net, talked in detail about communist movements all over the world besides the party manifesto, constituency profiles and the development work done there.

Of Bullets and Ballots

As the day of reckoning arrived some 4.5 million polling staff manned 7,73,667 polling booths to begin the massive exercise that among other things would consume 2,000 tonnes of paper and cost the nation close to Rs 800 crore.

Despite the intense wooing, only about 62 per cent of the 602.34 million electors turned up to vote in the four phase polling on February 16, 22, 23 and March 7 not counting the snow bound Ladakh and Mandi constituencies which voted in June. Many kept away because of indifference, but several others were robbed of their franchise by a fear of violence. In the midst of it all a dozen bombs exploded one after the other in Coimbatore on February 14 hours before BJP president Lal Krishna Advani was to address an election eve meeting. The serial blasts killed 60 and injured many more. Another four were killed in more blasts three days later as polling was postponed. As many were killed in Mumbai on February 27 as three bombs exploded in a series.

Like in the polls before, the Election Commission was flooded with charges of booth capturing, bogus voting and rigging from the sensitive states of Bihar, Haryana, Uttar Pradesh and West Bengal. As many as 2450 incidents of poll violence that claimed 65 lives were reported as against 2467 with 213 deaths last time. Repolls were ordered in 4733 booths, 3059 in Bihar alone where election was held afresh in whole of Patna. At 2825 repolls were far fewer last time with fresh voting in 1930 booths in Bihar. After Bihar which accounted for 26 deaths in 777 incidents of violence, 12 lives were lost in Andhra in 1430 incidents leading to a repoll in 302 booths. Only one person was killed in five incidents in UP, but repoll was ordered at 883 places. Five died in 64 incidents in West Bengal that led to repolls in 21 booths. Assam, where underground United Liberation Front of Assam (ULFA) had given a call to boycott the polls, escaped with eight deaths in 23 incidents causing fresh voting in 233 places. Another five persons were killed in Tripura, but the rest of the northeast was relatively peaceful. So was Haryana with only five repolls.

Everyone raised a hue and cry about criminalisation of politics, yet when it came to the crunch hardly any political party hesitated in nominating people with pending criminal cases. A four man panel set up by weekly *Outlook* identifed 72 Lok Sabha candidates facing criminal cases. Besides alleged dons like Kali Pandey, D.P. Yadav and Mohammad Shahabuddin, it named politicians facing corruption charges like Satish Sharma and Bhajan Lal of the Congress, Janata Dal chief Sharad Yadav and former Bihar chief minister Laloo Prasad Yadav accused in the Rs. 750 crore animal husbandry scam. The panel comprising former Supreme Court judge Kuldip Singh, former home secretary Madhav Godbole, former Maharashtra Governor C. Subramanium and social activist Agnivesh also named eight BJP candidates who stand accused in the Babri Masjid demolition case. Among them were party chief Advani, Murli Manohar Joshi and Uma Bharati, who all became ministers after the elections, saying these "criminal" cases against them were "politically motivated".

The New Face

The more things change, the more they look the same. Yet the 12th Lok Sabha was much different from the House of '96. For one, never before had the green carpeted chamber seen so many new faces—288 to be precise. As more than half the seats changed hands, Parliament was split right down the middle. There were some old faces too but many had donned new colours, like Rangarajan Kumaramangalam, who has travelled from the Congress to Tiwari Congress to BJP now. Reflective of the changed political complexion was the fact that one could count at least 36 parties instead of 28 last time.

Then again an average MP was older and more qualified, but the ratio between the sexes had not changed much. Close to half the members (48 per cent) were between 41 and 50 as against 44 per cent last time, but the number of those above 50 went up more than one and a half times, from 24 to 38 per cent.

There were about half as many MPs between 31 and 40 with their numbers declining from 22 per cent to 12 per cent. But the number of those under thirty dropped five times from one in ten to two in hundred. At 88, R. Veerappa, BJP MP from Bidar, Karnataka, was the oldest.

With more educated members entering the portals of Parliament, the ratio between graduates and post-graduates was reversed from 45: 35 to 36:45. Only 16 per cent instead of 18 per cent last time had had secondary education, though the per centage of MPs, who had not made it to the secondary level also went up marginally from two to three.

While P.V. Narasimha Rao was denied a ticket by his Congress Party for his failure to save the Babri Masjid, four other former Prime Ministers, Chandra Shekhar (SJP), H.D. Deve Gowda, I.K. Gujral and Atal Bihari Vajpayee made it. Prime Minister again, Vajpayee is the only politician to have won from six different constituencies—Balrampur (1957, 67), Gwalior (1971), New Delhi (1977, 80), Vidisha (1991), Lucknow (1991, 96, 98) and Gandhinagar (1996). Vajpayee lost in Balrampur in 1962 and Gwalior in 1984.

Besides eight former chief ministers, Laloo Prasad Yadav, Mayawati, Bhajan Lal, Mulayam Singh Yadav, Madan Lal Khurana, K. Karunakaran, K. Vijaya Bhaskara Reddy and Sharad Pawar, sons of four current state chiefs came in. But if Sukhbir Singh Badal (Punjab), Surender Singh (Haryana), Omar Abdullah (J&K) and Omak Apang (Arunachal Pradesh) made it to the Lok Sabha with their family names, Naveen Patnaik practically won Orissa for BJD-BJP alliance with the legacy of his late father, Biju Patnaik. Several other new entrants could well be called giant-killers. Among them Sartaj Singh (BJP) who vanquished Congress leader Arjun Singh in Hoshangabad and B.S. Hooda (Congress) who humbled former deputy Prime Minister Devi Lal in Rohtak. Uday Lal Anjana (Congress) got the better of Vajpayee's trouble shooter Jaswant Singh in Chittorgarh while Gurudas Kamat (Congress) humbled his political adviser, Pramod Mahajan in Mumbai North-East. Sompal Singh Shastri (BJP) punctured the ego of Ajit Singh, son of former Prime Minister Charan Singh, in Baghpat. Ayanur Manjunath (BJP)

Women in Lok Sabha

Voter Turnout in % *	
Women	: 58.02
Men	: 65.71
Overall	: 62.04

* based on data for 539 seats.

Success Ratio of Contestants

	Contested	Won	Success Ratio %
Women	274	43	15.69
Men	4476	500	11.17
Overall	4750	543	11.43

New Woman MPs by Party

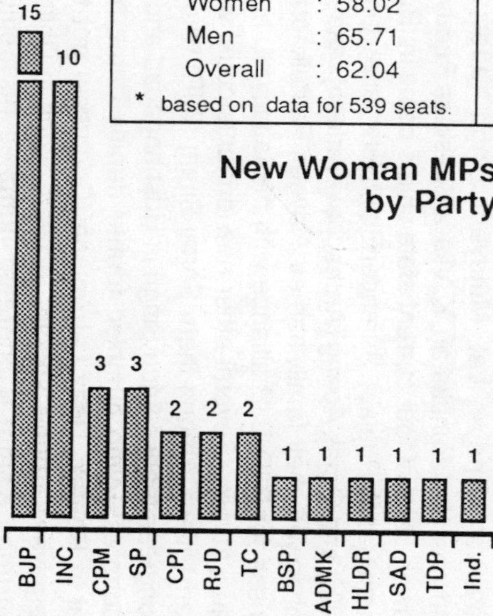

New Woman MPs by State

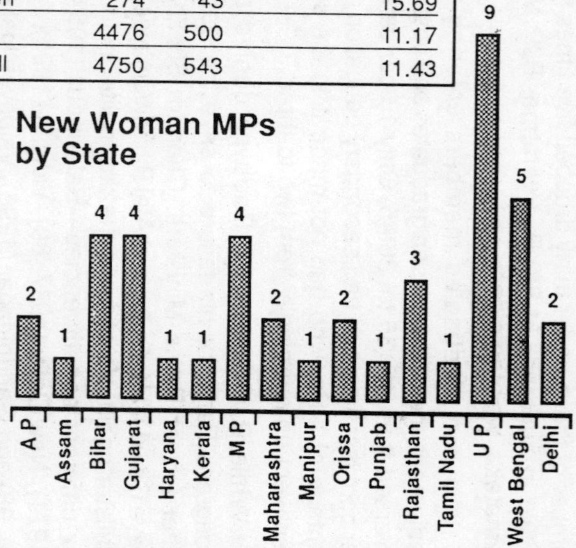

defeated former Karnataka Chief Minister S. Bangarappa in Shimoga, while Nakli Singh (BJP) got the better of BSP supremo Kanshi Ram in Saharanpur. Vithal Tupe vanquished former minister and sports administrator Suresh Kalmadi in Pune. First timer Mukhtar Abbas Naqvi won from Rampur on the BJP ticket to make it big straightaway as minister of state for information and broadcasting.

If the last Lok Sabha had some 40 members facing criminal cases, their number was not any less this time. Among the indicted politicians facing corruption charges, former Bihar chief minister Laloo Prasad Yadav defeated JD chief Sharad Yadav at Madhepura, former Haryana chief minister, Bhajan Lal made it from Karnal and former home minister Buta Singh came through from Jalore as an independent after being denied the Congress ticket. But former petroleum minister Satish Sharma failed to defend Rajiv Gandhi's Amethi seat from the onslaught of one-time family loyalist 'Raja' Sanjay Singh, now with BJP. Taslimuddin, who served briefly as minister of state for home in the UF government in 1996 before his past caught up with him, came through again from Kishanganj on the RJD ticket instead of JD. Also successful were alleged dons M.K. Subba (Congress) from Tezpur, Assam, Anand Mohan Singh (RJP) and M. Shahabuddin (RJD) from Sheohar and Siwan, Bihar. But former bandit queen Phoolan Devi (SP) lost her Mirzapur seat to BJP wrestler Virendra Singh.

From the silver screen came Vinod Khanna (BJP), Ambareesh (JD), R. Ramarajan (AIADMK) with victories in Gurdaspur (Punjab), Mandya (Karnataka) and Tiruchendur (Tamil Nadu).

There wasn't much change in the sex ratio—eight per cent instead of seven—even as 43 women, the highest so far made it to Lok Sabha instead of 40 in 1996. Chennai-based Dr. Beatrix D'Souza was nominated to fill one of the two Anglo-Indian seats raising the female representation to 44. Their numbers have gradually risen from 22 in 1952 to previously peak at 42 in 1984 after a dip in 1977 when only 19 could come through.

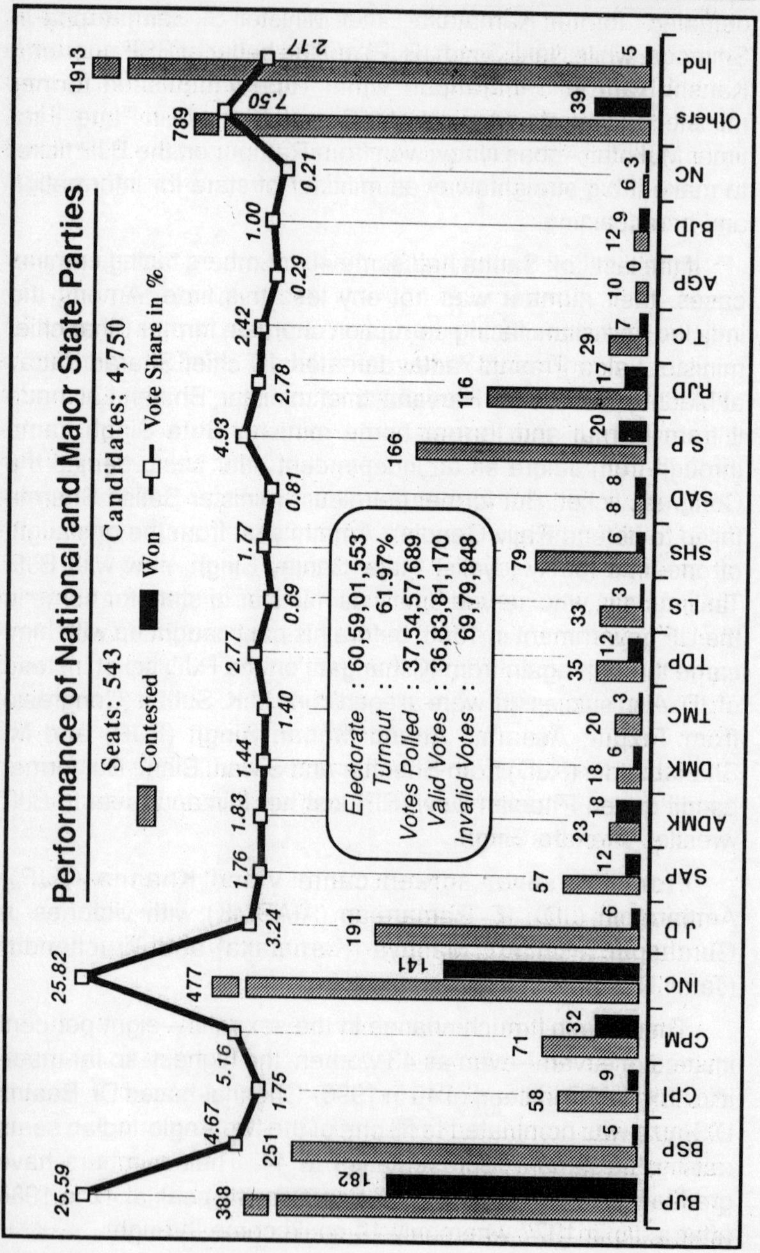

Performance of National and Major State Parties
Seats: 543
Candidates: 4,750
Contested
Won
Vote Share in %
Electorate : 60,59,01,553
Turnout : 61.97%
Votes Polled : 37,54,57,689
Valid Votes : 36,83,81,170
Invalid Votes : 69,79,848
BJP 388 182 25.59
BSP 251 5 4.67
CPI 58 9 1.75
CPM 71 32 5.16
INC 477 141 25.82
J D 191 6 3.24
SAP 57 12 1.76
ADMK 23 18 1.83
DMK 18 6 1.44
TMC 20 3 1.40
TDP 35 12 2.77
L S 33 3 0.69
SHS 79 6 1.77
SAD 8 8 0.81
S P 166 20 4.93
RJD 116 17 2.78
T C 29 7 2.42
AGP 10 0 0.29
BJD 12 9 1.00
NC 6 3 0.21
Others 789 39 7.50
Ind. 1913 5 2.17

Four of the winning women were inducted into the Vajpayee ministry. BJP spokesperson Sushma Swaraj as information and broadcasting minister, and Vasundhra Raje, Maneka Gandhi and Uma Bharati as junior ministers for external affairs, social welfare and human resource development respectively. BJP vice president, Vijaya Raje Scindia became the only woman to enter the Lok Sabha for the seventh time, while Geeta Mukhrjee (CPI) won for the sixth time in a row from Panskura in West Bengal. But Sukhbans Kaur Bhinder (Congress) after five consecutive wins in Gurdaspur lost to filmstar Vinod Khanna this time. Rebel Trinamul Congress leader Mamata Banerjee won for the third time from Calcutta South, while former IFS officer Meira Kumar (Congress) came in from Delhi. Former UP chief minister, Mayawati (BSP) too made it. Ila Pant (BJP), wife of former Congress defence minister K.C. Pant, came in from Naini Tal after humbling veteran politician N.D. Tiwari.

Just about half of the women (21) were members of the eleventh House too. BJP with 15 had the most women MPs, followed by Congress with ten. The CPM and SP had three each, while CPI, RJD and Trinamul Congress sent two each. Five other parties—AIADMK, BSP, HLD(R), Akali Dal and TDP—besides an independent made the rest. India's most populous state, UP returned nine women with West Bengal coming next with five. Bihar, Gujarat and Madhya Pradesh each sent four, while three came from Rajasthan. Three other states—Andhra, Maharashtra, Orissa—besides Delhi elected two women each, while six more came from Assam, Haryana, Kerala, Manipur, Punjab and Tamil Nadu. Ten States and six Union Territories went without female representation.

5
How India Voted

For the fourth time in four elections in a row since 1989 Indian voters threw up a hung House. It was said to be an election that no one wanted, an election totally devoid of issues. Yet for the first time more people came out to vote in a mid-term poll. At 62 per cent, the turnout was four per cent higher than in the 1996 general elections. But the verdict was none too clear at the national level. With the process of political realignments continuing through the 'nineties, the balance of power shifted further towards regional players. Among the seven national parties, the BJP and Congress between them picked up 323 seats with five other national parties left with only 64 seats, half of them with CPM alone. Thirty state parties bagged 100 of the remaining 156 seats as unrecognised old and new parties including Laloo Yadav's RJD and Mamata Banerjee's Trinamul Congress won 51. Only five of the 1900 independents made it.

But with the three major formations led by the BJP, the Congress and the United Front still falling short of the magic halfway mark of 272 in a House of 543, regional players like Jayalalitha's AIADMK and Chandrababu Naidu's TDP and small parties including some one-man outfits played a key role in the ensuing numbers game. In the event it took 18 odd parties to help Vajpayee cobble together a shaky government and a last minute dramatic switch by Naidu in a game of realpolitik to help it survive the first vote of confidence. It was again evident that there was no direct road to South Block any more and the key to power at the Centre lay in making friends with or without kinship. If strategic alliances helped BJP to break out of its moorings in north and central India into the south and the east, similar tie-ups helped the Congress upset the saffron applecart in

Party Performance

Bharatiya Janata Party

State/ UT/Region (Total Seats)	Contested	Won	Lost Deposit	1998 Vote %	1996 Vote %	Vote Swing %
All-India (543)	**388**	**182**	**57**	**25.59**	**23.39**	**+ 2.20**
North (151)	**134**	**78**	**4**	**34.59**	**31.32**	**+ 3.27**
Haryana (10)	6	1	0	18.89	19.74	- 0.85
H P (4)	4	3	0	51.43	39.62	+ 11.81
J & K (6)	6	2	4	28.59	19.04	+ 9.55
Punjab (13)	3	3	0	11.67	6.48	+ 5.19
Rajasthan (25)	25	5	0	41.65	42.36	- 0.71
U P (85)	82	57	0	36.49	33.44	+ 3.05
Chandigarh (1)	1	1	0	42.36	39.05	+ 3.31
Delhi (7)	7	6	0	50.73	49.62	+ 1.11
South (132)	**82**	**20**	**42**	**15.44**	**8.78**	**+ 6.66**
A P (42)	38	4	21	18.30	5.65	+ 12.65
Karnataka (28)	18	13	1	26.95	24.85	+ 2.10
Kerala (20)	20	0	20	8.02	5.61	+ 2.41
Tamil Nadu (39)	5	3	0	6.86	2.93	+ 3.93
A&N Islands (1)	1	0	0	35.53	24.25	+ 11.28
Lakshadweep (1)	-	-	-	-	-	-
Pondicherry (1)	-	-	-	-	4.42	- 4.42
East (142)	**77**	**29**	**11**	**17.99**	**13.34**	**+ 4.65**
Arunachal (2)	2	0	1	21.75	17.41	+ 4.34
Assam (14)	14	1	4	24.47	15.92	+ 8.55
Bihar (54)	32	20	0	24.03	20.54	+ 3.49
Manipur (2)	1	0	0	12.61	5.25	+ 7.36
Meghalaya (2)	2	0	2	9.01	9.13	- 0.12
Mizoram (1)	1	0	1	2.94	-	+ 2.94
Nagaland (1)	-	-	-	-	-	-
Orissa (21)	9	7	0	21.19	13.42	+ 7.77
Sikkim (1)	-	-	-	-	-	-
Tripura (2)	2	0	2	8.19	6.50	+ 1.69
West Bengal (42)	14	1	1	10.20	6.88	+ 3.32
West (118)	**95**	**55**	**0**	**36.46**	**33.33**	**+ 3.13**
Goa (2)	2	0	0	30.04	13.75	+ 16.29
Gujarat (26)	26	19	0	48.28	48.52	- 0.24
M P (40)	40	30	0	45.73	41.32	+ 4.41
Maharashtra (48)	25	4	0	22.49	21.81	+ 0.68
D & N Haveli (1)	1	1	0	53.73	42.42	+ 11.31
Daman & Diu (1)	1	1	0	41.96	40.45	+ 1.51

Maharashtra and check its march in Bihar. But nothing seemed to help the United Front which turned out to be the biggest loser with many of the partners fighting each other in several places.

BSP, which had emerged as a force to reckon with last time and won recognition as a national party, ploughed a lonely furrow and lost six seats even as it raised its vote share by 0.67 points above the four per cent in 1996, while 174 of its 251 candidates across the country forfeited their deposits. Sundry other parties won 18 seats, three less, with 6.19 per cent—a downswing of 4.71 per cent.

Anti-incumbency swings did not affect the fortunes of parties in power in states alone, but also in individual constituencies with more than half (277) of the 543 seats changing hands. Even as they made new conquests, they lost ground in old strongholds.The UF lost as many as 108 seats across the board, BJP and allies yielded 70 with the saffron party itself dropping 53. In the Congress alliance, it alone lost 71 seats.

BJP: Going Places with Friends

For once BJP with its allies emerged as the largest vote-getter with the 14 pre-poll partners together collecting 37.28 per cent to win 255 seats, a clear gain of 60 made with a ten per cent swing. BJP itself again finished at the top with 182 seats, 21 more than last time. It had displaced the Congress as the largest party in 1996, but this time it caught up with India's oldest party in terms of votes too. Thanks to an over five per cent swing, at 25.59 per cent it polled just about as much as the Congress whose share declined by another three points to 25.82 per cent, but then it had contested 89 seats less. The allies added another 11.69 per cent to the vote pie, though they too had fought each other at quite a few places, and brought in 73 more seats, a gain of 39. Except the Haryana Vikas Party of Bansi Lal and the Shiv Sena in Maharashtra, each ally bagged more seats, though Lakshmi Parvathi's TDP again came a cropper.

In the south, which sends 132 MPs to the Lok Sabha, the alliance won a round fifty, gaining 44 seats, 27 of them contributed by Jayalalitha's own Tamil grouping alone with 11.2 per cent votes. Hegde's Lok Shakti brought in three in Karnatka with 2.56

per cent. But the BJP itself picked up 20, a net gain of 14, with more than half the 29.61 per cent of the popular vote in the alliance kitty in the south. Though except Karnataka it won fewer seats than allies it polled 15.44 per cent - an upswing of 6.57 per cent. The allies brought in almost as many additional votes to make for a massive swing of 12.74 per cent. Only BJP lost a seat in Karnataka and Parvathi's TDP saw its vote share slashed to less than half- from 5.71 per cent to 2.56 per cent.

In the east too, BJP and allies picked up 55 of the 142 seats, a net gain of 29, with 36.18 per cent votes, almost double of the 18.59 per cent they polled separately last time. BJP again was the main vote-getter polling 17.93 per cent - an upswing of 4.62 points—to win 29 seats. Old ally Samata gained three seats in Bihar to add ten seats to the alliance tally with 5.91 per cent votes - a minor hike of 0.63 points. But Naveen Patnaik's Biju Janata Dal brought in nine with 3.68 per cent in Orissa and Mamata Banerjee's Trinamul seven with a vote share of 8.66 per cent in West Bengal.

In the north, the BJP alliance could gain no more than two seats with anti-incumbency and anti-prohibition votes in Rajasthan and Haryana offsetting modest gains in UP, Delhi and Himachal. A combined vote share of 38.96 per cent—up only 0.80 points—won the alliance 89 of the 151 seats. BJP itself gained three seats to win 78 with 34.59 per cent—a three per cent upswing. In Punjab, Badal's Shiromani Akali Dal brought in eight like last time with just about the same three per cent vote share. Samata with less than half a per cent added two in UP even as its share went down by 1.97 per cent but that was because it contested only eight seats this time. The only loser was Bansi Lal's Haryana Vikas Party which could retain just one of its three seats as its vote share dropped by about half a point to 0.89 per cent.

But the west on the whole was a disaster with heavy losses in Maharashtra spoiling the good show in Gujarat and Madhya Pradesh, where the BJP went alone. In Maharashtra both BJP and Shiv Sena gained a few votes, but conceded 15 seats to end up with a regional tally of 61 in 118 with 44.9 per cent votes-an upswing of 3.72 points. BJP's own 55 seats—a net loss of six—were picked up with 36.46 per cent votes-around three per cent more than last time. But ally Shiv Sena lost nine in Maharashtra to add only six with 8.30 per cent votes—just a wee bit more.

However, the gains in the southern and eastern coastal belts far outweighed the ups and downs in BJP's traditional strongholds in the north and the west.

Altogether the alliance lost 70 seats, but gained 130 to end up with a net gain of 60 seats as the allies held on to 125 seats. The BJP itself lost 53, but wrested 21 more as it retained 108 other seats. Though it snatched 35 seats from the Congress, it yielded back 32 to it. Again it snatched 10 seats from the SP, but lost 13 to it. Major gains were thus made at the cost of the Janata Dal (10) and BSP (6) though it conceded three to the latter. Among the allies Shiv Sena lost nine, Haryana Vikas Party two while Badal's Akali Dal gave up one for JD's Punjabi Prime Minister Inder Kumar Gujral. BJP again registered the best success ratio (46.90 per cent) and the lowest rate (14.50 per cent) of deposit losers—with 182 of its 388 candidates winning and only 56 unable to save their security. BJP's highest support came in tiny Dadra and Nagar Haveli where it polled 53.73 per cent followed by Delhi with 50.73 per cent. Its worst was in Mizoram where it could poll no more than 2.94 per cent. Among the allies, only one in five of Samata's 57 candidates succeeded while 35 (61.40 per cent) lost deposits. Samata did its best in Bihar with 10 of its 21 candidates winning with a vote share of 8.71 per cent. Both its candidates won in UP with 0.79 per cent. Elsewhere it hardly got any votes worth the name.

Overall, not only did the BJP alliance win more general seats—205 out of 423 or 48.46 per cent, but surprisingly also 50 of the120 or 41.67 per cent of the reserved seats. With 36 seats, 24 of BJP itself, the alliance won 45.57 per cent of the 79 SC seats with about a third of the total votes. While BJP polled 24.23 per cent, six seat winning allies brought in 8.55 per cent. Only in ST seats, it took second place to the Congress, though there too it won over a third (34.15 per cent) of the 41 seats with BJP alone taking all the alliance 14 with 33.60 per cent votes as against 25 per cent in the general category.

Party Performance
Samata Party

State/ UT/Region (Total Seats)	Contested	Won	Lost Deposit	1998 Vote %	1996 Vote %	Vote Swing %
All-India (543)	**57**	**12**	**35**	**1.76**	**2.17**	**-0.41**
North (151)	**8**	**2**	**6**	**0.46**	**2.43**	**-1.97**
Haryana (10)	-	-	-	-	19.01	- 19.01
H P (4)	-	-	-	-	0.04	-0.04
J & K (6)	-	-	-	-	-	-
Punjab (13)	-	-	-	-	-	-
Rajasthan (25)	6	0	6	0.06	0.85	- 0.79
U P (85)	2	2	0	0.79	0.93	- 0.14
Chandigarh (1)	-	-	-	-	17.59	-17.59
Delhi (7)	-	-	-	-	0.12	-0.12
South (132)	**14**	**0**	**14**	**0.03**	**0.02**	**-0.01**
A P (42)	5	0	5	0.02	0.04	- 0.02
Karnataka (28)	4	0	4	0.08	-	+ 0.08
Kerala (20)	1	0	1	0.00	0.01	- 0.01
Tamil Nadu (39)	4	0	4	0.01	0.01	0.00
A&N Islands (1)	-	-	-	-	-	-
Lakshadweep (1)	-	-	-	-	-	-
Pondicherry (1)	-	-	-	-	-	-
East (142)	**25**	**10**	**5**	**5.91**	**5.29**	**+0.62**
Arunachal (2)	-	-	-	-	-	-
Assam (14)	-	-	-	-	-	-
Bihar (54)	21	10	1	15.74	14.45	+ 1.29
Manipur (2)	1	-	1	0.59	1.74	- 1.15
Meghalaya (2)	-	-	-	-	-	-
Mizoram (1)	-	-	-	-	-	-
Nagaland (1)	-	-	-	-	-	-
Orissa (21)	2	0	2	0.08	1.55	- 1.47
Sikkim (1)	-	-	-	-	-	-
Tripura (2)	-	-	-	-	-	-
West Bengal (42)	1	0	1	0.00	0.01	- 0.01
West (118)	**10**	**0**	**10**	**0.15**	**0.06**	**+0.09**
Goa (2)	-	-	-	-	-	-
Gujarat (26)	2	0	2	0.07	0.09	- 0.02
M P (40)	8	0	8	0.38	0.06	+ 0.32
Maharashtra (48)	-	-	-	-	0.05	- 0.05
D & N Haveli (1)	-	-	-	-	-	-
Daman & Diu (1)	-	-	-	-	-	-

In politics, two and two do not always make four, but somehow they did this time. Voters were apparently none too put off by marriages of convenience. For instance, supporters of traditionally anti-Brahmin AIADMK did back BJP with the *Hindutva* tag. A post-poll study conducted by the Centre for the Study of Developing Societies (CSDS) suggested that while BJP still got over half the votes (56 per cent) of the upper castes, more OBCs (42 per cent) supported the saffron alliance than either the Congress or the United Front. BJP's OBC votes were largely picked from the United Front, which was backed by over a third of them in 1996. The study also suggested that younger, richer and better educated as also more men than women tended to back BJP. But the alliances helped BJP widen its base among the poor and in the rural areas.

Congress: A Gamble that Failed

Pulling down the UF government was a gamble that did not work for the Congress despite the media hype over the arrival of Sonia Gandhi on the scene. For the trouble, it just got three seats more, but a near three per cent downswing brought its vote share down to a historic low of 25.82 per cent. If it was any consolation it also managed with a whisker to stay on as the single party with most votes. But then with 477 candidates it had contested more seats than anyone else. An understanding with Laloo's RJD in Bihar and a strategic alliance with RPI and SP in Maharashtra, however, did help the combine to pile up 166 seats, 25 more than last time, with 29.77 per cent votes, just about the same as the smaller alliance polled in 1996.

Largely going it alone, except in Maharashtra, Bihar and Kerala, Congress made substantial gains in Assam, Maharashtra and Rajasthan, but lost much ground in West Bengal and Tamil Nadu thanks to its failure to please two ladies—Mamata Banerjee and Jayalalitha. It also suffered in states where it was in power, Himachal Pradesh, Madhya Pradesh and Orissa, as also in Gujarat where it had backed Vaghela's RJP government till the other day. Sonia factor apparently did help, but it's difficult to say how many votes she actually won for the party through her hectic campaign. Results indicate that the constituencies she visited witnessed a three per cent swing in favour of the

Party Performance
Indian National Congress

State/ UT/Region (Total Seats)	Contested	Won	Lost Deposit	1998 Vote %	1996 Vote %	Vote Swing %
All-India (543)	**477**	**141**	**153**	**25.82**	**28.80**	**-2.98**
North (151)	**137**	**24**	**76**	**19.01**	**20.36**	**-1.35**
Haryana (10)	10	3	3	26.02	22.64	+ 3.38
H P (4)	4	1	0	41.90	54.33	- 12.43
J & K (6)	6	1	2	19.42	27.46	- 8.04
Punjab (13)	8	0	0	25.85	35.10	- 9.25
Rajasthan (25)	25	18	2	44.45	40.51	- 3.94
U P (85)	76	0	69	6.02	8.14	- 2.12
Chandigarh (1)	1	0	0	38.70	29.79	+ 8.91
Delhi (7)	7	1	0	42.64	37.29	+ 5.35
South (132)	**125**	**41**	**36**	**28.79**	**31.15**	**-2.36**
A P (42)	42	22	1	38.46	39.66	- 1.20
Karnataka (28)	28	9	0	36.22	30.29	+ 5.93
Kerala (20)	17	8	0	38.67	38.01	+ 0.66
Tamil Nadu (39)	35	0	35	4.78	18.26	- 13.48
A&N Islands (1)	1	1	0	35.91	58.22	- 22.31
Lakshadweep (1)	1	1	0	51.55	51.71	- 0.16
Pondicherry (1)	1	0	0	32.12	39.97	- 7.85
East (142)	**105**	**24**	**39**	**18.75**	**30.52**	**-11.77**
Arunachal (2)	2	0	1	23.90	28.83	- 4.93
Assam (14)	13	10	1	38.97	31.64	+ 7.33
Bihar (54)	21	5	10	7.27	12.99	- 5.72
Manipur (2)	2	0	1	18.60	40.17	- 21.57
Meghalaya (2)	2	2	0	47.62	53.64	- 6.02
Mizoram (1)	1	0	0	34.86	42.50	- 7.64
Nagaland (1)	1	1	0	86.70	62.31	+ 24.39
Orissa (21)	21	5	0	41.04	44.90	- 3.86
Sikkim (1)	1	0	0	33.11	-	+ 33.11
Tripura (2)	2	0	0	42.12	34.13	+ 7.99
West Bengal (42)	39	1	26	15.20	40.09	- 24.89
West (118)	**110**	**52**	**2**	**40.43**	**34.05**	**+6.38**
Goa (2)	2	2	0	31.59	34.37	- 2.78
Gujarat (26)	25	7	0	36.49	38.69	- 2.20
M P (40)	40	10	0	39.40	31.02	+ 8.38
Maharashtra (48)	41	33	0	43.64	34.78	+ 8.86
D & N Haveli (1)	1	0	1	4.13	55.62	- 51.49
Daman & Diu (1)	1	0	1	1.98	50.62	- 48.64

Congress. And where she did not go, there was a similar swing against it.

In the north, with no allies, Congress was completely wiped out in Uttar Pradesh. It could not even hold on to Amethi, Rajiv Gandhi's own constituency. In all, it lost 19 seats, but gained 12 to end up with a net deficit of seven and only 24 in its kitty. Polling about 19 per cent, it lost about 1.38 per cent votes in the region.

Down south, it gained four seats with a better show in Andhra Pradesh to win 41 seats with 28.79 per cent despite an adverse regional swing of 2.36 per cent. In Kerala, long-standing United Democratic Front (UDF) partners Muslim League and Kerala Congress hung on to their two and one seats to give the alliance 44 seats and raising its regional vote share to nearly 30 per cent.

In the east, though the Congress itself lost 13 seats in West Bengal and Orissa, the alliance gainea five seats with Laloo's RJD bringing in 17 and Vaghela's RJP picking up another in Bihar. The combine won 42 seats in all with 28.90 per cent votes, indicating a deceptively small downswing of 1.57 per cent. But in fact, the Congress ran into a massive adverse swing of 11.69 per cent that cost it 25 seats and brought down its regional vote share to 18.78 per cent. A tie-up with RJD in Bihar and a better show in Assam helped it recover 12 seats. RJD and RJP together added a little over ten per cent to the alliance vote pie.

It was the west, which really brought good cheer to the Congress-RPI combine winning 56 seats with 42.12 per cent with an upswing of 6.28 per cent. Considering that SP too was an ally in Maharashtra, their combined vote was even higher—43.56 per cent making for a 6.74 per cent regional swing. But essentially, it was a Congress show. Gaining 28 seats and conceding 11, it picked up 52 seats, 17 more than last time with 40.34 per cent votes—an upswing of 6.49 per cent. RPI lost a few votes, but thanks to the alliance won four seats with 1.78 per cent.

In all the Congress gained 72 seats, 32 of them from BJP alone, but lost three more to it. Other gains came from JD and

TDP (nine each), Shiv Sena (eight) and AGP (five). Apart from 35 lost to BJP, it also conceded seven seats to TDP, six each to Trinamul and BJD, three to CPM and two to CPI. Eight other parties took away 12 more to take its losses to 71. It also retained 69 seats. Less than 30 per cent of the Congress' 477 candidates emerged successful and 152 or about one third lost their deposits. In terms of votes, Congress did its best in Nagaland to win 86.70 per cent support and its worst in Daman and Diu where its support dropped to less than two per cent.

Congress could win only a fifth of the 79 SC seats as against over 45 per cent by BJP and about 26.5 per cent by the UF. It took the second place behind BJP in general seats with success in 31.30 per cent. Only in tribal areas, it finished ahead of the pack with 43.90 per cent success in 41 ST seats. While it polled 37.16 per cent in ST seats, its vote share was 19.78 per cent in SC areas. In the general category, Congress with 26 per cent polled about one per cent more than BJP.

According to a CSDS study, Congress managed to hold on to whatever support it had among the OBCs, but lost some support among both the Adivasis and the Dalits, particularly among STs in Madhya Pradesh. Sonia's apology over Babri Masjid may have stemmed the outflow of Muslim votes, but did not win it more support. The Muslim vote was more or less equally divided between the Congress and the UF. The study suggested that the Congress was preferred more by the elderly, the poor and less educated and the women.

United Front: Mixed Luck

Cobbled together after the 1996 poll again threw up a hung House, the United Front generally stuck together during its 20-month rule under two Prime Ministers of the Janata Dal. The verdict of '98 changed all the equations within. Janata Dal, which spearheaded the Front, was nearly wiped out, but the Left stood its ground to emerge as the largest block even as regional parties suffered erosion in their support bases. The UF turned out to be the worst loser with its tally reduced to 99 won with 22.18 per cent votes in the face of an adverse swing of 6.33 per cent. And whatever little hopes it still may have had of clinging on to power were dashed by convenor Chandrababu Naidu of TDP first declaring the Congress as its "prime enemy" and then switching support to the Vajpayee government.

JD lost 40 seats across the board to join the ranks of also rans with just six seats as the four left parties—CPM, CPI, Forward Bloc and RSP—took the lead position with 48 wins though they too conceded four seats. Mulayam Singh Yadav's SP alone did battle to keep BJP at bay in Uttar Pradesh to finish second with three gains and 20 seats. Among the regional parties, AGP was completely wiped out in Assam, the DMK-TMC combine was cut to size in Tamil Nadu with 28 losses reducing its tally to nine. Only Naidu's TDP did relatively well in Andhra to finish with 12, still four less than last time. UF as a whole suffered the most in the south and the east, where it lost 46 and 34 seats respectively. It gained six seats in the north largely thanks to Mulayam, but could again make no headway in the west, where it again drew a blank.

Practically going it alone in UP with even some UF constituents in opposition in 25 odd constituencies, Yadav's SP won 20 of the Front's 25 seats in the north with its own vote share of 16.45 per cent, indicating an upswing of 4.70 per cent and a gain of four seats. National Conference which had boycotted the polls last time brought in three seats and Tiwari Congress member Sisram Ola kept his Jhunjhunu seat under the Congress Secular banner. JD lost all the three seats it had, but former Prime Minister Inder Kumar Gujral gained Jalandhar for it with Akali support and much criticism. The 2.58 per cent decline in JD vote reduced the UF swing to less than three per cent even as its combined vote share in the region went up to 19.75 per cent.

But the south was a disaster with the DMK-TMC combine losing 28 in Tamil Nadu, the JD dropping 13 in Karnataka and TDP yielding four in Andhra. Only the CPM retained its tally of six with a straight fight with the Congress led UDF in Kerala limiting the left losses to only one in the region. UF's 37 seats in the region came with the support of 35.54 per cent voters indicating a near eleven per cent decline.

Party Performance
Janata Dal

States / UTs (Total Seats)	Contested	Won	Lost Deposit	1998 Vote %	1996 Vote %	Vote Swing %
All-India (543)	**191**	**6**	**156**	**3.24**	**8.08**	**-4.84**
North (151)	**54**	**1**	**51**	**1.23**	**3.82**	**-2.59**
Haryana (10)	4	0	4	0.38	1.54	- 1.16
H P (4)	3	0	3	0.88	0.22	+ 0.66
J & K (6)	1	0	1	0.50	17.63	- 17.13
Punjab (13)	1	1	0	4.18	2.66	+ 1.52
Rajasthan (25)	17	0	16	2.31	2.63	- 0.32
U P (85)	23	0	23	0.47	4.26	- 3.79
Chandigarh (1)	-	-	-	-	0.93	- 0.93
Delhi (7)	5	0	4	2.46	4.24	- 1.78
South (132)	**32**	**4**	**10**	**5.79**	**8.31**	**-2.52**
A P (42)	1	1	0	0.87	-	+ 0.87
Karnataka (28)	28	3	10	21.69	34.91	- 13.22
Kerala (20)	2	0	0	3.90	4.40	- 0.50
Tamil Nadu (39)	-	0	0	-	1.53	- 1.53
A&N Islands (1)	-	-	-	-	-	-
Lakshadweep (1)	1	0	0	48.45	48.29	+ 0.16
Pondicherry (1)	-	-	-	-	-	-
East (142)	**53**	**1**	**44**	**3.94**	**15.40**	**- 11.46**
Arunachal (2)	1	0	1	1.89	-	+ 1.89
Assam (14)	1	0	1	0.12	0.65	- 0.53
Bihar (54)	35	1	27	8.72	31.88	- 23.16
Manipur (2)	-	-	-	-	1.76	- 1.76
Meghalaya (2)	-	-	-	-	-	-
Mizoram (1)	-	-	-	-	-	-
Nagaland (1)	-	-	-	-	-	-
Orissa (21)	16	0	15	4.93	30.05	- 25.12
Sikkim (1)	-	-	-	-	-	-
Tripura (2)	-	-	-	-	0.29	- 0.29
West Bengal (42)	-	-	-	-	0.40	- 0.40
West (118)	**52**	**0**	**51**	**1.77**	**1.97**	**-0.20**
Goa (2)	-	-	-	-	-	-
Gujarat (26)	15	0	14	2.94	0.42	+ 2.52
M P (40)	18	0	18	1.22	1.05	+ 0.17
Maharashtra (48)	19	0	19	1.67	3.30	- 1.63
D & N Haveli (1)	-	-	-	-	-	-
Daman & Diu (1)	-	-	-	-	-	-

East again was a nightmare with every partner with the exception of CPM and RSP losing at least one seat. JD again was the worst loser as it was almost wiped out in Bihar and Orissa. Only railway minister Ram Vilas Paswan hung on to his Hajipur seat as 25 others went down like ninepins and its vote share plunged down by over 11 points to less than four per cent. AGP lost all its five seats in Assam, while the left conceded four seats. SP too lost a seat. Thanks to its good showing in West Bengal, the left turned out to be the biggest vote getter for the Front. CPM alone won 26 seats with about 14 per cent votes, while CPI, Forward Bloc and RSP added another ten seats and five per cent votes. Taken together, the United Front faced a massive adverse swing of 14.24 per cent which brought down its combined share to 25.82 per cent.

From the west, there was nothing to write home about with JD, SP, CPI and CPM gathering 3.78 per cent, just about the same as last time. Except that SP was actually an ally of the Congress in Maharashtra and as such its 1.44 per cent votes should not count as UF share. JD dropped about a quarter per cent of its vote, but still finished ahead of the others with 1.76 per cent votes.

In all, the UF lost 108 seats with JD conceding the most, 42. It made only two gains and retained four to finish with a tally of six for an all India vote share of 3.25 per cent, a downswing of 4.84 points. JD lost 11 to Laloo's rival RJD, ten to BJP, six to its ally Samata and nine to Congress. Three were lost to Biju Janata Dal in Orissa and two to Lok Shakti in Karnataka and one to an independent. Its only gain was one from the Congress besides the one gifted by the Akali Dal to Gujral. With a success rate of 3.16 per cent JD did only slightly better than BSP (2 per cent) among the national parties but it had the highest proportion of deposit losers—151 out of 190 or 81.55 per cent. JD did its best in Karanataka where it won three seats with 21.69 per cent, while 8.86 per cent votes gave it only one seat in Bihar, but even its highest vote share of 48.45 per cent could not win it the Lakshadweep seat.

The DMK-TMC lost 29 seats. But DMK snatched the Pondicherry seat from the Congress to limit its own losses to

Party Performance
Communist Party of India

State/ UT/Region (Total Seats)	Contested	Won	Lost Deposit	1998 Vote %	1996 Vote %	Vote Swing %
All-India (543)	**58**	**9**	**40**	**1.75**	**1.97**	**- 0.22**
North (151)	**14**	**0**	**13**	**0.55**	**0.46**	**+ 0.09**
Haryana (10)	1	0	1	0.15	0.36	- 0.21
H P (4)	1	0	1	0.56	0.42	+ 0.14
J & K (6)	-	-	-	-	-	-
Punjab (13)	1	0	0	3.40	1.60	+ 1.80
Rajasthan (25)	5	0	5	0.62	0.19	+ 0.43
U P (85)	6	0	6	0.18	0.38	- 0.20
Chandigarh (1)	-	-	-	-	-	-
Delhi (7)	-	-	-	-	0.12	- 0.12
South (132)	**10**	**5**	**1**	**2.86**	**2.86**	**0.00**
A P (42)	3	2	0	2.56	2.39	+ 0.17
Karnataka (28)	1	0	1	0.06	0.38	- 0.32
Kerala (20)	4	2	0	8.32	8.22	+ 0.10
Tamil Nadu (39)	2	1	0	2.45	2.33	+ 0.12
A&N Islands (1)	-	-	-	-	-	-
Lakshadweep (1)	-	-	-	-	-	-
Pondicherry (1)	-	-	-	-	-	-
East (142)	**25**	**4**	**17**	**2.98**	**3.30**	**- 0.32**
Arunachal (2)	-	-	-	-	-	-
Assam (14)	1	0	1	0.95	-	+ 0.95
Bihar (54)	15	0	11	3.40	5.08	- 1.68
Manipur (2)	2	1	1	20.47	4.01	+ 16.46
Meghalaya (2)	2	0	2	1.44	1.41	+ 0.03
Mizoram (1)	-	-	-	-	-	-
Nagaland (1)	-	-	-	-	-	-
Orissa (21)	2	0	2	0.99	0.34	+ 0.65
Sikkim (1)	-	-	-	-	-	-
Tripura (2)	-	-	-	-	-	-
West Bengal (42)	3	3	0	3.64	3.81	- 0.17
West (118)	**9**	**0**	**9**	**0.29**	**0.58**	**- 0.29**
Goa (2)	-	-	0	-	0.92	- 0.92
Gujarat (26)	1	0	1	0.09	0.09	0.00
M P (40)	6	0	6	0.66	0.73	- 0.07
Maharashtra (48)	2	0	2	0.07	0.61	- 0.54
D & N Haveli (1)	-	-	-	-	-	-
Daman & Diu (1)	-	-	-	-	-	-

11. TMC and DMK lost 15 and 11 seats respectively to AIADMK and its Tamil allies besides three to BJP. Together polling 2.85 per cent, the combine lost 1.47 points in the national vote pie.

SP lost a dozen, but gained 15 to finish with three more. It gained 13 from BJP but gave back ten. Taking two more from BSP, it conceded one each to BSP and Samata. SP's 20 seats were won with a 4.94 per cent vote share, 1.64 points more than last time. TDP lost eleven, nine to Congress and two to BJP, but snatched seven from the Congress to limit its losses to four. TDP's dozen seats were won by 2.78 per cent, a small drop of 0.19 points.

The Left dropped nine, but won back five to cut down its losses to four. All the five gains were made at the cost of Congress, which won back three. It conceded two each to BJP and RJD and a seat apiece to UMF, MDMK and Trinamul. The left's 48 seats were won with a combined vote share of 7.8 per cent, a little downswing of 1.27 points. CPM alone contributed 29, same as last time, with 5.17 per cent votes indicating an erosion of 0.93 points in its support base. With 32 of its 71 candidates winning CPM's success rate of 45.07 per cent was second only to that of BJP (46.61 per cent), though the proportion of its deposit losers (28.17 per cent) was almost double that of the saffron party. CPI recorded a success rate of 15.52 per cent with 9 of its 58 candidates getting through, but 40 or nearly 69 per cent failed to save their security deposit. In terms of votes, CPM's best came in Tripura where it won both the seats with 48.80 per cent followed by West Bengal with success in 24 of the 32 seats with 35.41per cent and Kerala with six wins out of nine with 21 per cent votes. CPI did its best in Manipur with one win in two with 20.47 per cent votes followed by Kerala where 8.32 per cent votes brought it two victories. In West Bengal all its three candidates won with 3.64 per cent votes, while in Andhra two of the three won with 2.56 per cent.

AGP lost all its five seats in Assam to Congress. Only the National Conference and Secular Congress brought three and one gains to the United Front as new entrants.

UF, which had emerged as the main OBC block in 1996, still did its best in 79 SC constituencies, winning 26.58 per cent of

Party Performance
Communist Party of India (Marxist)

State/ UT/Region (Total Seats)	Contested	Won	Lost Deposit	1998 Vote %	1996 Vote %	Vote Swing %
All-India (543)	**71**	**32**	**20**	**5.16**	**6.12**	**-0.96**
North (151)	**8**	**0**	**6**	**0.48**	**0.76**	**-0.28**
Haryana (10)	1	0	1	0.34	-	+0.34
H P (4)	-	-	-	-	0.95	-0.95
J & K (6)	-	-	-	-	-	-
Punjab (13)	3	0	3	1.06	2.68	-1.62
Rajasthan (25)	2	0	1	1.28	0.44	+0.84
U P (85)	2	0	1	0.23	0.66	-0.43
Chandigarh (1)	-	-	-	-	2.33	-2.33
Delhi (7)	-	-	-	-	0.27	-0.27
South (132)	**16**	**6**	**3**	**4.49**	**4.94**	**-0.45**
A P (42)	3	0	0	2.89	2.91	-0.02
Karnataka (28)	1	0	1	0.04	0.38	-0.34
Kerala (20)	9	6	0	21.00	21.16	-0.16
Tamil Nadu (39)	2	0	1	0.63	1.82	-1.19
A&N Islands (1)	1	0	1	5.67	14.32	-8.65
Lakshadweep (1)	-	-	-	-	-	-
Pondicherry (1)	-	-	-	-	-	-
East (142)	**42**	**26**	**7**	**14.11**	**15.36**	**-1.25**
Arunachal (2)	-	-	-	-	-	-
Assam (14)	2	0	1	3.27	3.94	-0.67
Bihar (54)	4	0	4	0.40	0.84	-0.44
Manipur (2)	-	-	-	-	-	-
Meghalaya (2)	-	-	-	-	-	-
Mizoram (1)	-	-	-	-	-	-
Nagaland (1)	-	-	-	-	-	-
Orissa (21)	2	0	2	0.41	1.69	-1.28
Sikkim (1)	-	-	-	-	-	-
Tripura (2)	2	2	0	48.80	52.41	-3.61
West Bengal (42)	32	24	0	35.41	36.70	-1.29
West (118)	**5**	**0**	**4**	**0.29**	**0.53**	**-0.24**
Goa (2)	-	-	-	-	-	-
Gujarat (26)	-	-	-	-	0.02	-0.02
M P (40)	2	0	2	0.11	0.05	+0.06
Maharashtra (48)	3	0	2	0.61	1.10	-0.49
D & N Haveli (1)	-	-	-	-	-	-
Daman & Diu (1)	-	-	-	-	-	-

them with over 23 per cent votes. It was still ahead of the Congress which retained its 20.25 per cent share, but BJP overtook it to take the top slot with 45.57 per cent SC seats. It fared at its worst in the 41 ST seats winning only 14.63 per cent with a little over 12 per cent votes. Finishing a poor third after BJP with Congress in the lead with 43.90 per cent seats in SC areas, in general category too, it was left far behind with a seat share of 16.90 per cent. While the left front together collected the most votes in reserved areas—9.64 per cent in SC and 8.41 per cent in ST—SP was the UF's largest vote-getter in SC seats with 6.43 per cent. JD came third after CPM (5.27 per cent) with 4.24 per cent. In ST areas too CPM with 3.72 per cent was ahead of JD with 2.91 per cent.

A CSDS survey suggested that UF had the most support among Muslims (30 per cent), second only to Congress, followed by OBCs (21 per cent), STs (18 per cent) and the least among the upper castes (11 per cent). The support for the UF still came from the underprivileged with more illiterates, elderly and women backing it like the Congress.

Others: Also Rans

Kanshi Ram's BSP hoping to play the kingmaker chose to stay aloof from the three major formations, but appeared to be in danger of losing its newly acquired status of a national party. With only four wins in UP and one in Haryana, BSP found its national tally reduced by six with ten losses and four gains. Six of the seats were lost to BJP from which it took back three. Two went to SP, which too conceded one. A seat apiece were taken by the Akali Dal and an independent. Party supremo Kanshi Ram himself was humbled in Saharanpur, UP, by a college teacher Nakli Singh of BJP. Buy polling 4.68 per cent votes, BSP raised its share in the national vote pie by 0.67 points. Three of the five seats it won came from SC areas (3.80 per cent) with 8.49 per cent votes and two from the general (0.48 per cent) with 4.23 per cent. No seat came its way in tribal areas though it polled 1.45 per cent votes in ST seats. BSP was the least successful among the national parties with only two per cent of its 251 candidates winning and 176 or 70.12 per cent losing their deposits. In terms of votes, BSP still did its best in

Party Performance

Bahujan Samaj Party

State/ UT/Region (Total Seats)	Contested	Won	Lost Deposit	1998 Vote %	1996 Vote %	Vote Swing %
All-India (543)	**251**	**5**	**176**	**4.67**	**4.02**	**+0.65**
North (151)	**125**	**5**	**58**	**14.13**	**13.29**	**+ 0.84**
Haryana (10)	3	1	1	7.68	6.59	+ 1.09
H P (4)	1	0	1	1.15	0.69	+ 0.46
J & K (6)	4	0	4	4.98	5.95	- 0.97
Punjab (13)	4	0	0	12.65	9.35	+ 3.30
Rajasthan (25)	22	0	21	2.12	1.35	+ 0.77
U P (85)	85	4	25	20.90	20.61	+ 0.29
Chandigarh (1)	-	-	-	-	4.10	- 4.10
Delhi (7)	6	0	6	2.34	-	+ 2.34
South (132)	**39**	**0**	**39**	**0.28**	**0.07**	**+ 0.21**
A P (42)	15	0	15	0.21	0.04	+ 0.17
Karnataka (28)	6	0	6	0.56	0.15	+ 0.41
Kerala (20)	7	0	7	0.13	0.15	- 0.02
Tamil Nadu (39)	10	0	10	0.23	-	+ 0.23
A&N Islands (1)	-	-	-	-	-	-
Lakshadweep (1)	-	-	-	-	-	-
Pondicherry (1)	1	0	1	0.63	0.87	- 0.24
East (142)	**25**	**0**	**24**	**0.33**	**0.26**	**+ 0.07**
Arunachal (2)	-	-	-	-	-	-
Assam (14)	-	-	-	-	-	-
Bihar (54)	3	0	2	0.53	0.63	- 0.10
Manipur (2)	-	-	-	-	-	-
Meghalaya (2)	-	-	-	-	-	-
Mizoram (1)	-	-	-	-	-	-
Nagaland (1)	-	-	-	-	-	-
Orissa (21)	8	0	8	0.32	-	+ 0.32
Sikkim (1)	-	-	-	-	-	-
Tripura (2)	-	-	-	-	-	-
West Bengal (42)	14	0	14	0.24	0.11	+ 0.13
West (118)	**62**	**0**	**55**	**3.42**	**3.22**	**+ 0.20**
Goa (2)	-	-	-	-	-	-
Gujarat (26)	-	-	-	-	0.38	- 0.38
M P (40)	35	0	28	8.70	8.18	+ 0.52
Maharashtra (48)	27	0	27	0.75	0.29	+ 0.46
D & N Haveli (1)	-	-	-	-	-	-
Daman & Diu (1)	-	-	-	-	-	-

UP with four wins in 85 with 20.90 per cent. Punjab gave it 12.66 per cent votes but no seats as did Madhya Pradesh where it polled 8.70 per cent. Its only other win came in Haryana with its three candidates polling 7.68 per cent.

The 18 remaining seats were won by five independents and sundry small parties polling 6.19 per cent, indicating a loss of three seats and 4.71 per cent votes. They won three seats each in the SC (3.80 per cent) and ST (7.32) areas, while 12 came in the general(2.85 per cent) category. Others and independents won eight seats each in the northern and eastern zones, picking up one apiece in the other two regions. Of the 860 candidates fielded by 139 registered parties, including breakaway factions like the RJD and Trinamul, 734 or 85.35 per cent lost their deposits. A hundred of 465 fielded by 30 state parties within or without the three alliances, won. But 203 or 43.66 per cent of them too lost their deposits. The plight of independents was still worse with 1892 of the 1913 candidates, or 99.11 per cent unable to keep theirs. In all 3545 candidates, including 182 women, lost their deposits with the highest 807 in Uttar Pradesh, which again had the highest number of 1037 candidates.

A hike In deposit amount from Rs. 500 to Rs. 10,000 for general seats and from Rs. 250 to Rs. 5,000 for reserved seats brought about a five-fold decrease in the number of independents —from 10634 or 76.23 per cent of the total to 1913 or 40.27 per cent. A total of 4750 candidates stood for election, making for an average of 8.75 in each of the 543 constituencies. There were four straight contests, 14 triangular and 38 four-cornered ones. Over ten candidates stood in 176 seats, while those with 6 to 8 aspirants numbered the highest at 186. As many as 34 candidates stood in a constituency in Andhra, 29 in another in Jammu and Kashmir and 24 in a third in Uttar Pradesh.

Only 271 women entered the fray and a record 43 made it, just three more than last time and only one higher than the previous best of 42 in 1984. Though in hard numbers fewer women participated this time, their proportion was higher and their success rate more than doubled from 6.7 per cent to 15.9 per cent. Over the years female representation in the Lok Sabha has been gradually rising from 22 in the first House when

Party Performance
Regional Parties

State/UT (Total Seats)	Party	Contested	Won	Lost Deposit	'98 State Vote %	'96 State Vote %	State Vote Swing %
AP (42)	TDP	35	12	1	31.97	32.59	-0.62
	TDPNTR	**5**	**0**	**3**	**1.20**	**10.66**	**-9.46**
Arunachal Pr. (2)	ANC	2	2	0	52.47	-	+52.47
Assam (14)	**AGP**	**10**	**0**	**3**	**12.72**	**27.17**	**-14.45**
Bihar (54)	RJD	38	17	2	26.58	-	+26.58
	JMM	**8**	**0**	**4**	**2.45**	**3.01**	**-0.56**
Goa (2)	MGP	2	0	1	13.17	26.77	-13.60
	UGDP	**2**	**0**	**0**	**24.88**	**22.66**	**+2.22**
Gujarat (26)	RJP	20	0	13	10.21	-	+10.21
Haryana (10)	**HVP**	**4**	**1**	**0**	**11.60**	**15.19**	**-3.59**
	HLDR	7	4	0	25.90	-	+25.90
HP (4)	**HVC**	**4**	**0**	**4**	**3.57**	**-**	**+3.57**
J&K (6)	NC	6	3	0	36.25	-	+36.25
Karnataka (28)	**LS**	**10**	**3**	**1**	**11.50**	**-**	**+11.50**
Kerala (20)	KEC	1	0	0	2.20	2.23	-0.03
	KCM	**1**	**1**	**0**	**2.40**	**2.66**	**-0.26**
	MUL	2	2	0	5.01	5.08	-0.07
Maharashtra (48)	**SHS**	**22**	**6**	**0**	**19.66**	**16.83**	**+2.83**
	RPI	4	4	0	4.14	4.92	-0.78
	PWP	**2**	**1**	**1**	**0.86**	**1.54**	**-0.68**
Manipur (2)	MSC	2	1	0	25.39	-	+25.39
	MPP	**1**	**0**	**0**	**15.44**	**6.70**	**+8.74**
Meghalaya (2)	UDP	2	0	1	25.49	-	+25.49
Mizoram (1)	**MNF**	**1**	**0**	**0**	**26.85**	**37.63**	**-10.78**
Orissa (21)	BJD	12	9	0	27.50	-	+27.50
Punjab (13)	**SAD**	**8**	**8**	**0**	**32.93**	**28.72**	**+4.21**
Sikkim (1)	SDF	1	1	0	65.72	72.15	-6.43
Tamil Nadu (39)	**ADMK**	**22**	**18**	**0**	**25.89**	**7.84**	**+18.05**
	DMK	17	5	0	20.08	25.77	-5.69
	TMC	**20**	**3**	**0**	**20.19**	**27.00**	**-6.81**
	MDMK	5	3	0	6.26	4.50	+1.76
	PMK	**5**	**4**	**0**	**6.05**	**1.89**	**+4.16**
UP (85)	SP	81	20	9	28.70	20.84	+7.86
West Bengal (42)	**TC**	**29**	**7**	**3**	**24.43**	**-**	**+24.43**
Pondicherry (1)	ADMK	1	0	0	25.10	-	+25.10
	DMK	**1**	**1**	**0**	**41.11**	**39.91**	**+1.20**

they made up only 4.4 per cent of the total strength. The House of 1977 had only 19, the least number of women ever. Women fared best in 1957 when 27 of the 45 candidates or 60 per cent made it. Their worst came in 1996 when a record 599 jumped into the fray, but only 6.7 per cent got through.

Vallabh Kathiriya of the BJP defeated Vithal Radadiya of the RJP with the largest margin of 3,54,183 votes in Rajkot in Gujarat. Another BJP candidate beat a Congress nominee by 3,04,022 votes in Surat. They were the only two to win with margins exceeding three lakhs, while four did so in 1996. Prime Minister to be Atal Bihari Vajpayee defeated his SP rival in Lucknow with the 15th highest margin of 2,16,263. He was one of the 15 candidates to win with margins between two and three lakhs as against 32 last time.

In Rajmahal, Bihar, BJP's Shom Marandi pipped his Congress rival by just nine votes, the lowest margin in the 1998 poll. Independent Lallungmuana defeated another Congress candidate by 41 votes in Mizoram and in Mumbai South Central Shiv Sena's Mohan Rawale slipped past an SP nominee by 153 votes. Nine candidates defeated their rivals by less than 1000 votes and four with 1-2,000 margins.

Former Prime Minister P V Narasimha Rao, who was denied a ticket this time by the Congress for his failure to save the Babri Masjid, holds the record for the highest margin of victory. Coming to Lok Sabha through a by-election in Nandyal, Andhra Pradesh, in November 1991 he trounced his nearest rival by 5,80,297 votes. All his rivals lost their deposits too. The earlier record was held by Ram Vilas Paswan of Janata Dal who won by a margin of 5,04,448 from Hajipur in Bihar in 1989.

For the first time in a mid-term poll 62.04 per cent of the 602.34 million voters exercised their franchise with Lakshadweep registering the highest turnout of 85.10 per cent. Tripura followed with 80.86 per cent with West Bengal close behind with 79.17 per cent. Jammu and Kashmir recorded the lowest turnout of 44.31 per cent. But despite a boycott call by some insurgent groups, 45.41 per cent voters turned out in Nagaland. In no other state or Union Territory was the turnout lower than51.29 per cent recorded in Delhi. The highest turnout in a single constituency was recorded at Barrackpore in West Bengal with 88 per cent and the lowest at Anantnag in Jammu and Kashmir with 28.09 per cent.

Of the 287.53 million women voters 58.02 per cent turned out. Though this was four points lower than the national average, Lakshadweep recorded the highest particiption by the fair sex at 87.70 per cent , which was even better than men. Tripura women came next with 80.47 per cent followed by 79.50 per cent in Dadra-Nagar Haveli. Women's turnout was lowest in Jammu & Kashmir at 34.64 per cent.

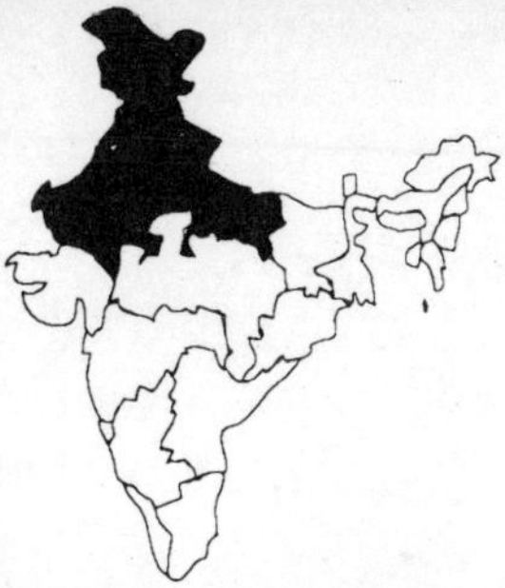

NORTH

Seats: 151	Candidates: 1756

Electorate : 17,56,33,372
Turnout : 57.26%
Votes Polled : 10,05,66,895
Valid Votes : 9,91,92,521
Invalid Votes : 13,57,585

Party	Contested	Won	Lost Deposit	1998 Vote %	1996 Vote %	Vote Swing %
BJP + Allies	**154**	**89**	**10**	**38.96**	**38.16**	**+ 0.80**
BJP	134	78	4	34.59	31.32	+ 3.27
SAP	8	2	6	0.46	2.43	- 1.97
SAD	8	8	0	3.03	3.03	0.00
HVP	4	1	0	0.88	1.38	- 0.50
INC	**137**	**24**	**76**	**19.01**	**20.36**	**- 1.35**
UF Parties	**193**	**25**	**107**	**19.78**	**16.67**	**+ 3.11**
J D	54	1	51	1.23	3.82	- 2.59
CPI	14	0	13	0.55	0.46	+ 0.09
CPM	8	0	6	0.48	0.76	- 0.28
S P	106	20	34	16.27	11.63	+ 4.64
AIICS	5	1	3	0.46	-	+ 0.46
N C	6	3	0	0.79	-	+ 0.79
BSP	**125**	**5**	**58**	**14.13**	**13.29**	**+ 0.84**
Others	**1147**	**8**	**1,127**	**8.12**	**11.52**	**- 3.40**

6
The North: Desert Surprise

Despite setbacks in Rajasthan and Haryana, BJP alliance retained its preeminent position in the north winning 89 of the 151 seats up for grabs in the region. Congress practically going it alone, ended up with a net loss of seven as it ran into adverse swings all over except in the desert state. SP of Mulayam Singh Yadav alone checked the saffron surge in UP to pick up four more seats for the United Front even as JD dropped two and the National Conference brought in three.

BJP and allies polled about 39 per cent votes to pick up just two more seats than last time with the saffron party itself winning 78 seats for 34.59 per cent. Holding on to 47 seats, it snatched 30 more seats from its rivals, but lost 27 others to finish with only three more on the slate. If a divided opposition and UP Governor Romesh Bhandari's controversial acts helped it a bit in India's most populous state, an anti-incumbency wave in Rajasthan evened the odds. Among its allies, Shiromani Akali Dal gained a seat and lost another to bring in the same number of eight seats with 3.03 per cent of the regional vote. Samata Party too gained one with its 0.45 per cent vote share, but Haryana Vikas Party of Bansi Lal lost two as it polled 0.89 per cent. Shiv Sena's 21 candidates, some fighting against alliance partners, brought in another 0.23 per cent votes.

As many as 14 of BJP's 30 gains in the north were from the Congress, which in turn took back 11. It gained nine from SP and four from BSP, but gave away 13 and four respectively to them. It gained two more from the Tiwari faction of Congress and one from JD. Swings for BJP ranged from 8.98 per cent in Himachal, 5.19 per cent in Punjab, to 1.11 per cent in Delhi.

Those against it ranged from 0.71 per cent in Rajasthan to 0.85 per cent in Haryana. Overall, BJP gained 3.08 points in the north raising its vote share from 31.33 per cent 34.41 per cent.

Losing everywhere except in Rajasthan, Congress picked up 24 seats, seven less than last time for a regional vote share of 19.01 per cent. Besides 14 lost to BJP, it conceded three to the National Conference, now back in the poll fray, and one each to Chautala's Haryana Lok Dal (Rashtriya) and former Congressman Buta Singh, who was denied ticket, in Rajasthan. Apart from the 11 won back from BJP, its only other gain came from Janata Dal. Its worst ever performance came in UP, where it could not even hold on to Rajiv Gandhi's Amethi constituency despite Sonia Gandhi's campaign visits. It also suffered in Himachal Pradesh where it was in power, but the Sonia factor apparently helped it chalk out an impressive win in Rajasthan.

For the United Front, SP won 20 seats , all in UP, to add four to its kitty with its own vote share of 16.28 per cent. National Conference brought in three, all picked up from Congress with 0.56 per cent votes. Losing two seats, JD took one for 1.24 per cent. Former Prime Minister Chandrashekhar in Ballia and former TIwari faction minister Sis Ram Ola in Rajasthan completed the UF tally of 25 with less than half a per cent vote share each. Counting 0.56 per cent and 0.48 per cent contributed by CPI and CPM respectively, the UF vote share in the north added up to about 20 per cent.

Among others, BSP with 14.13 per cent ended up fourth in the popularity stakes even as it dropped four seats, losing four to BJP, two to SP and one each to Akali Dal and an independent, but wresting back three from BJP and one from SP. Chautala's party's four wins gave Haryana Lok Dal (Rashtriya) a 1.83 per cent share in the regional pie, while163 independents including three winners earned 3.02 per cent. Rest of the 2.62 per cent were shared by a host of smaller parties.

Seven national parties cornered 70.37 per cent of the regional vote, while 22.80 per cent went to state parties, including Samajwadi Party in UP, Akali Dal in Punjab, National Conference in Jammu and Kashmir, Haryana Vikas Party and Haryana Lok

Dal and Himachal Vikas Congress. Of the rest, smaller parties took 3.81 per cent with 3.02 per cent going to the independents.

As many as 1756 candidates tried their luck in 151 constituencies. They included 1543 in 119 general seats, 195 in 29 SC and 18 in three ST seats.

Electorate	:	1,10,78,895
Turnout	:	69.04%
Votes Polled	:	76,49,388
Valid Votes	:	75,52,804
Invalid Votes	:	94,751

HARYANA

Seats: 10	Candidates: 140

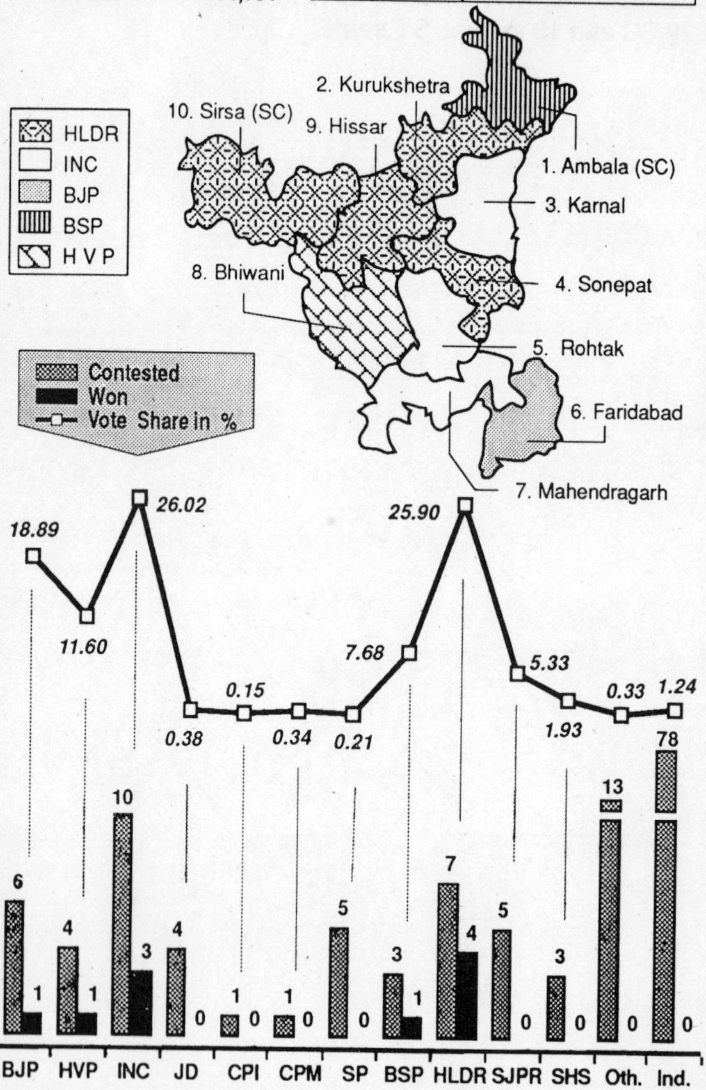

Haryana: Bottle Kicks Back HVP

Chief Minister Bansi Lal's prohibition policy proved costly for his Haryana Vikas Party and coalition ally, the BJP as the alliance received a drubbing in the state losing five seats in the face of a negative swing of 4.44 per cent. The Congress, which had lost power in the state in 1996 in the simultaneous assembly poll, took away a large chunk of the shifted vote (3.38 per cent) to gain two seats from the BJP. But it was former chief minister Om Prakash Chautala's Haryana Lok Dal (Rashtriya) which made the most of this voter disenchantment to win four seats snatching two from the HVP, one from the Congress and unseating an independent. But Chautala's father, Devi Lal lost again to Bhupendra Singh Hooda of the Congress. It was the third defeat in a row for the Tau, 83, a former deputy Prime Minister on his home turf. Bansi Lal's son Surender Singh won from Bhiwani defeating his own brother and a grandson of Devi Lal. Critical of his father's prohibition policy, he had won from Tosham in 1977 too when Bansi Lal lost in the anti-Congress wave.

The BJP-HVP alliance still finished at the top of the heap with a combined vote share of 30.49 per cent , but it won them only two seats with each taking one to finish with a net loss of five. Though BJP won only one of the six seats it contested, it dropped only 0.85 per cent of its votes to finish with 18.89 per cent as against 19.74 per cent in 1996. But HVP in losing two seats to HLDR saw its vote share go down by 3.59 points from 15.19 per cent to 11.60 per cent. The Congress pushing its vote share from 21.88 per cent to 26.02 per cent finished higher than any single party, but it could add only one seat to its 1996 tally with only three of its ten candidates emerging successful. Three of its nominees even lost their deposit. It gained two seats from BJP, but lost one to HLDR.

New entrant HLDR came a close second with 25.90 per cent winning four of the six seats it contested and immediately queered the pitch for rival Bansi Lal by offering its support to the BJP led coalition at the Centre.

HARYANA

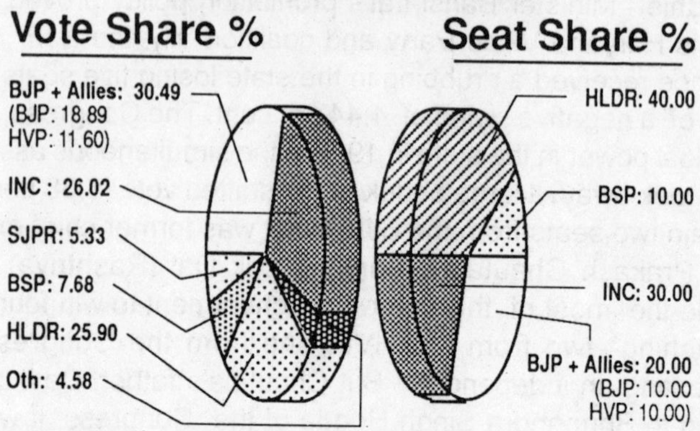

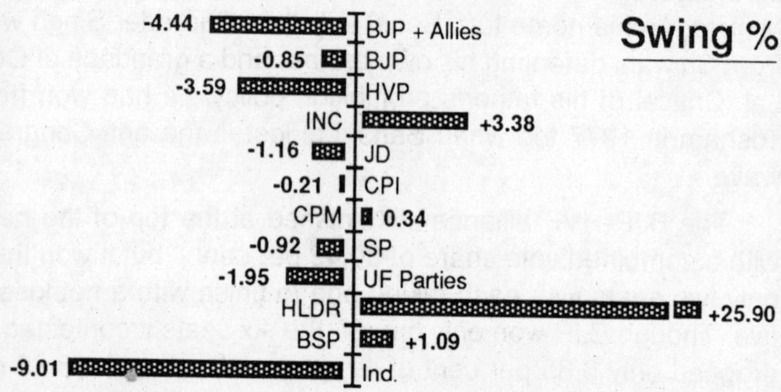

GAINS & LOSSES

Party	Seats Won '96	Seats Won '98	Reta-ined	Gain-ed	Gained From:	Lost	Lost to:	Net + / -
BJP	4	1	1	-	-	3	INC-2, BSP-1	-3
HVP	3	1	1	-	-	2	HLDR-2	-2
INC	2	3	1	2	BJP-2	1	HLDR-1	+1
BSP	0	1	-	1	BJP-1	-	-	+1
HLDR	0	4	-	4	HVP-2, INC-1, IND-1	-	-	+4
IND	1	0	-	-	-	1	HLDR-1	-1
Total	10	10	3	7		7		

BSP, which had drawn a blank last time for 6.59 per cent votes snatched an SC seat from the BJP as it raised its vote share by a little over one point to 7.68 per cent—3.70 per cent coming from the winning seat. The other SC seat went to HLDR for a vote share of 4.18 per cent or 21.78 per cent.of the total SC vote as against 18.58 per cent of the BSP. But it was the BJP which got the maximum SC votes at 30.94 per cent ahead of the Congress with 26.46 per cent. But neither could win any of the two SC seats they both had contested.

Janata Dal contesting four seats again drew a blank as its vote share plunged to a minuscule 0.38 per cent from 1.54 per cent in 1996 and 12.49 per cent five years before that. Among the other also rans were the Shiv Sena (1.93 per cent), which chose to field three candidates against its ally BJP, the CPM (0.34 per cent) and CPI (0.15 per cent).

Of the six women candidates only Kailasho Devi of HLDR won with 43.57 per cent votes in Kurukshetra. Former Congress minister at the Centre Selja lost in Sirsa though she polled 29.48 per cent votes. Four other women candidates lost their deposits.

Women, who had brought Bansi Lal to power in 1996, again turned out in large numbers (65.07 per cent) though a little less than the total of 69.04 per cent. But the result brought no cheer to the fair sex. The chief Minister who till the other day was proclaiming that he would quit rather than modify or relax prohibition, turned his state wet again from April 1, ending the 21 month experiment which cost it an annual revenue loss of Rs. 800 crore.

HIMACHAL PRADESH

Seats: 4	Candidates: 22

Electorate : 36,25,295
Turnout : 66.40%
Votes Polled : 24,07,218
Valid Votes : 23,80,668
Invalid Votes : 26,508

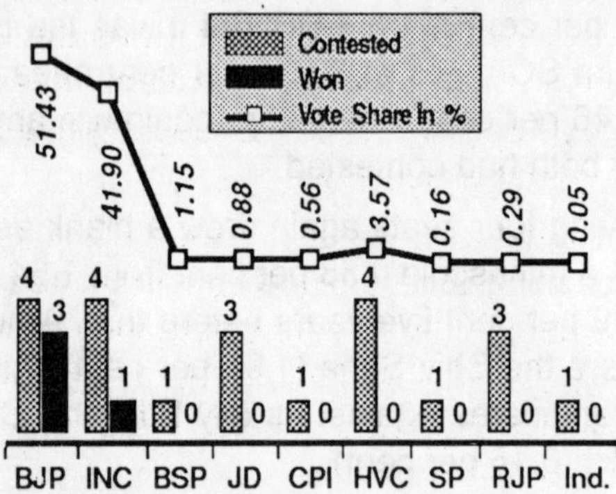

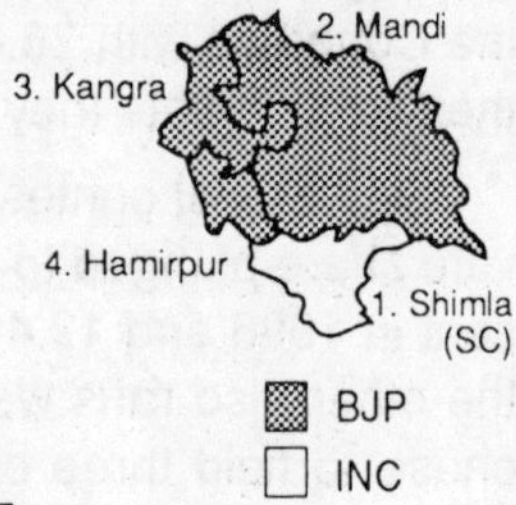

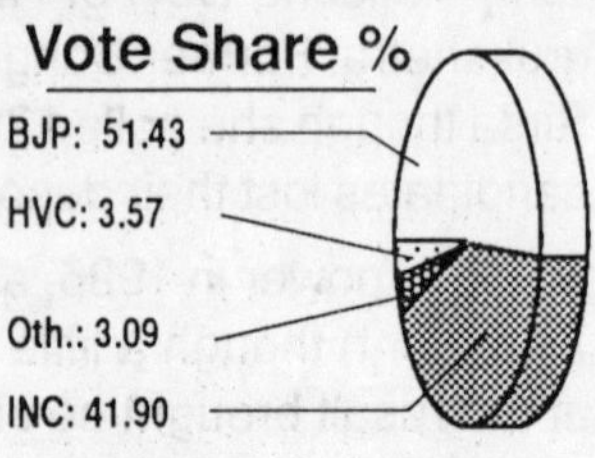

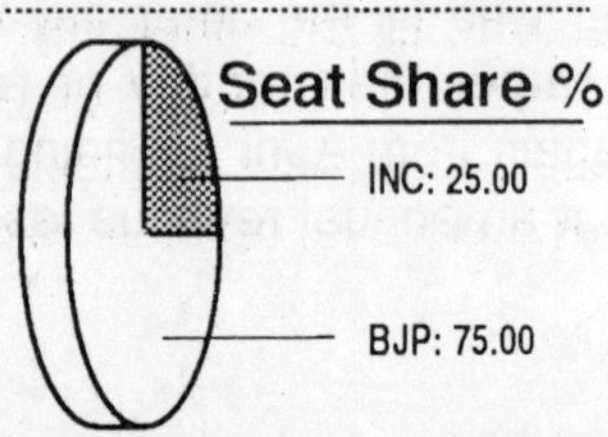

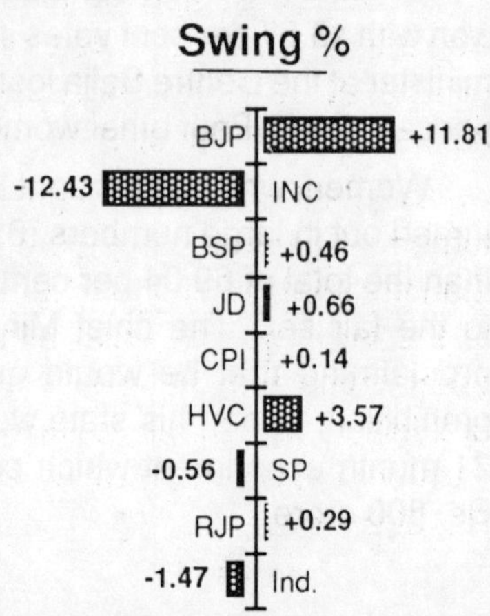

GAINS & LOSSES

Party	Seats Won '96	Seats Won '98	Reta-ined	Gain-ed	Gained From:	Lost	Lost to:	Net +/-
BJP	0	3	-	3	INC-3	-	-	+3
INC	4	1	1	-	-	3	BJP-3	-3
Total	**4**	**4**	**1**	**3**		**3**		

HIMACHAL PRADESH: A Gamble That Failed

Less than two years after making a clean sweep of all the four seats in the state, the Congress not only lost three of them, but was also dislodged from power as party chief minister Virbhadra Singh lost out in yet another gamble. In the simultaneous Assembly poll that he called nine months before schedule, the Congress emerged a whisker short of the half-way mark to allow BJP to rule Shimla with the help of scam tainted former communications minister Sukh Ram's Himachal Vikas Congress.

In the three Lok Sabha seats which went to the polls in February, Congress saw its vote share drop by 10.76 points from 54.33 per cent in 1996 to 43.57 per cent as it lost two seats to BJP. Loss of Mandi later brought its share further down to 41.90 per cent with an adverse swing of 12.44 per cent. While former BJP chief minister Shanta Kumar regained the Kangra seat he had lost to Sat Mahajan of Congress in 1996, party colleague Suresh Chandel wrested the Hamirpur seat with a 50.47per cent vote. Congress, however retained the Shimla SC seat with 42.58 per cent votes in a five-cornered contest instead of the 56.25 per cent last time. BJP share was 42.58 per cent in the lone SC seat.

Sukh Ram, who played the kingmaker in the state with his four MLAs, was a candidate in the Mandi seat but retired in favour of BJP before the poll in June. BJP took the seat to raise its vote share to 51.43 per cent, marking a near 12 per cent swing in its favour. He had won it for the Congress in 1984, only to lose it in 1989. He wrested it in 1991 and retained it in 1996.

The Janata Dal, which again drew a blank marginally increased its vote share from a minuscule 0.22 per cent to 0.88 per cent. The BSP finished with1.15 per cent, CPI with 0.56 per cent, and SP with just 0.16 per cent. Sukh Ram's HVC finished ahead of them all with 3.57 per cent votes . Except three candidates each of the Congress and BJP all other eleven candidates lost their deposits. No woman contested the poll in the state though at 71.15 per cent their turnout much higher than the total of 66.40 per cent.

JAMMU & KASHMIR

Seats: 6	Candidates: 86

Electorate : 50,21,994
Turnout : 44.31%
Votes Polled : 22,25,187
Valid Votes : 21,62,972
Invalid Votes : 61,297

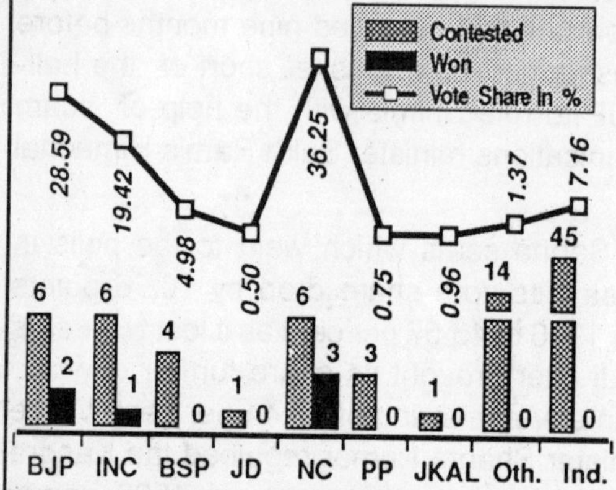

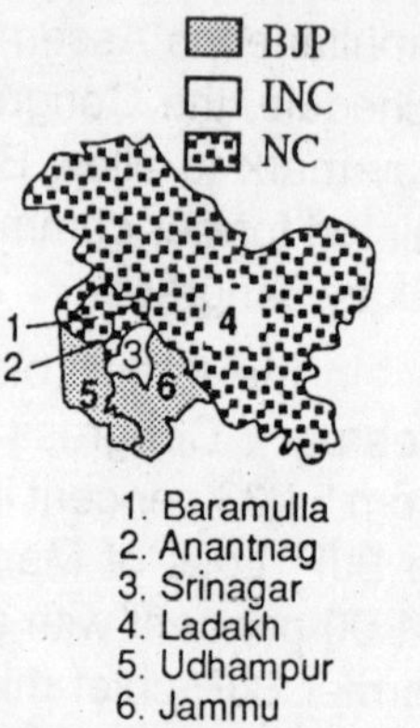

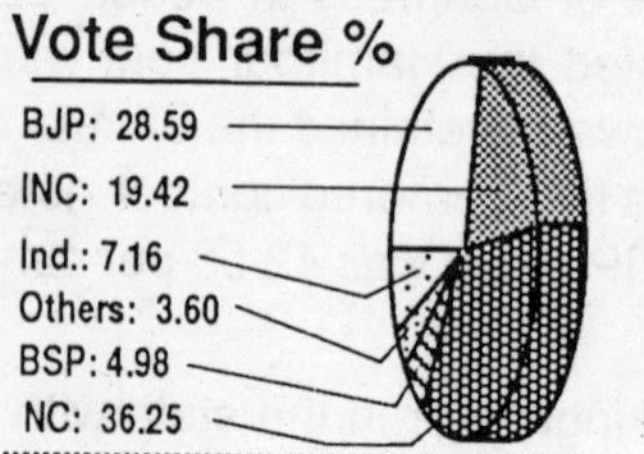

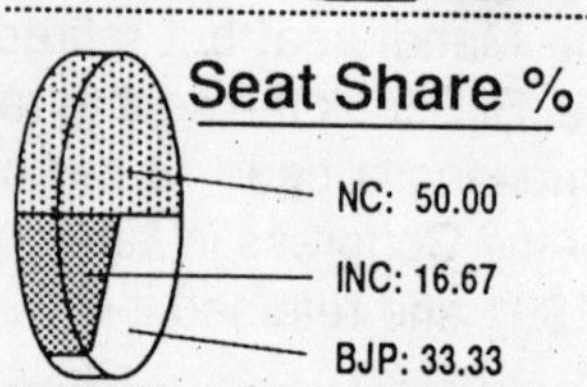

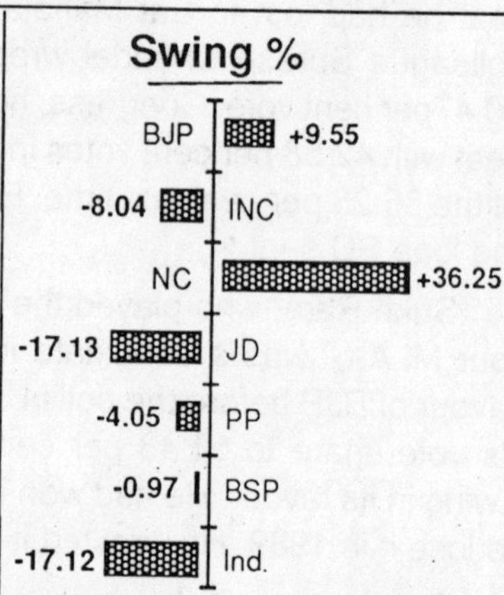

GAINS & LOSSES

Party	Seats Won '96	Seats Won '98	Retained	Gained	Gained From:	Lost	Lost to:	Net +/-
BJP	1	2	1	1	INC-1	0	-	+1
INC	4	1	0	1	JD-1	4	NC-3, BJP-1	-3
JD	1	0	0	0	-	1	INC-1	-1
NC	-	3	-	3	INC-3	-	-	+3
Total	6	6	1	5		5		

JAMMU & KASHMIR: Return of the National Conference

The National Conference of Chief Minister Farooq Abdullah returned to the poll fray after its 1996 boycott to wrest Baramulla and Srinagar seats from the Congress. But former union home minister Mufti Mohamad Sayeed, now back in Congress took Anantnag from his old party JD as Jammu was wrested by the BJP. Later NC snatched the Ladakh seat from the Congress in June to raise its tally to three with 36.25 per cent votes.

National Conference topped the popularity stakes with three wins, all gains from the Congress. BJP won two seats with 28.59 per cent—9.55 points up from 1996 to overtake the Congress. But its four loser candidates could not even save their deposits. Congress could win only one seat with 19.42 per cent—an eight point drop from 27.46 per cent last time. One of its candidates too lost his deposit. JD which lost its lone seat saw its vote share plummet from 17.63 per cent to a minuscule 0.50 per cent. Four BSP candidates again lost their deposits, but the party more or less maintained its vote share as it slid marginally from 5.95 per cent to 4.98 per cent. Sundry other small parties polled between 0.05 per cent and 1.35 per cent. Fortyfive independents together polled 7.16 per cent. All but one of them lost deposits as did 21 party candidates among a total of 87 candidates in the fray.

The lone woman candidate Hafiza Begum lost her deposit in Srinagar. Just a little over one-third of women voters turned out (34.64 per cent)—about ten points less than the total of 44.31 per cent.

Electorate	:	1,53,44,540
Turnout	:	60.07%
Votes Polled	:	92,17,137
Valid Votes	:	91,16,139
Invalid Votes	:	99,413

PUNJAB

Seats: 13	Candidates: 102

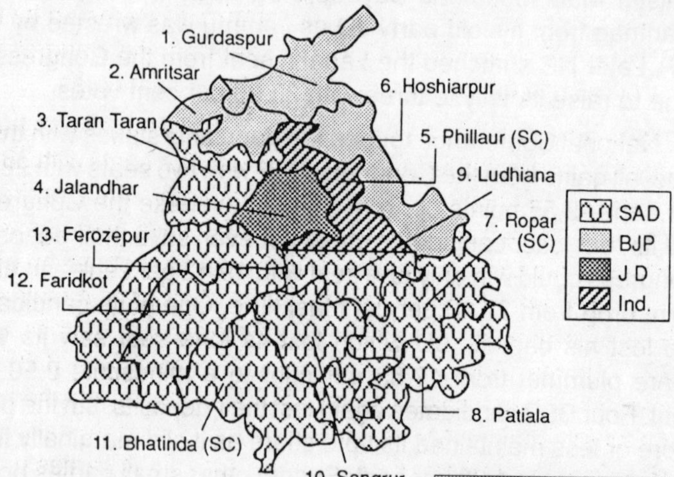

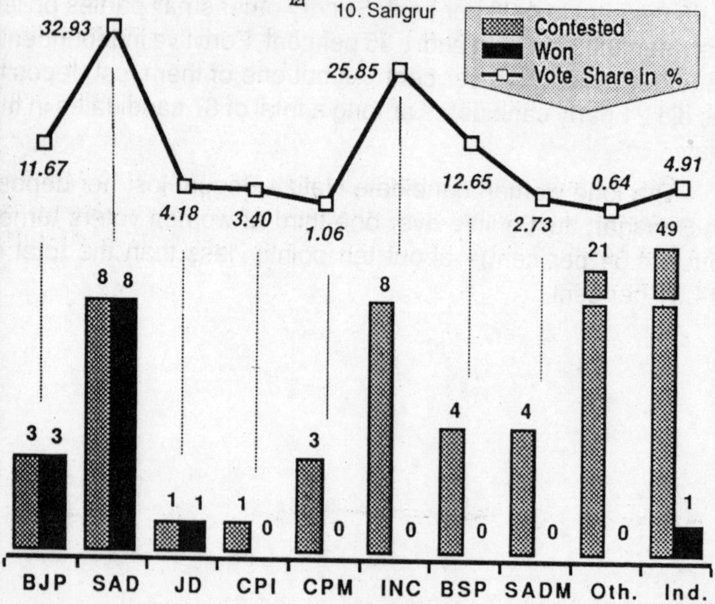

PUNJAB: BJP-SAD Make Hay as Badal Shines

Aided by an over nine per cent swing, the SAD-BJP combine swept the Lok Sabha polls as the alliance government in the state completed one year of rule under farmer friendly Chief Minister Parkash Singh Badal. While the Congress drew a blank in a repeat performance of 1977, former Prime Minister Inder Kumar Gujral gained a seat for JD winning Jalandhar with the backing of SAD and its ally BJP, which shed its reservations on the issue at the last minute.

The alliance won all the eleven seats it contested with a combined vote share of 44.6 per cent with SAD providing 32.93 per cent and BJP 11.67 per cent. While the SAD's own share from eight seats won by it went up by 4.21 points, BJP added 5.19 per cent to its 6.48 per cent share with three wins to reach 11.67 per cent. All the seats won by BJP were gains, two from Congress and one from BSP. SAD too snatched a seat from BSP but conceded the Jalandhar seat to JD for Gujral to finish with the same tally of eight. Prominent SAD winners included Surjit Singh Barnala from Sangrur and Badal's son Sukhbir Singh from Faridkot. They both found a berth in the Vajpayee government, but Prem Singh Lalpura was expelled from the party as he declined to take oath as an MP unless he was made a minister.

Congress which had the highest vote share of 35.10 per cent for a single party last time dropped 9.25 points to finish with 25.85 per cent as it lost two seats to BJP. Its eight losers included former union ministers R.L. Bhatia and Sukhbans Kaur Bhinder, who had to bite the dust in Amritsar and Gurdaspur respectively. Bhinder lost to film star Vinod Khanna of the BJP, who romped home with a margin of 1.06 lakh with the promise of building a bridge on the Ravi that cuts through Gurdaspur constituency.

Gujral's victory on the *Punjabiyat* ticket with a 1.2 lakh margin raised the JD share from 2.66 per cent to 4.18 per cent. BSP too increased its vote share by 3.30 points to finish third in the popularity stakes with 12.65 per cent as against 9.35 per cent last time, but failed to win a seat. CPI share went up by 1.8

PUNJAB

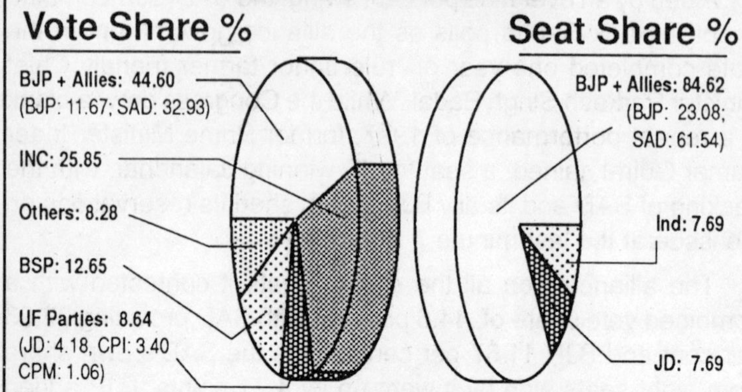

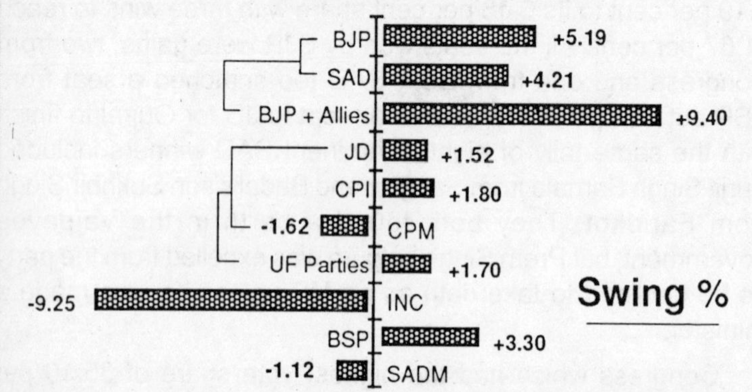

GAINS & LOSSES

Party	Seats Won '96	Seats Won '98	Retained	Gained	Gained From:	Lost	Lost to:	Net +/-
BJP	0	3	-	3	INC-2, BSP-1	-	-	+3
SAD	8	8	7	1	BSP-1	1	JD-1	0
INC	2	0	-	-	-	2	BJP-2	-2
BSP	3	0	-	-	-	3	BJP-1, SAD-1, Ind.-1	-3
JD	0	1	-	1	SAD-1	-	-	+1
Ind.	0	1	-	1	BSP-1	-	-	+1
Total	13	13	7	6		6		

points from 1.60 to 3.40 per cent, while all the three CPM candidates lost their deposits as the party votes dropped from 2.68 per cent to 1.06 per cent. Fifty independents cornered 4.91 per cent votes.

In the three SC constituencies, SAD topped with a 36.16 per cent share ahead of BSP with 28 per cent and CPI with 15.17 per cent. Both failed to get a seat and the third SC seat went to independent Satnam Singh Kainth in Phillaur. Seven independents together polled 17.59 per cent votes in the SC seats.

Of the nine women candidates only one got elected, while seven lost their deposits. The lone winner was Satwinder Kaur of SAD from Ropar. Over 58 per cent women turned out as against 60 per cent of the total electorate.

Electorate	:	2,97,51,400
Turnout	:	60.26%
Votes Polled	:	1,79,27,276
Valid Votes	:	1,76,50,528
invalid Votes	:	2,73,397

RAJASTHAN

Seats: 25	Candidates: 219

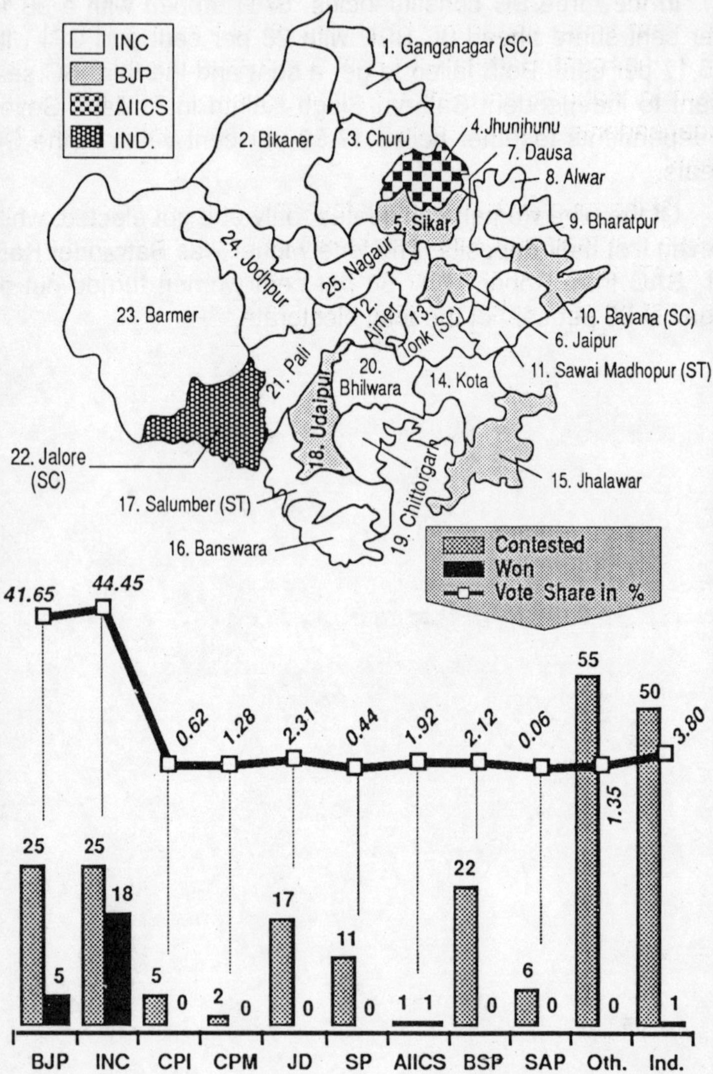

RAJASTHAN: Desert Warms Congress Cockles

An anti-incumbency wave, a near four per cent swing in its favour and the Sonia factor together helped Congress win 18 of the 25 seats in Rajasthan in a repeat of its 1980 performance. But a less than one per cent (0.71 per cent) drop in its vote share cost the ruling BJP seven seats whereas both had emerged with honours even in 1996 with 12 seats each. Former union ministers Buta Singh and Sis Ram Ola won their seats on their own. Denied a ticket by the Congress Buta Singh contested as an independent from Jalore and Ola made a one-man Congress(S) outfit after the return of the breakaway Tiwari faction to the party fold.

With 44.45 per cent votes, 3.94 points more than last time, Congress snatched away nine seats from the BJP, but also lost two to it and the Jalore (SC) seat to Buta Singh to finish with a net gain of six. Prominent Congress winners included former ministers Balram Jakhar from Sikar, Rajesh Pilot from Dausa and Natwar Singh from Bharatpur. But another former minister Girija Vyas lost her Udaipur seat.

Jaswant Singh, who served as finance minister in BJP's short-lived government at the Centre in 1996 lost in Chittorgarh, from where he had won twice in the past. This cost him the FM's chair and he ended up being deputy chairman of the Planning Commission. All the other national parties except Samata and JD marginally increased their modest vote shares, but could not win any seats. BSP share went up from 1.35 per cent to 2.12 per cent as all but one of its 22 candidates lost their deposits. So did 16 of the 17 Janata Dal candidates as the party polled 2.31 per cent votes—0.30 points less than last time. Six Samata, five CPI and a CPM candidate also lost their deposits. All but two of the 50 independents could not save theirs even as they together collected 3.80 per cent votes. In the four SC seats, the Congress polled 37.15 per cent votes, just a little behind BJP with 38.26 per cent. But in three ST constituencies, it polled over 50 per cent votes to finish much ahead of BJP with 36.24 per cent. JD won 9.49 per cent of ST votes and CPI with 2.49 per cent.

RAJASTHAN

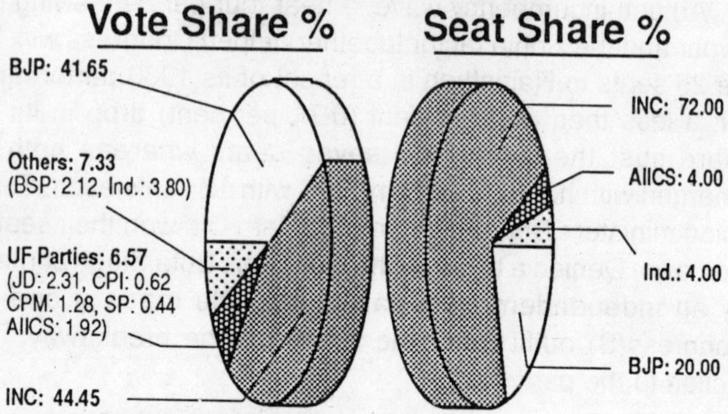

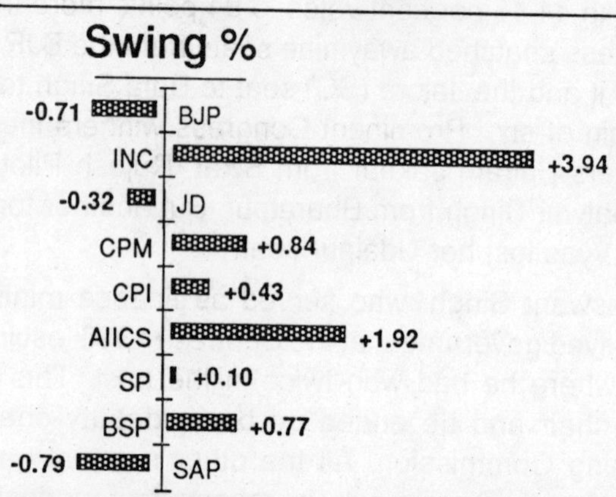

GAINS & LOSSES

Party	Seats Won '96	Seats Won '98	Retained	Gained	Gained From:	Lost	Lost to:	Net +/-
BJP	12	5	3	2	INC-2	9	INC-9	-7
INC	12	18	9	9	BJP-9	3	BJP-2, Ind.-1	+6
AIICT	1	0	-	-	-	1	AIICS-1	-1
AIICS	-	1	-	1	AIICT-1	-	-	+1
Ind.	0	1	-	1	INC-1	-	-	+1
Total	25	25	12	13		13		

Only three of the 20 women candidates succeeded including Vasundhra Raje of the BJP who won from Jhalawar to become minister of state for external affairs in the Vajpayee government. Two Congresswomen won from Ajmer and Sawai Madhopur. Sonia Gandhi's campaign is said to have brought out a record 55.27 per cent of women though their turnout was still lower than the total of 60.26 per cent.

Electorate	:	10,19,82,480
Turnout	:	55.50%
Votes Polled	:	5,65,99,934
Valid Votes	:	5,58,29,573
Invalid Votes	:	7,62,312

UTTAR PRADESH

Seats: 85 | **Candidates: 1037**

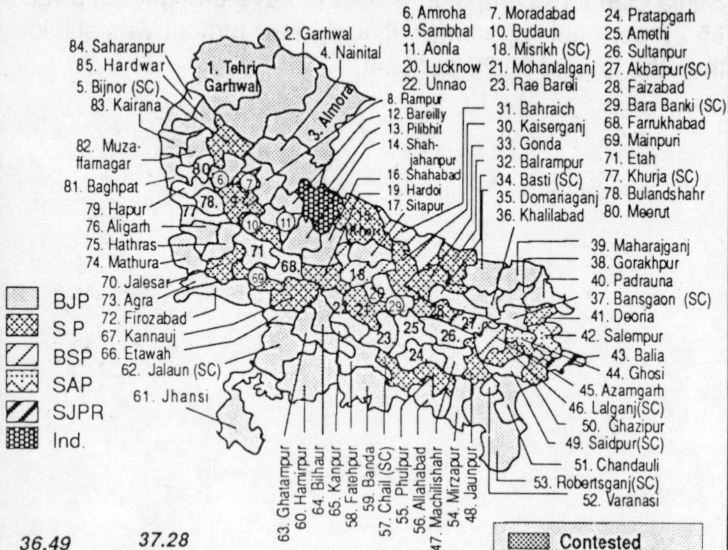

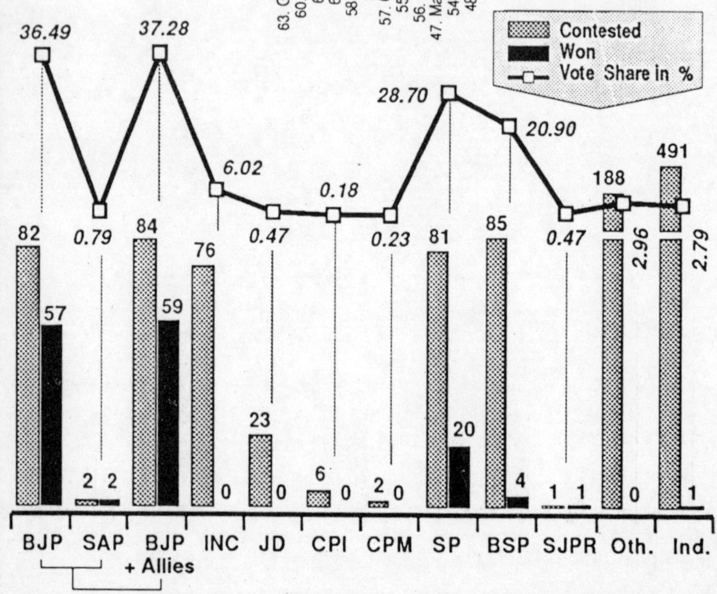

UTTAR PRADESH: Divided Front Helps BJP

Aided by an over three per cent swing and a divided opposition, BJP romped home with 57 of the 85 seats even as the SP gave it a tough fight. But the Congress was completely wiped out as it had been once before in the Janata wave of 1977. Apart from the three-way split in the opposition vote, BJP apparently also gained from Governor Romesh Bhandari's controversial attempt to remove chief minister Kalyan Singh on the eve of polling for the second round as the swing in favour of BJP increased from 1.9 per cent to 4.4 per cent between the two rounds. But even as BJP raised its vote share from 33.44 per cent to 36.49 per cent, it lost 15 seats, 13 to SP alone and two to BSP. However 20 gains, including nine from SP and five from Congress raised its tally by five. Other BJP gains came from BSP(3), Tiwari Congress(2), and JD(1).

BJP winners included Sanjay Singh, who humbled Satish Sharma in Rajiv Gandhi's Amethi constituency, former defence minister K.C. Pant's wife Ila Pant, who pipped Congress heavyweight Narain Dutt Tewari and a little known college teacher, Nakli Singh who floored the BSP supremo Kanshi Ram in Saharanpur. Sompal Singh Shastri chose to challenge Jat leader Ajit Singh in his citadel of Baghpat and won. So did Mukhtar Abbas Naqvi, who defeated Noor Bano of Congress to get a berth in the Vajpayee government as a first timer Muslim MP in saffron colours.

With the Nehru-Gandhi bastion of Amethi breached, the Congress rout was complete in the state as its vote share slipped another 2.12 points to its lowest ever 6.02 per cent. All the five seats it had held in the last House were snatched away by BJP.

The SP alone gave a tough fight to BJP as it increased its vote share by a hefty 7.86 per cent from 20.84 per cent to 28.70per cent to finish with a tally of 20, a net gain of four. Holding on to five seats, it actually snatched 13 seats from BJP and two from BSP only to concede 11 others, nine to BJP and one each to BSP and Samata Party.

BSP, which chose to contest all the 85 seats, marginally increased its vote share from 20.61 per cent to 20.90 per cent,

UTTAR PRADESH

Vote Share % / Seat Share %

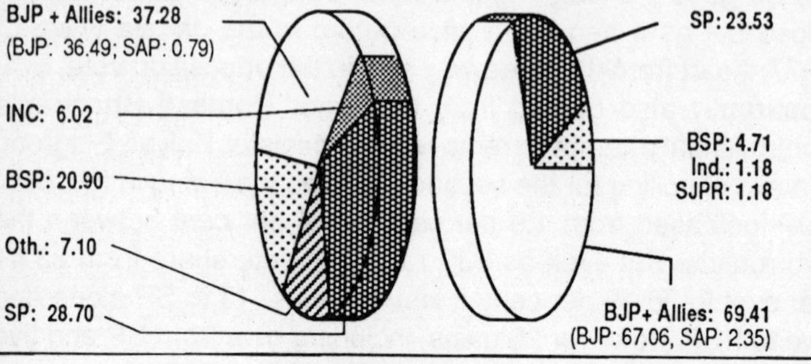

Swing %

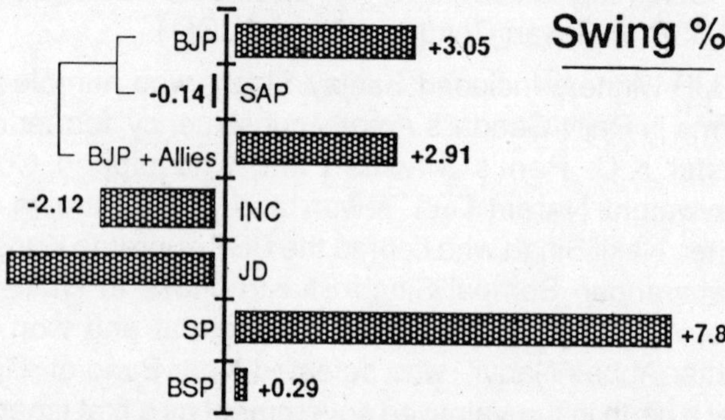

GAINS & LOSSES

Party	Seats Won '96	Seats Won '98	Retain-ed	Gain-ed	Gained From:	Lost	Lost to:	Net +/-
BJP	52	57	37	20	SP-9, INC-5, JD-1; BSP-3, AIICT-2	15	SP-13, BSP-2	+5
SAP	1	2	0	2	SP-1, Ind.-1	1	SJPR-1	+1
INC	5	0	0	0	-	5	BJP-5	-5
SP	16	20	5	15	BJP-13, BSP-2	11	BJP-9, SAP-1, BSP-1	+4
JD	2	0	0	0	-	2	BJP-1, Ind.-1	-2
AIICT	2	0	0	0	-	2	BJP-2	-2
BSP	6	4	1	3	BJP-2, SP-1	5	BJP-3, SP-2	-2
SJPR	0	1	0	1	SAP-1	-	-	+1
Ind.	1	1	0	1	JD-1	1	SAP-1	0
Total	85	85	43	42		42		

but ended up with a net loss of two seats in its tally of four seats. Retaining only one of its old seats, BSP gained two seats from BJP and one from SP, but lost three to the saffron party and two to SP.

None of Janata Dal's 23 candidates could make it as its vote share dropped from 4.26 per cent to a minuscule 0.47 per cent. Both the Samata Party candidates won snatching a seat from SP and another from an independent. But former Prime Minister Chandra Shekhar chose to contest as the lone candidate of his Samajwadi Janata Party instead of Samata and won again for the sixth time since 1977 from Ballia though with a much reduced margin of 29,484. Of the 491 independent candidates only Maneka Gandhi retained her Pilibhit seat with the backing of BJP. She had won it for the JD last time. Besides 2.79 per cent polled by the independents, 188 candidates of smaller parties cornered another 2.95 per cent votes.

Of the 18 SC constituencies, BJP won 11 with 37.1 per cent votes, SP took five with 30.29 per cent and two went to BSP for 25.32 per cent. Congress polled about four per cent votes in 17 SC seats, but without success.

Only nine of the 56 women candidates won with 40 of them even failing to save their deposits. A little over half of the women voters turned out, over 5 per cent less than the state average of 55.50 per cent.

Electorate : 82,97,622
Turnout : 51.29%
Votes Polled : 42,55,606
Valid Votes : 42,17,082
Invalid Votes : 37,603

DELHI

Seats: 7 | Candidates: 132

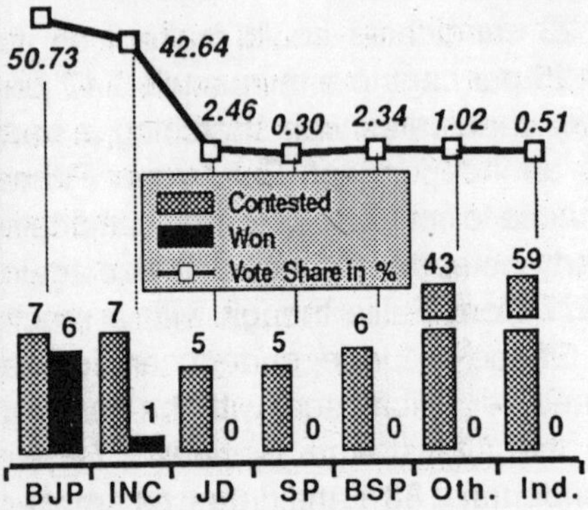

Vote Share %

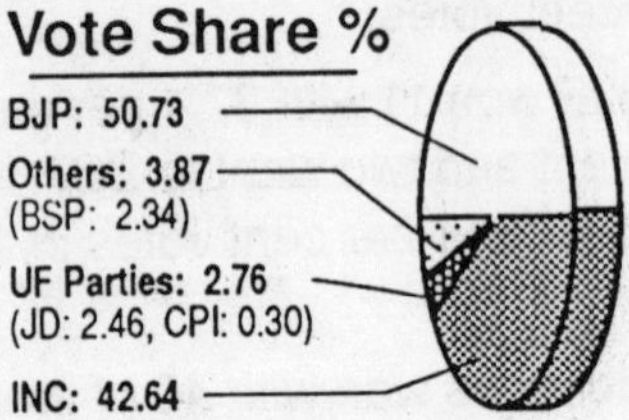

Seat Share %

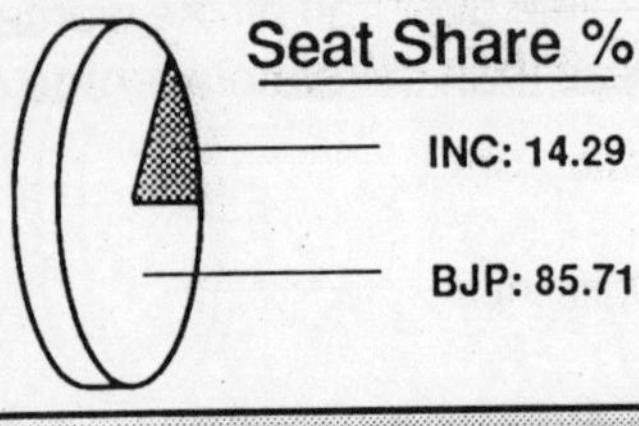

Swing %

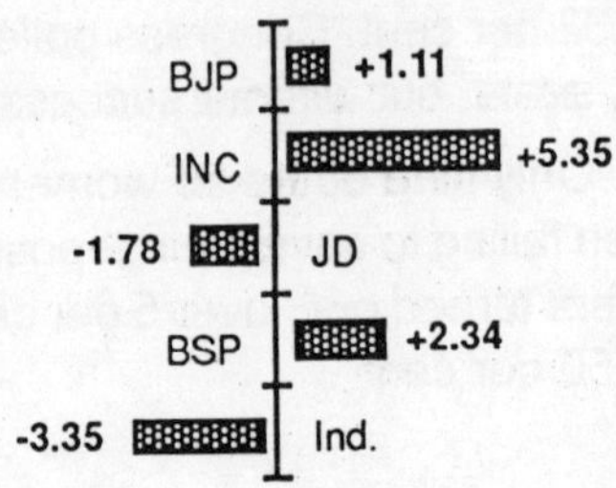

GAINS & LOSSES

Party	Seats Won '96	Seats Won '98	Retained	Gained	Gained From:	Lost	Lost to:	Net +/-
BJP	5	6	5	1	INC-1	0	-	+1
INC	2	1	1	0	-	1	BJP-1	-1
Total	7	7	6	1		1		

DELHI: BJP Keeps Capital on Hold

BJP consolidated its position in the capital winning all but one of the seven seats as it took its vote share above the halfway mark in the city which has seen the pendulum swing between the erstwhile Jan Sangh and the Congress since 1962. Though it polled 50.73 per cent-up 1.11 points from 49.62 per cent last time— the popularity gap between it and Congress was reduced from 12 per cent to 8 per cent as the rival too raised its vote share by 5.35 points from 37.29 per cent to 42.64 per cent.

Holding on to five seats, BJP regained Chandni Chowk from Congress, but could not dislodge Meira Kumar, daughter of former deputy Prime Minister Jagjivan Ram from the Karol Bagh SC constituency. But Congress vote share came down by 8.80 points from 51.44 per cent to 42.64 per cent. While BJP share went up from 37.21 per cent to 50.73 per cent, BSP and JD were way behind with 2.34 per cent and 2.46 per cent votes respectively.

Former Jammu and Kashmir Governor, Jagmohan again won from prestigious New Delhi constituency defeating R.K. Dhawan of the Congress while BJP spokesperson Sushma Swaraj retained her South Delhi seat. Madan Lal Khurana, who had lost his chief ministership because of the *Hawala* case, came again to Parliament from Delhi Sadar. Both Khurana and Swaraj found a place in the Vajpayee cabinet.

Among others, Janata Dal polled 4.24 per cent in five seats and lost deposits in all of them. A CPI candidate collected 0.12 per cent, three Samata nominees an equal number and CPM a little more with 0.27 per cent. With votes ranging between 68 and 12,000 (SP), all but 14 of the 523 candidates, including 378 independents forfeited their deposits.

Only two of the ten women candidates—Swaraj and Kumar—emerged successful and seven of them lost their deposits. At 48.52 per cent women's turnout was slightly less than the total of 51.29 per cent.

Electorate : 5,31,146
Turnout : 53.69%
Votes Polled : 2,85,149
Valid Votes : 2,82,755
Invalid Votes : 2,304

CHANDIGARH

Seats: 1	Candidates: 18

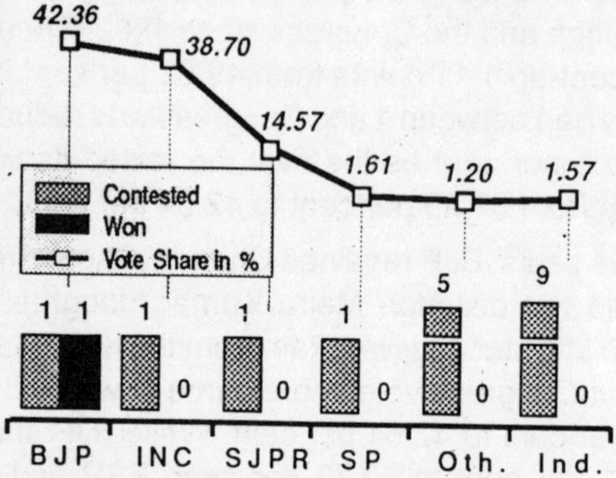

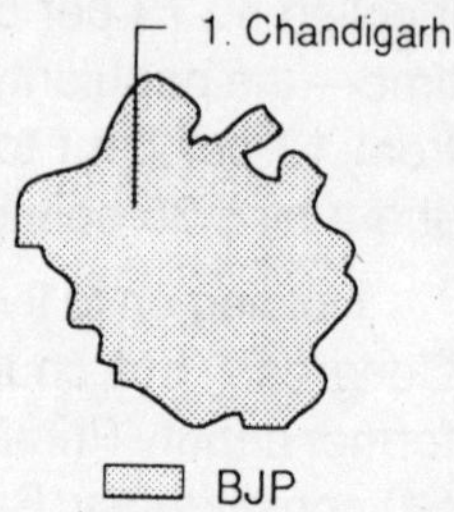

Vote Share %

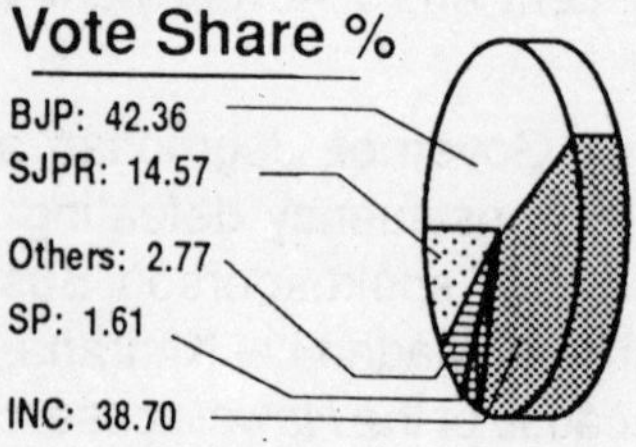

Seat Share %

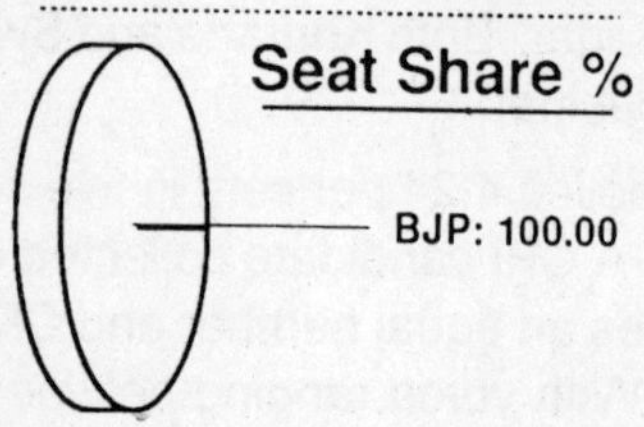

Swing %

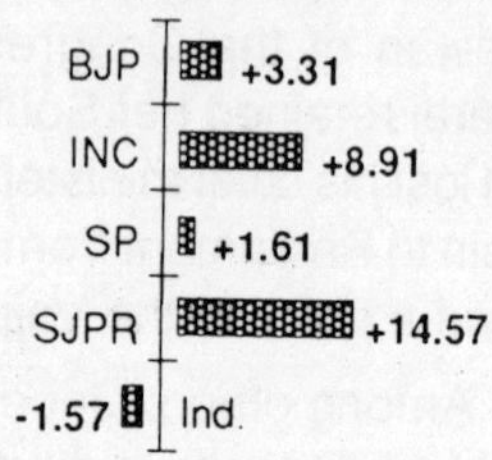

GAINS & LOSSES

Party	Seats Won '96	Seats Won '98	Reta-ined	Gain-ed	Gained From:	Lost	Lost to:	Net +/-
BJP	1	1	1	0	-	0	-	0
Total	1	1	1	0		0		

CHANDIGARH: BJP Stays Put

BJP's Satya Pal Jain won the Union Territory again to record his party's second triumph since 1967, when its forerunner Jan Sangh took the seat, and raise the party vote share by 3.31 points from 39.05 per cent to 42.36 per cent. His Congress rival's determined bid to unseat Jain came a cropper even as he increased the party share to 38.70 per cent, up 8.91 points from 29.79 per cent last time. An SJP(R) candidate playing spoilsport took away 14.57 per cent votes in the 18-cornered contest, but still lost his deposit. So did candidates of six sundry parties and nine independents. Among them SP polled 1.61 per cent, Laloo Yadav's Rashtriya Janata Dal a mere 498 votes (0.22 per cent), and four others between 283 and 1026 votes (0.10-0.36 per cent). The independents polled 1.57 per cent.

The Jan Sangh won the seat in 1967 with 48.7 per cent only to lose it in 1971 with 23.3 per cent. As BJP it gradually raised its share from 5.6 per cent in 1984 to 39.05 per cent in 1996 to score its first win. Congress won the seat four times between 1971 and 1991, losing it to Janata Party (66.1 per cent) in 1977 and Janata Dal (42.1 per cent) in 1989. Congress did its best in 1971 when it polled 66.9 per cent and its worst in 1967 with 23 per cent.

There were only two women candidates. Both lost their deposits. At 52.93 per cent, women's participation was almost equal to the seat average of 53.69 per cent.

7
The South: Saffron Surge

At long last, BJP broke out of its north and central Indian moorings to make a great impact across the Vindhyas thanks to strategic alliances all over the Southern region which sends 132 members to the Lok Sabha. For once BJP and allies took the top slot with 50 seats picked up with 29.65 per cent votes, three-fourths more than the16.92 per cent they together polled last time. This swing of 12.73 points raised their tally of six more than eight times with 44 gains across three states.

The Congress alliance finishing six behind too managed to add four seats to its tally despite an adverse swing of 2.41 per cent, which reduced its regional vote share from 32.37 per cent to 29.96 per cent. With a tally of 37 picked up with 37.01 per cent votes, it was the UF which turned out to be the biggest loser even as various alliance partners together polled much more than the other two formations. Its regional vote share was 7.36 points higher than that of BJP and 7.05 points above the Congress. An anti-establishment vote cost it 46 seats with swings against its various constituents adding up to over seven per cent (-7.49 per cent). TMC topped the list of UF losers with 17. JD came next with 13 and DMK followed with 11. TDP lost four, but when it came to the crunch, its 12 winners too sided with the rival BJP alliance in the crucial confidence vote.

BJP's own success story was made up of 14 gains with a swing of 6.66 per cent. In a region where it had picked up a measly half a dozen seats with 8.78 per cent vote, it now had a score in hand with 15.44 per cent. Losing just one seat to the Congress in Karnataka, it gained in all 15 seats in the region, four in Andhra, eight in Karnataka and three in Tamil Nadu. Five of the BJP gains came from JD in Karnataka where it also dislodged Karnataka Congress leader S Bangarappa, now heading another rebel outfit Karnataka Vikash Party. In Andhra,

SOUTH

Seats: 132	Candidates: 1023

Electorate : **14,99,32,210**
Turnout : **63.96%**
Votes Polled : **9,58,96,004**
Valid Votes : **9,40,53,022**
Invalid Votes : **18,12,476**

Party	Contested	Won	Lost Deposit	1998 Vote %	1996 Vote %	Vote Swing %
BJP + Allies	**151**	**50**	**65**	**29.65**	**16.92**	**+ 12.73**
BJP	82	20	42	15.44	8.78	+ 6.66
ADMK	23	18	0	7.16	2.33	+ 4.83
PMK	5	4	0	1.65	0.58	+ 1.07
MDMK	5	3	0	1.70	1.35	+ 0.35
TRC	1	1	0	0.38	-	+ 0.38
JP	5	1	4	0.30	0.30	0.00
LS	11	3	2	2.58	-	+ 2.58
NTRTDP	5	0	3	0.41	3.56	- 3.15
SAP	14	0	14	0.03	0.02	+ 0.01
INC + Allies	**129**	**44**	**37**	**29.96**	**32.37**	**- 2.41**
INC	125	41	36	28.79	31.15	- 2.36
KCM	1	1	0	0.38	0.42	- 0.04
MUL	3	2	1	0.79	0.80	- 0.01
UF Parties	**146**	**37**	**24**	**37.01**	**44.50**	**- 7.49**
J D	32	4	10	5.79	8.31	- 2.52
CPI	10	5	1	2.86	2.86	0.00
CPM	16	6	3	4.49	4.94	- 0.45
KEC	1	0	0	0.35	0.35	0.00
RSP	1	1	0	0.42	0.39	+ 0.03
ICS	3	0	1	0.44	0.37	+ 0.07
LDF-Ind.	2	0	0	0.63	0.37	+ 0.26
DMK	18	6	0	5.64	7.87	- 2.23
TMC	20	3	0	5.50	8.03	- 2.53
TDP	35	12	1	10.84	10.87	- 0.03
S P	8	0	8	0.05	0.14	- 0.09
BSP	**39**	**0**	**39**	**0.28**	**0.07**	**+ 0.21**
Others	**558**	**1**	**554**	**3.10**	**6.14**	**- 3.04**

it wrested four from the Congress and in Tamil Nadu it took two from the TMC and one from the DMK.

BJP allies too gained with AIADMK making the most of it. Jayalalitha's party, which was completely wiped out in 1996, came back this time with 18 victories, picking up ten from the TMC and eight from DMK in Tamil Nadu for a regional vote share of 7.16 per cent indicating a swing of 4.83 per cent in her favour. Four other partners of Jayalalitha, namely PMK(4), MDMK(3), Rajiv Congress and Janata Party (one each), brought in nine more gains from the state while Hegde's Lok Shakti added three in Karnataka.

But unlike BJP, which practically gained all the way, Congress picked up 20 new seats, but lost 16 others to finish with a net gain of four despite an adverse swing of 2.36 points, which reduced its vote share from 31.15 per cent to 28.79 per cent. Half the 20 Congress gains came from Andhra, nine from TDP and one from CPM. Seven more came from Karnataka, six from JD and one from BJP. Rest of the other three came from Kerala with JD, CPI and an independent contributing one each. Of its 16 losses, ten again came from Andhra with seven going to TDP, two to BJP and one to JD. Three more were lost in Karnataka, two to BJP and one to Lok Shakti. CPI and CPM wrested one each in Kerala and DMK snatched the Pondicherry seat. Muslim League retained its two seats in Kerala as did Kerala Congress (Mani) its only seat in the state to complete the alliance tally of 44 in the south.

Among the UF partners, the biggest loser was TMC, whose tally was reduced from 20 to three in Tamil Nadu. JD came next with 14 losses, 13 of them in Karnataka alone, where it conceded six to Congress, five to BJP and two to Lok Shakti. It lost another seat to Congress in Kerala, but gained one from it in Andhra to finish with a net loss of 13 with an adverse swing of 2.53 points reducing its regional share to 5.50 per cent from 8.03 per cent. DMK lost a dozen seats in Tamil Nadu, but wrested Pondicherry from Congress to limit its losses to 11 in the face of an adverse regional swing of 2.23 per cent. TDP lost four in Andhra and CPI one in Tamil Nadu. CPM retained its tally of six even as it lost 0.46 per cent votes to end up with 4.49 per cent votes. Polling 10.84 per cent and 2.86 per cent TDP and CPI more or less retained their slices in the vote pie.

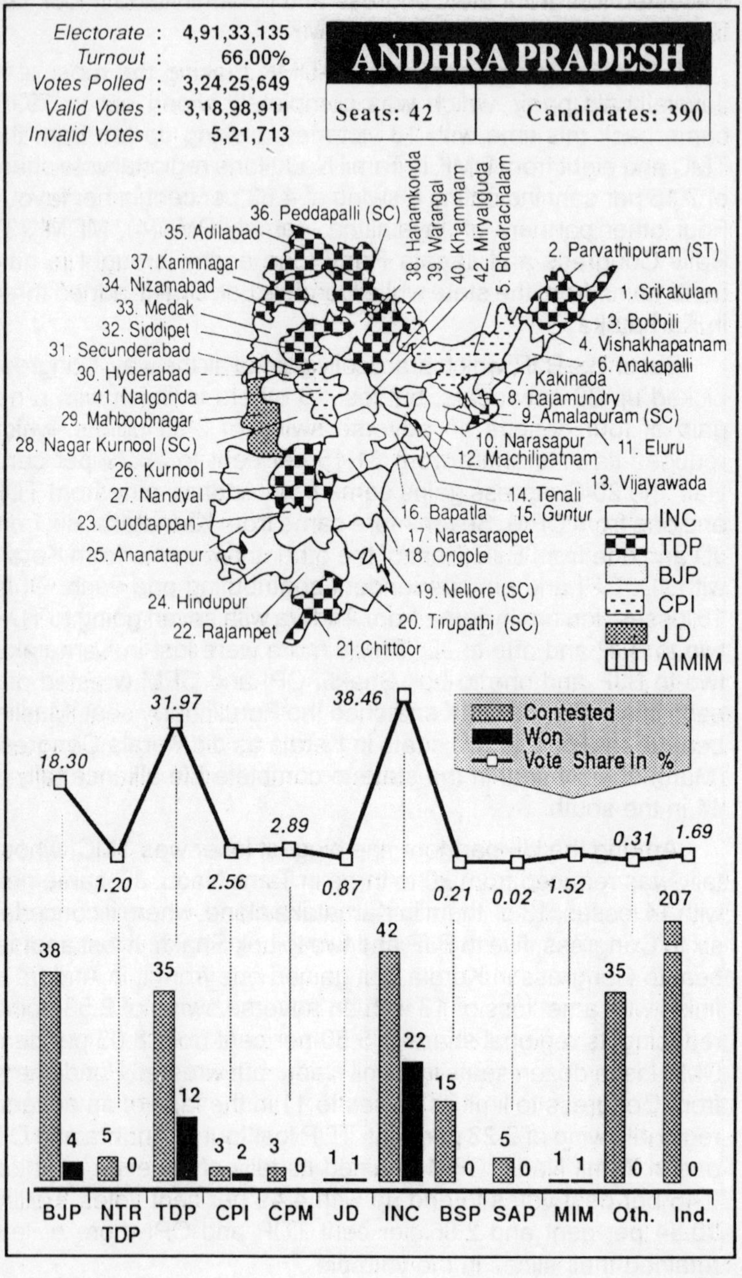
Electorate : 4,91,33,135
Turnout : 66.00%
Votes Polled : 3,24,25,649
Valid Votes : 3,18,98,911
Invalid Votes : 5,21,713
ANDHRA PRADESH
Seats: 42
Candidates: 390
36. Peddapalli (SC)
35. Adilabad
37. Karimnagar
34. Nizamabad
33. Medak
32. Siddipet
31. Secunderabad
30. Hyderabad
41. Nalgonda
29. Mahboobnagar
28. Nagar Kurnool (SC)
26. Kurnool
27. Nandyal
23. Cuddappah
25. Ananatapur
24. Hindupur
22. Rajampet
21.Chittoor
38. Hanamkonda
39. Warangal
40. Khammam
42. Miryalguda
5. Bhadrachalam
2. Parvathipuram (ST)
1. Srikakulam
3. Bobbili
4. Vishakhapatnam
6. Anakapalli
7. Kakinada
8. Rajamundry
9. Amalapuram (SC)
10. Narasapur
11. Eluru
12. Machilipatnam
13. Vijayawada
14. Tenali
15. Guntur
16. Bapatla
17. Narasaraopet
18. Ongole
19. Nellore (SC)
20. Tirupathi (SC)
INC
TDP
BJP
CPI
J D
AIMIM
Contested
Won
Vote Share in %
18.30
1.20
31.97
2.56
2.89
0.87
38.46
0.21
0.02
1.52
0.31
1.69
38
4
5
0
35
12
3
2
3
0
1
1
42
22
15
0
5
0
1
1
35
0
207
0
BJP
NTR TDP
TDP
CPI
CPM
JD
INC
BSP
SAP
MIM
Oth.
Ind.

ANDHRA PRADESH : BJP Gains a Foothold

Thanks to a strategic alliance with the TDP led by N.T Rama Rao's widow Lakshmi Parvathi and a massive 12.65 per cent swing in its favour, BJP made major inroads in Andhra winning four seats with a record 18.30 per cent of the popular vote.

In raising its vote share more than threefold, BJP snatched two seats each from the Congress and chief minister Chandrababu Naidu's rival TDP. But in propelling BJP forward Parvathi's party not only again came a cropper, but also saw its vote share slashed to about a ninth of the 10.66 per cent it won in 1996. Apparently a bulk of the Parvathi vote went to BJP and there was little erosion in the vote banks of either the Congress or TDP. Though the latter did drop four seats with a marginal 0.59 per cent cut in its share, Congress maintained its tally of 22 as its vote too came down only a notch—1.20 points to be exact—from 39.66 per cent to 38.46 per cent .

While Congress did finish with honours even, it also lost ten seats, seven to TDP, two to BJP and one to JD. But it snatched nine from TDP and one from CPM to make up for the losses. Naidu's TDP lost 11, nine to Congress and two to BJP as its vote share slipped from 32.59 per cent to 31.97 per cent. But it wrested back seven from the Congress, while keeping five of its own, to limit its net loss to four. JD too gained a seat from the Congress with its 0.87 per cent vote as the UF information and broadcasting minister S. Jaipal Reddy defeated the PCC president S. Mallikarjun in a triangular contest.

Of the two leftist parties, CPI retained its two seats with just a marginal 0.17 per cent rise in its vote share from 2.39 per cent to 2.56 per cent. But CPM lost its only seat to the Congress as its votes declined by a minuscule 0.02 points to 2.89 per cent. The local All India Majlis-e-Ittehadul Muslimeen retained its only seat with a 1.52 per cent vote share. Over 200 independents polled 1.69 per cent, but all in vain.

In coastal Andhra, which provides 19 seats, Congress picked up four more to take its tally to 12, BJP opened its score with wins in Rajahmundry and Kakinada, while TDP lost six seats. But in Telengana region with 15 seats, Congress lost four seats,

ANDHRA PRADESH

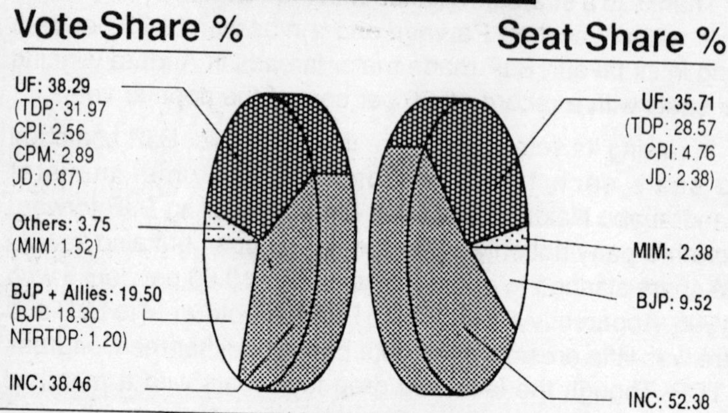

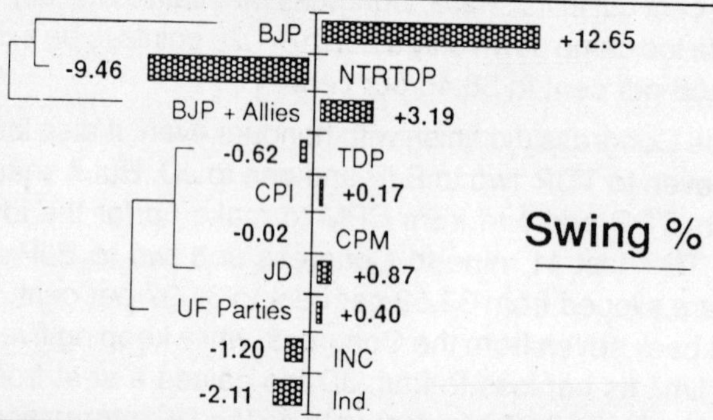

GAINS & LOSSES

Party	Seats Won '96	Seats Won '98	Retained	Gained	Gained From	Lost	Lost to	Net +/-
BJP	0	4	-	4	TDP-2, INC-2	-	-	+4
TDP	16	12	5	7	INC-7	11	INC-9, BJP-2	-4
CPI	2	2	2	-	-	-	-	0
CPM	1	0	-	-	-	1	INC-1	-1
JD	0	1	-	1	INC-1	-	-	+1
INC	22	22	12	10	TDP-9, CPM-1	10	TDP-7, BJP2, JD-1	0
MIM	1	1	1	-	-	-	-	0
Total	42	42	20	22		22		

two each to TDP and BJP, while in Rayalseema with eight seats, Congress and TDP maintained their respective positions.

Of the six SC seats, Congress and TDP won three with 37.39 per cent and 32.79 per cent votes respectively. At 38.03 per cent Congress share was higher than either CPI or TDP who shared the two ST seats with 20.65 per cent and 23.67 per cent with seven independents and others taking away 17.63 per cent votes.

Only two of the 18 women, one each from the Congress and TDP , won as 12 others lost their deposits. At 62.62 per cent women's turn out was over three points lower than the state average of 66 per cent.

Prominent winners included three former Congress chief ministers, K. Vijay Bhaskar Reddy from Kurnool, N. Janardan Reddy from Bapatla and N. Bhaskar Rao from Khammam. Losers included union ministers B.B. Ramaiah from Eluru and U. Venkateswarulu from Bapatla and P.V. Rajeshwara Rao, a son of former Prime Minister P.V. Narasimha Rao.

Electorate : 3,30,98,338
Turnout : 64.92%
Votes Polled : 2,14,89,089
Valid Votes : 2,11,02,670
Invalid Votes : 3,71,878

KARNATAKA

Seats: 28 | Candidates: 200

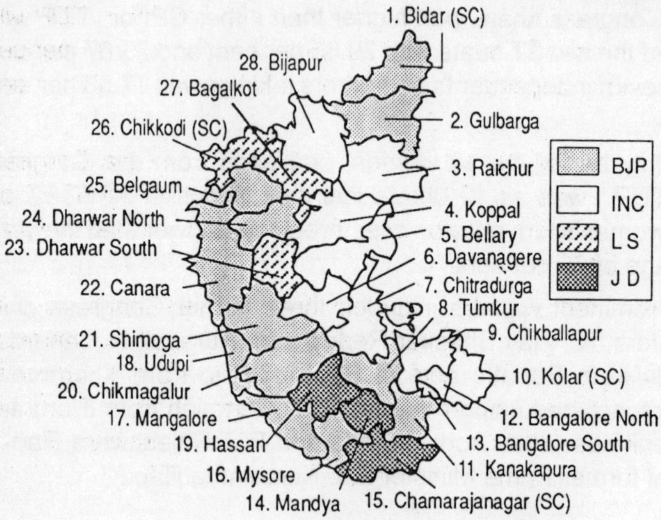

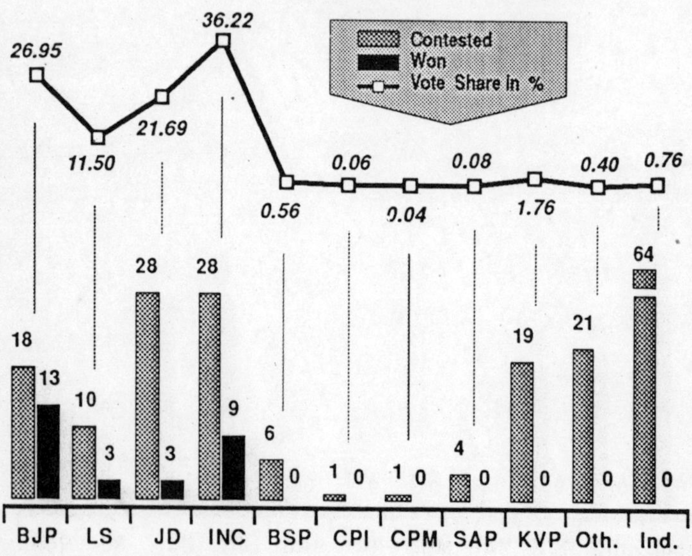

KARNATAKA: BJP Rides High on Lok Shakti

An alliance with former chief minister Rama Krishna Hegde's Lok Shakti, projection of Vajpayee as the able Prime Minister to head a stable government and the anti-incumbency vote against the Janata Dal government of J.H. Patel brought rich dividends to the BJP. Unlike other southern states where it rode piggyback on the allies, BJP itself took the lion's share of 13 seats with 26.95 per cent votes, up 2.1 points over 1996 when it could win only six seats with 24.85 per cent. Ally Lok Shakti itself could win only three of the ten seats it contested, but it probably tilted the balance in favour of BJP as it polled 11.50 per cent votes. Together the combine cornered 16 seats with a joint vote share of 38.45 per cent.

While BJP's own eight gains came from JD (5), Congress (2) and Karnataka Congress (1) of former chief minister Bangarappa, Lok Shakti gained two from JD and one from Congress. BJP also lost a seat to Congress. Bangarappa, who had returned to the Congress only to leave again on poll eve himself lost in his own backyard of Shimoga to Ayanur Manjunath of BJP by a hefty 1.59 lakh votes. Except him, all the other 18 candidates of his newly floated Karnataka Vikash Party lost their security deposits.

A united Congress, no longer saddled with the burden of incumbency and spurred by the Sonia factor also put up a creditable performance by raising its tally from five to nine thanks to a 5.93 per cent swing in its favour. Raising its share from 30.29 per cent to 36.22 per cent, the highest in the state for a single party, Congress wrested six seats from JD and one from BJP. But it also lost two to BJP and one to Lok Shakti to finish with a net gain of four.

JD was the worst loser in dropping 13 of the 16 seats it held in 1996. Yielding six to Congress, five to BJP and two to Lok Shakti, it was left hanging on to only three as a massive 13.22 per cent swing reduced its vote share from 34.91 per cent to 21.69 per cent. Its left partners, CPI and CPM could not win a seat again as they both suffered a 0.66 point erosion in their combined vote share of 0.76 per cent.

KARNATAKA

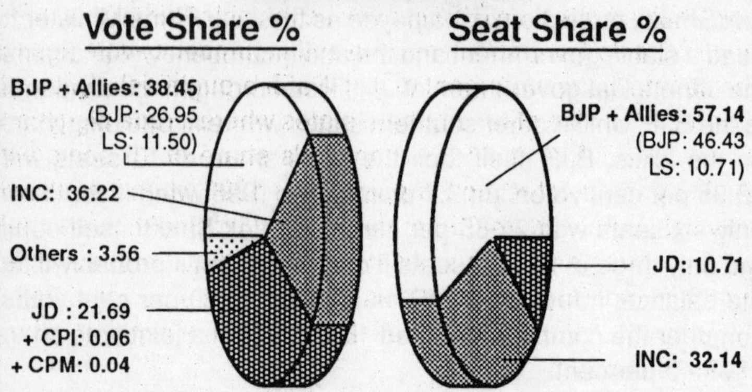

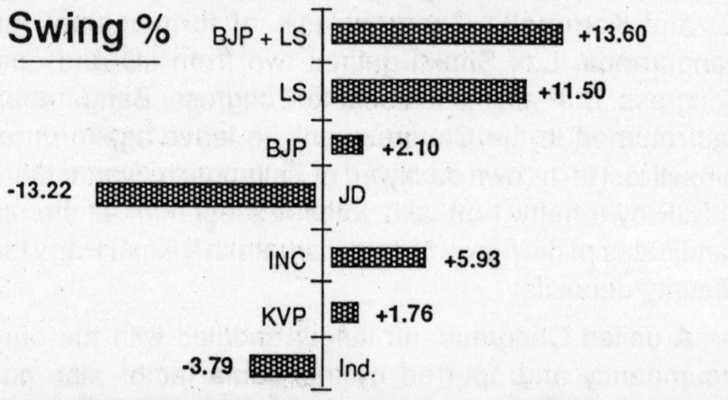

GAINS & LOSSES

Party	Seats Won '96	Seats Won '98	Reta-ined	Gain-ed	Gained From:	Lost	Lost to:	Net +/-
BJP	6	13	5	8	INC-2, JD-5, KCP-1	1	INC-1	+7
LS	0	3	-	3	INC-1, JD-2	-	-	+3
INC	5	9	2	7	BJP-1, JD-6	3	BJP-2, LS-1	+4
JD	16	3	3	0	-	13	BJP-5, INC-6, LS-2	-13
KCP	1	0	0	-	-	1	BJP-1	-1
Total	28	28	10	18		18		

The four SC seats were shared equally by the BJP, Lok Shakti, Congress and JD with 19.54 per cent, 15.66 per cent, 32.54 per cent, and 27.98 per cent respectively. Twenty other candidates, including 12 independents shared the remaining 4.28 per cent of the reserved pie. None of the ten women candidates could make it with seven unable to save their deposits. Losers included former minister Margaret Alva in Kanara. At 60.96 per cent women's turn out was about four points lower than the state average of 64.92 per cent.

Former Prime Minister H.D. Deve Gowda who had vowed to "rise from the ashes" after the Congress pulled the rug from under him, barely managed to win by 31,654 votes from native Hassan. But son H.D. Kumaraswamy lost in Kanakpura to BJP's M. Srinivas, a three-time MLA who was a minister in the Hegde government in 1983. Film star Ambareesh defeated G Madegowda of the Congress with 1.8 lakh votes to win Mandya for JD.

Electorate : 2,11,88,712
Turnout : 70.67%
Votes Polled : 1,49,73,020
Valid Votes : 1,48,61,825
Invalid Votes : 1,08,833

KERALA

Seats: 20	Candidates: 120

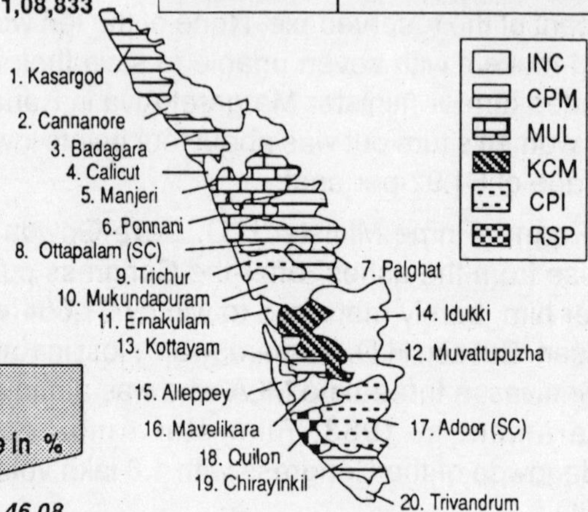

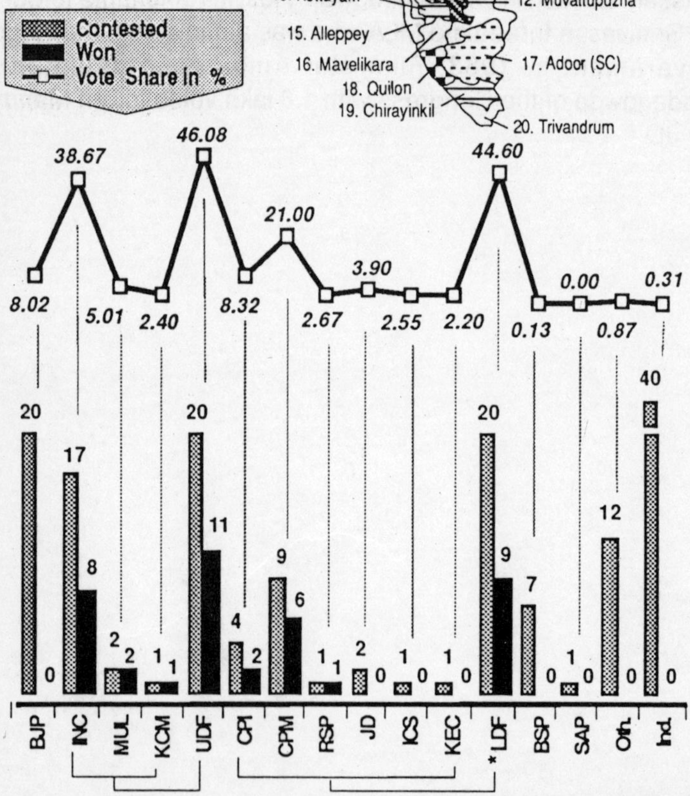

* including two LDF backed independents who polled 3.96% of the votes.

KERALA: Honours Even

The Congress-led United Democratic Front (UDF) recovered a bit of the lost ground in Kerala, where it had gone out of power in the simultaneous assembly polls in 1996, winning 11 of the 20 seats, just one more than last time, even as it cornered 46.08 per cent—a swing of just 0.30 points.

Itself polling 38.67 per cent votes, just 0.66 points more than last, Congress retained five seats, wrested a seat each from CPI, JD and an independent in Ernakulam, but lost one apiece to the two leftist parties to finish with a net gain of one. Allies Muslim League and Kerala Congress retained their two and one seats with 5.01 per cent and 2.40 per cent votes respectively.

The rival Left Democratic Front, polling about the same as last time at 38.09 per cent, retained its share of nine with CPM and CPI gaining a seat each from Congress, but CPI and JD also losing a seat each to it. CPM won six seats for the front with 21 per cent—0.16 points less—CPI brought in two with 8.32 per cent—up 0.10 points—and RSP one with 2.67 per cent. JD and Kerala Congress won no seats but added 3.90 per cent—down 0.50 points—and 2.20 per cent to its vote bank.

BJP not only failed to open its account, but all its 20 candidates lost their deposits even as it raised its vote share to 8.02 per cent up 2.41 points from 5.61 per cent it polled in 1996. The leftist parties won one each of the two SC seats with 23.73 per cent votes for the CPI and 23.94 per cent for CPM. Congress polled 45.02 per cent in the two seats, but could not win either. BJP which too contested both the seats nevertheless polled about seven per cent votes.

Of the ten women candidates in fray, four from BJP, three from LDF, one Congress and two independents, only one, A.K. Premajam of CPM won from Badagara. Six others lost their deposits. At 70.71 per cent women's participation was a wee bit higher than the state average of 70.67 per cent.

Former chief minister K. Karunakaran, who had lost in Thrissur last time, won from Thiruvananthapuram, but his son K Muraleedharan defeated in Kozhikode in 1996, lost in his father's

KERALA

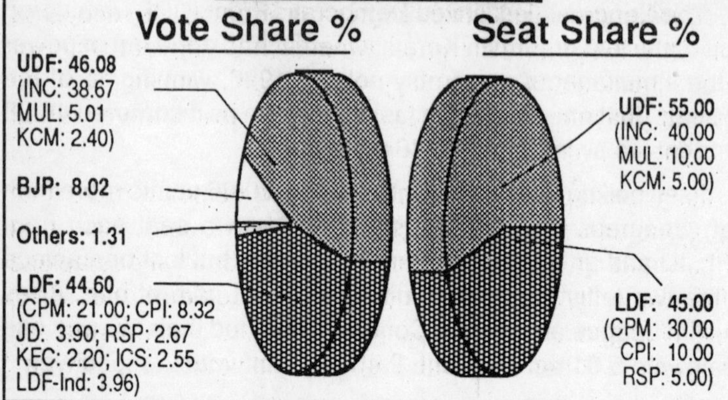

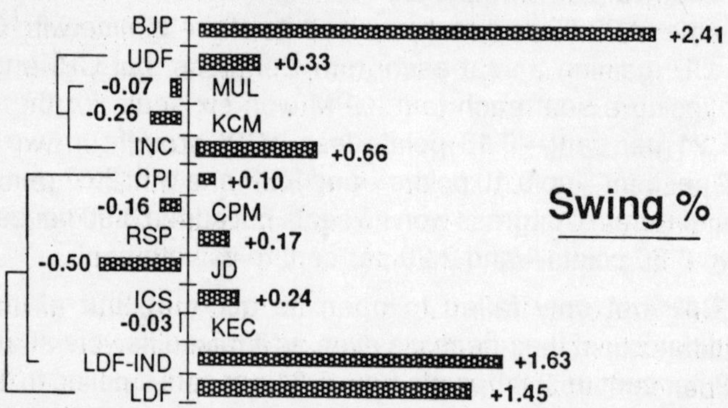

GAINS & LOSSES

Party	Seats Won '96	'98	Reta-ined	Gain-ed	Gained From:	Lost	Lost to:	Net + / -
INC	7	8	5	3	JD-1; IND-1; CPI-1	2	CPM-1; CPI-1	+1
MUL	2	2	2	-	-	-	-	0
KCM	1	1	1	-	-	-	-	0
CPM	5	6	5	1	INC-1	-	-	+1
CPI	2	2	1	1	INC-1	1	INC-1	0
JD	1	0	-	-	-	1	INC-1	-1
RSP	1	1	1	-	-	-	-	0
IND	1	0	-	-	-	1	INC-1	-1
Total	20	20	15	5		5		

old constituency. Union labour minister M.P. Veerendra Kumar lost to P. Shankaran of the Congress in Kozhikode.

TAMIL NADU

Electorate	:	4,55,77,788
Turnout	:	57.95%
Votes Polled	:	2,64,11,498
Valid Votes	:	2,56,03,798
Invalid Votes	:	7,99,153

Seats: 39 | **Candidates: 296**

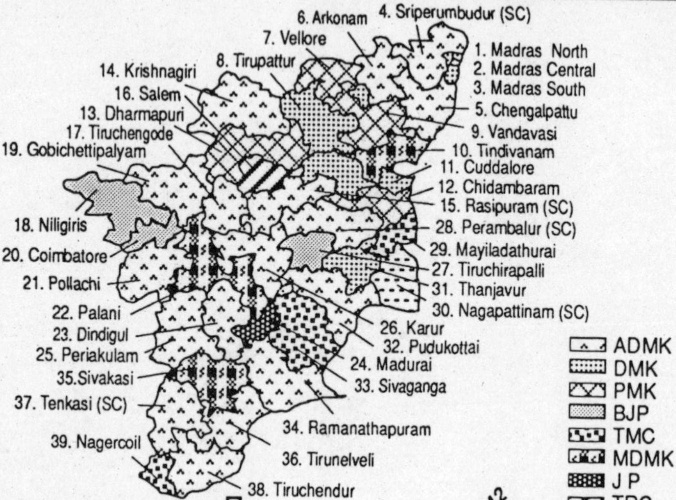

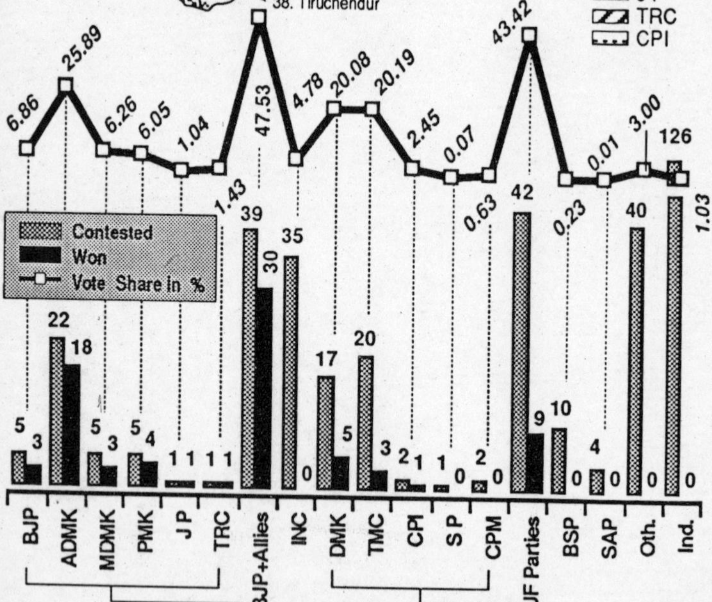

TAMIL NADU: Amma Rocks the Boat

A strategic alliance with Jayalalitha's AIADMK and its smaller partners and a series of blasts that ripped through Coimbatore hours before BJP president Lal Krishna Advani was due to address a poll eve rally rocked the DMK-TMC boat in Tamil Nadu. In the event helped by a massive 29.41 per cent swing, the AIADMK-BJP combine cornered 30 of the 39 seats with close to half the popular vote—47.53 per cent to be precise. As confounded psephologists, few of whom could read the writing on the wall, wondered whom had the alliance helped more—BJP or AIADMK. The result pitchforked Jayalalitha, *Puratchi Thalaivi* or revolutionary leader to her supporters, into the position of kingmaker in distant New Delhi.

AIADMK took the largest slice of the alliance pie winning 18 seats, ten wrested from the TMC and eight from DMK, with 25.89 per cent votes—a more than three-fold rise in its 7.84 per cent share in 1996. Nine other seats went to Jayalalitha' allies Pattali Makkal Katchi (PMK) 4, Marumalarchi Dravida Munnetra Kazhagam (MDMK) 3, Tamizhaga Rajiv Congress (TRC) and Janata Party, one each. BJP opened its account in the state with three of its five candidates winning with 6.86 per cent of the popular vote—a swing of 3.93 points over its 2.93 per cent share last time. While BJP took two seats from TMC and one from DMK, PMK (6.05 per cent) wrested two each from them, and MDMK (6.26 per cent) gained one each from DMK, TMC and CPI. Both TRC (1.43 per cent) and Subramaniam Swamy's Janata (1.04 per cent) took a seat each from TMC.

The rival DMK-TMC combine which had swept the poll last time with CPI to capture all the 39 seats with a record 55.10 per cent vote lost 30 seats—all to BJP and allies—as it ran into an adverse swing of 12.34 per cent. DMK itself lost 12 seats, eight to AIADMK, two to PMK and one each to BJP and MDMK as its own vote share fell by 5.69 points from 25.77 per cent to 20.08 per cent. Partner TMC's losses were even greater as it conceded 17 of its 20 seats with a drop of 6.81 points from its previous vote share of 27per cent. This time it polled only 20.19 per cent. CPI too lost one of its two seats even as it marginally increased its vote share from 2.33 per cent to 2.45 per cent. CPM which

TAMIL NADU

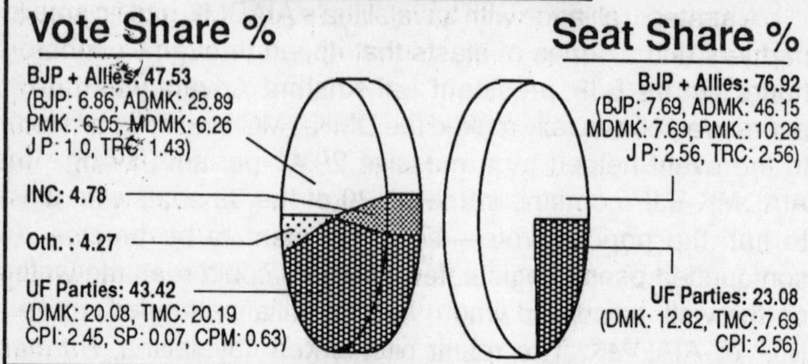

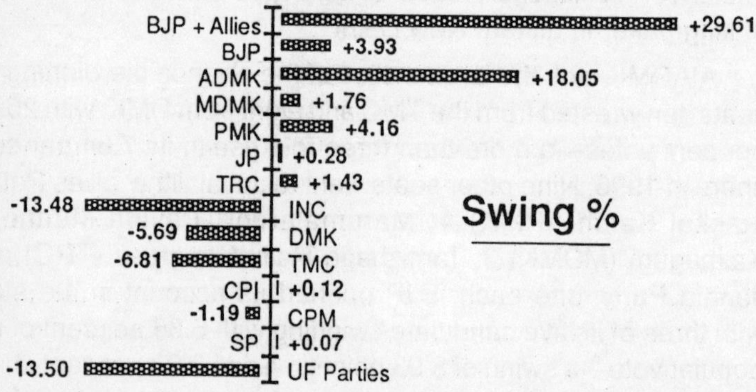

GAINS & LOSSES

Party	Seats Won '96	Seats Won '98	Retain-ed	Gain-ed	Gained From:	Lost	Lost To:	Net +/-
BJP	0	3	0	3	TMC-2, DMK-1	-	-	+3
ADMK	0	18	0	18	TMC-10, DMK-18	-	-	+18
MDMK	0	3	0	3	TMC-1, DMK-1, CPI-1	-	-	+3
PMK	0	4	0	4	TMC-2, DMK-2	-	-	+4
JP	0	1	0	1	TMC-1	-	-	+1
TRC	0	1	0	1	TMC-1	-	-	+1
DMK	17	5	5	0	-	12	ADMK-8, PMK-2 MDMK-1, BJP-1	-12
TMC	20	3	3	0	-	17	ADMK-10, TRC-1 MDMK-1, JP-1 PMK-2, BJP-2	-17
CPI	2	1	1	0	-	1	MDMK-1	-1
Total	39	39	9	30		30		

had fielded two candidates on its own in opposition to the alliance lost deposit in one as its vote share fell from 1.82 per cent to 0.63 per cent.

The Congress, which had helped one or the other of the rival Kazhagams to come to power in the state until the 1996 split over then Prime Minister P.V. Narasimha Rao's decision to continue ties with a tainted Jayalalitha, not only came a cropper again, but also saw its vote share slashed by 13.48 points—from 18.26 per cent to a mere 4.78 per cent as all its 35 candidates lost their deposits.

Five of the seven SC seats were won by AIADMK with 40.92 per cent votes. Two other were shared by PMK and CPI with seven per cent and 8.58 per cent of the SC votes. The Congress share in the reserved seats was 5.14 per cent, while DMK took away 14.42 per cent and ally TMC 20.14 per cent.

Only one of the 13 women candidates, Dr V. Saroja of the AIADMK won in Rasipuram even as eleven others lost their deposits. At 55.19 per cent women's participation was not much lower than the state average of 57.95 per cent.

Former Union finance minister P. Chidambaram won his Sivaganga seat again but with a reduced margin of 59,141, but three of his TMC ministerial colleagues, M. Arunachalam, S.R. Balasubramaniam and Dhanashkodi Adithyan lost. Two DMK ministers Murasoli Maran and T.R. Balu also retained their seats. A little known knitwear exporter C.P. Radhakrishnan of BJP won Coimbatore with the highest margin of 1.44 lakh. Tamil filmstar R. Ramarajan of AIADMK vanquished four time MP, R.D Athithan of TMC in the temple town of Tiruchendur.

Electorate : 2,32,013
Turnout : 63.66%
Votes Polled : 1,47,698
Valid Votes : 1,45,836
Invalid Votes : 1,850

ANDAMAN & NICOBAR ISLANDS

Seats: 1	Candidates: 6

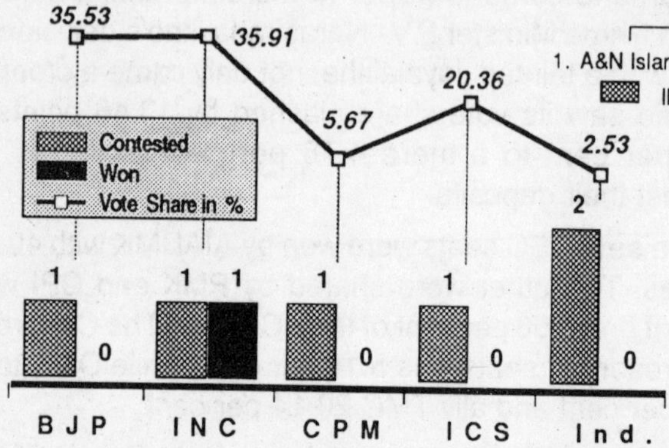

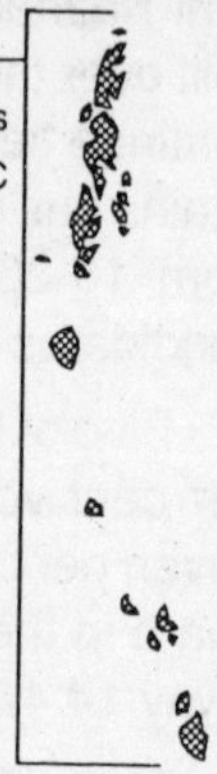

Vote Share %

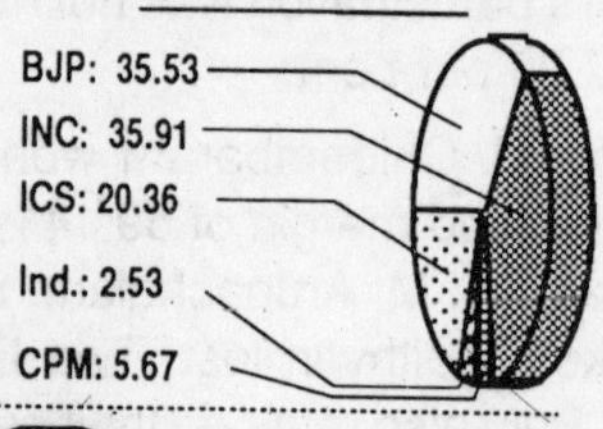

Seat Share %

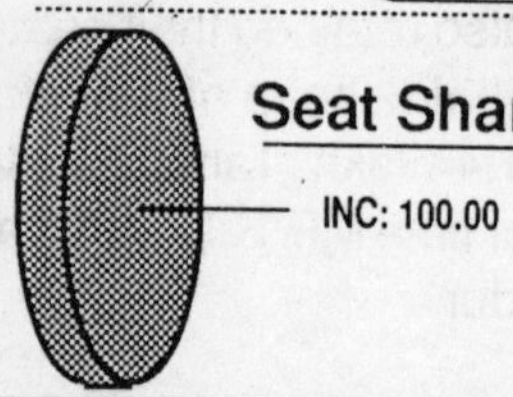

Swing %

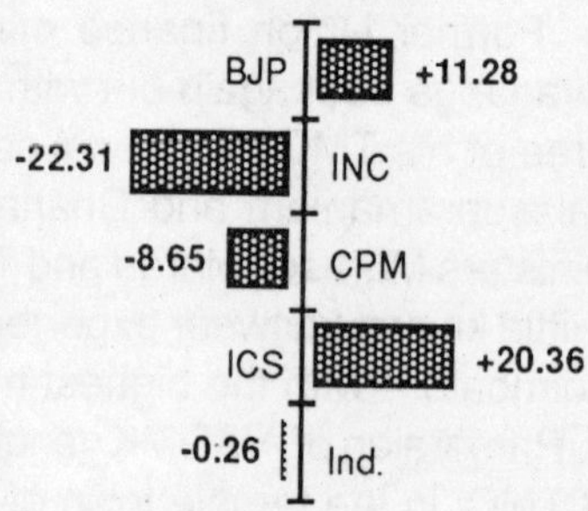

GAINS & LOSSES

Party	Seats Won '96	Seats Won '98	Reta-ined	Gain-ed	Gained From:	Lost	Lost to:	Net + / -
INC	1	1	1	0	-	0	-	0
Total	**1**	**1**	**1**	**0**		**0**		**0**

ANDAMAN & NICOBAR ISLANDS:
Congress Goes On and On

Manoranjan Bhakta kept the Congress flag flying in the 3,000 picturesque islands as he won the lone seat for the sixth time in a row to record the party's ninth straight win since the first Lok Sabha poll in 1967. But the going was tough this time as his BJP rival reduced the margin to just 544 votes. As the Congress share went plunging to its lowest ever of 35.91 per cent—a massive 22.31 points drop from 58.22 per cent last time, BJP almost caught up with 35.53 per cent. The saffron party which had polled 4.85 per cent in its first foray in 1991 raised it to 24.25 per cent last time and added another 11.28 per cent now. Congress did its best in 1971 when K.R Ganesh polled 61.5 per cent and its previous worst came in 1989 when it polled 47.2 per cent.

A candidate of Indian Congress (Socialist) finished third with 20.36 per cent votes. CPM slipped to the fourth position with only 5.67 per cent votes and to add insult to injury lost its deposit too. CPM which had polled its highest ever of 44.14 per cent in 1991 lost a massive 30 per cent in 1996 to poll 14.32 per cent. It suffered a further erosion of 8.65 points this time. Two independents also failed to save their deposits as they together collected 2.53 per cent votes.

Electorate	:	**36,738**
Turnout	:	**85.10%**
Votes Polled	:	**31,264**
Valid Votes	:	**31,064**
Invalid Votes	:	**198**

LAKSHADWEEP

Seats: 1	Candidates: 2

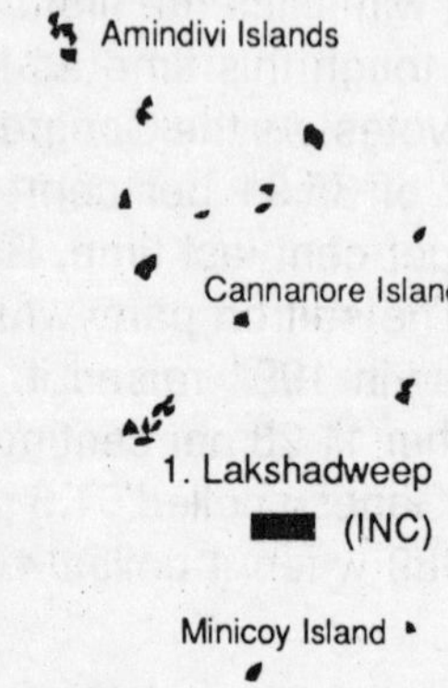

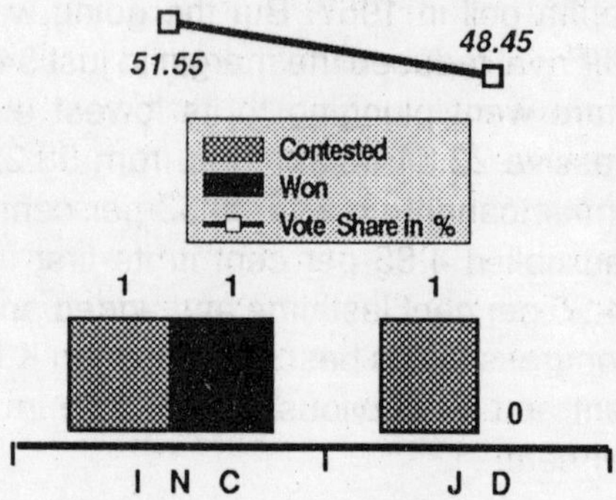

Vote Share %

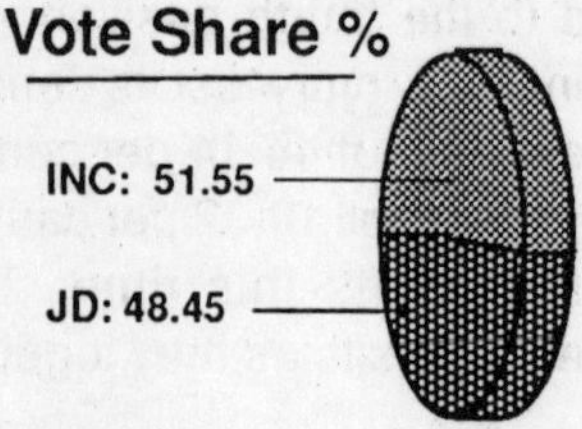

Swing %

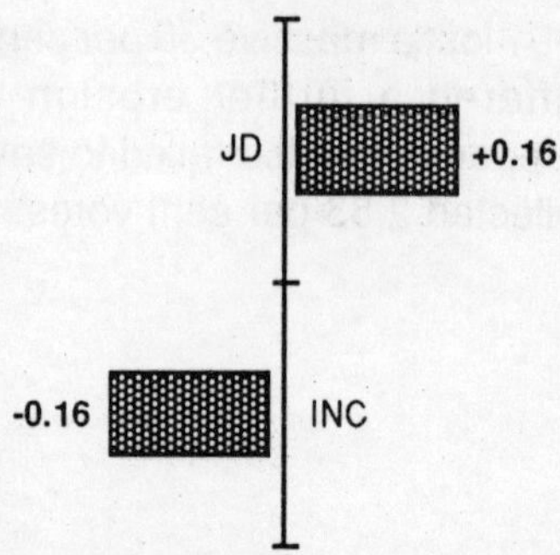

Seat Share %

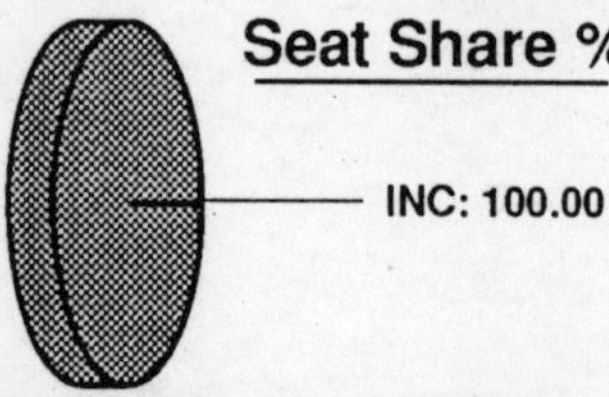

GAINS & LOSSES

Party	Seats Won '96	Seats Won '98	Reta-ined	Gain -ed	Gained From:	Lost	Lost to:	Net + / -
INC	1	1	1	0	-	0	-	0
Total	**1**	**1**	**1**	**0**		**0**		

LAKSHADWEEP: Sayeed Keeps Going

P.M. Sayeed did it again. For the ninth time in a row, he won the smallest Lok Sabha constituency, all but twice for the Congress. He contested the first poll as an independent in 1967, was returned unopposed in the second and stood for the rival Urs Congress in 1980. Except in 1967, when he beat another independent, A.T. Arnakad, Sayeed has always faced Mohammed Koya as his opponent, thrice as an independent, as a nominee of Janata Party in 1980 and that of Janata Dal since 1991. This time Sayeed won with 964 votes, 70 less than last time, but thrice as much as in 1991 when he just scraped through with 281 votes. In per centage terms, Congress votes went down by 0.16 points to 51.55 per cent, while the JD vote went up by as much to 48.45 per cent. Sayeed did his best for the Congress in 1967 when he polled 58.6 per cent and his worst in 1991 when he polled 50.6 per cent. In 1980, when he won the seat for Urs Congress with 56.4 per cent votes, Congress(I) polled just 3.9 per cent.

Electorate : 6,65,486
Turnout : 62.78%
Votes Polled : 4,17,786
Valid Votes : 4,08,918
Invalid Votes : 8,851

PONDICHERRY

Seats: 1 | Candidates: 9

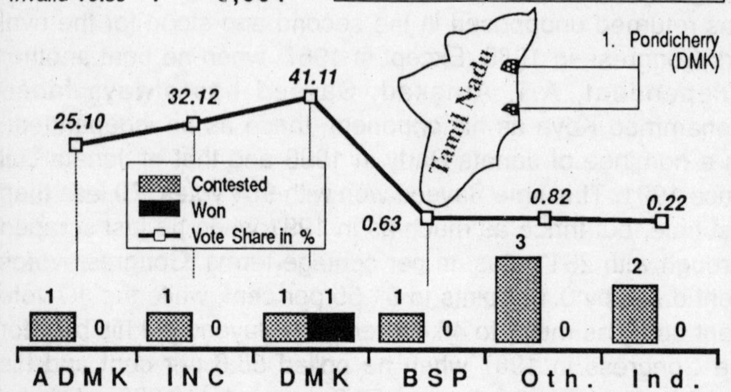

Vote Share %

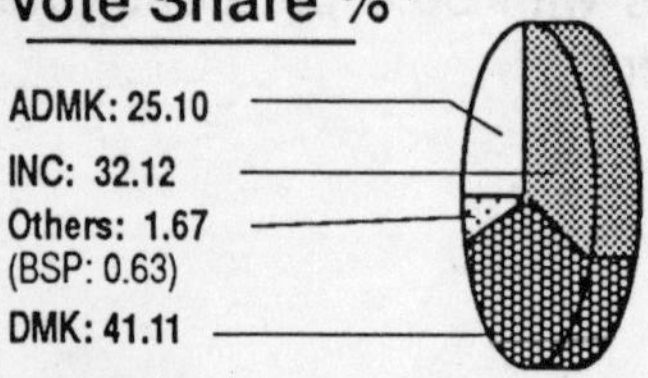

Seat Share %

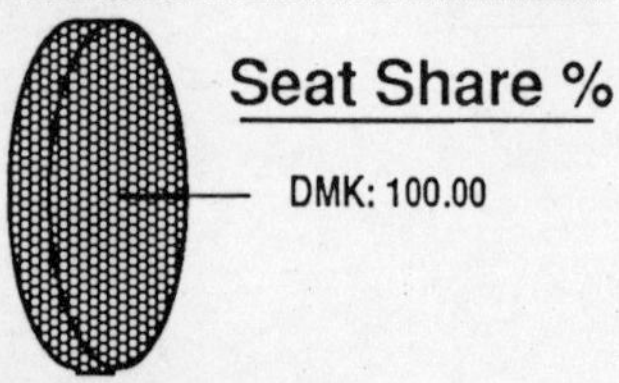

Swing %

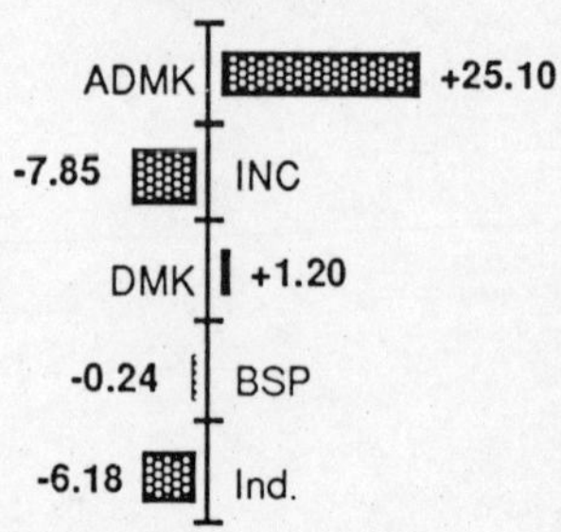

GAINS & LOSSES

Party	Seats Won '96	Seats Won '98	Retained	Gained	Gained From:	Lost	Lost to:	Net +/-
DMK	0	1	-	1	INC-1	-	-	+1
INC	1	0	0	-	-	1	DMK-1	-1
Total	1	1	0	1		1		

PONDICHERRY: DMK Upsets Congress

DMK's S Arumhugham finally avenged his 1991 defeat by just 284 votes at the hands of sitting Congress MP, M.O.H. Farook. Although at 41.11 per cent, he polled just 1.21 points more than last time, he won mainly because the rival AIADMK parted company with Congress and took away 25.10 per cent of the opposition vote. It was to date the best performance by DMK, which had finished runner-up four times since 1980.

Congress which had always won the seat since 1967, except once in 1977 when AIADMK took it, saw its vote share slashed by 7.85 points to 32.12 per cent.

The Congress did its best in 1980 when it polled 66.5 per cent. Its previous lowest was in 1967 when it polled 39.8 per cent. AIADMK won the seat in 1977 with 53.3 per cent.

Six other candidates, including those of BSP and Laloo Yadav's Rashtriya Janata Dal, together polling 1.67 per cent all lost their deposits. BJP which had last time more than doubled its vote share from 1.97 per cent to 4.42 per cent left it to the new-found ally AIADMK to do the battle in Pondicherry.

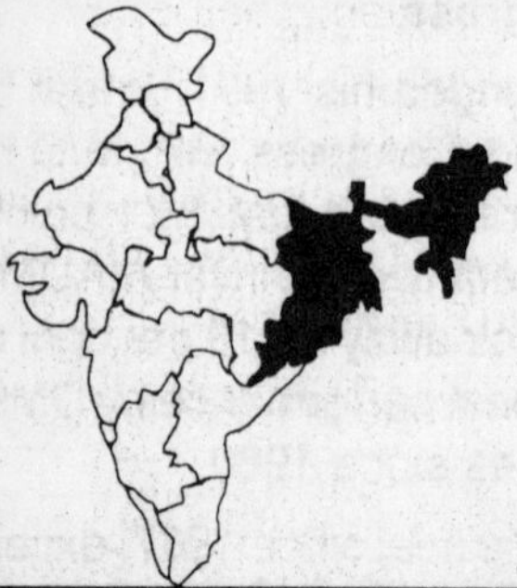

EAST

Seats: 142	Candidates: 1034

Electorate : 14,97,04,535
Turnout : 67.81%
Votes Polled : 10,16,29,811
Valid Votes : 9,97,65,280
Invalid Votes : 18,38,059

Party	Contested	Won	Lost Deposit	1998 Vote %	1996 Vote %	Vote Swing %
BJP + Allies	**156**	**55**	**32**	**36.63**	**18.63**	**+ 18.00**
BJP	77	29	11	17.99	13.34	+ 4.65
SAP	25	10	5	5.91	5.29	+ 0.62
BJD	12	9	0	3.69	-	+ 3.69
TC	29	7	3	8.94	-	+ 8.94
LS	13	0	13	0.10	-	+ 0.10
INC + Allies	**166**	**42**	**63**	**29.21**	**30.52**	**- 1.31**
INC	105	24	39	18.75	30.52	- 11.77
RJD	58	17	22	10.10	-	+ 10.10
RJP	3	1	2	0.36	-	+ 0.36
UF Parties	**166**	**37**	**97**	**25.85**	**40.24**	**- 14.39**
J D	53	1	44	3.94	15.40	- 11.46
CPI	25	4	17	2.98	3.30	- 0.32
CPM	42	26	7	14.11	15.36	- 1.25
RSP	4	4	0	1.64	1.78	- 0.14
FBL	4	2	1	1.22	1.28	- 0.06
SP	28	0	25	0.89	0.50	+ 0.39
AGP	10	0	3	1.07	2.62	- 1.55
BSP	**25**	**0**	**24**	**0.33**	**0.26**	**+ 0.07**
Others	**521**	**8**	**491**	**7.98**	**10.35**	**- 2.37**

8
The East: Changing Colour

Thanks to strategic alliances, BJP at long last succeeded in breaking into the eastern region with major successes in Bihar, Orissa and West Bengal. And though it didn't make much of an impact in the northeast in terms of seats, its candidates succeeded in making their presence felt with substantial votes. True, in two of the three eastern states, the allies took a larger share of seats and votes, but the 29 combined gains made BJP the dominant player in the region with the alliance winning 55 of the 142 seats. A mixed run, a good show in Assam offsetting poor performances in Orissa and West Bengal, coupled with Laloo's luck in Bihar, helped the Congress-led alliance tot up 42 seats, a gain of five, with 29.21 per cent votes. It was a divided United Front which turned out to be the worst loser—34 across the board—leaving it with a tally of 37 as its regional vote share tumbled from 40.24 per cent to 25.85 per cent votes.

Picking up 36.63 per cent votes, BJP alliance turned out to be the biggest vote catcher in the eastern region with a combined swing of 18 per cent. Leading the pack of allies was BJP with 17.99 per cent with an upswing of 4.65 points. Trinamul contributed 8.94 per cent followed by Samata with 5.91 per cent, up 0.63 points, and Biju Janata Dal bringing up the rear with 3.68 per cent. Pro-BJP swings ranged from 3.23 per cent in West Bengal and 3.49 per cent in Bihar to 7.78 per cent in Orissa.

The alliance made its greatest pickings in Orissa where it gained 16 seats with a swing of 35.27 per cent. West Bengal brought eight gains with a swing of 27.75 per cent and Bihar added six more seats with a swing of 4.78 per cent. Northeast brought no gains, but BJP traded a seat in Assam with another.

BJP itself gained 16 seats, eight from the Congress, four from JD and one each from CPM, Samata, Samajwadi Party and Jharkhand Mukti Morcha. But it also lost three seats each to the Congress and RJD to finish with a net gain of ten. Biju Janata Dal gained nine, six from the Congress and three from JD in Orissa, while Trinamul snatched half a dozen from the Congress and one from the Forward Bloc in West Bengal.

Though the Congress alliance gained five seats with a combined vote of 29.21 per cent despite an adverse swing of 1.31 per cent, Congress itself lost 13 seats across the region. Running into a negative swing of 11.77 per cent which brought its vote share down from 30.52 per cent to 18.75 per cent, Congress yielded 25 seats in all. Eight of these went to BJP, six each to BJD and Trinamul, two to CPM and one each to CPI, Manipur State Conress and an independent in Mizoram. But it recovered a dozen—five from AGP, three from BJP, two independents and one each from JD and CPI.

Winning 23 seats in Bihar, the alliance gained 21 with Laloo's RJD bringing in 17 with a regional vote share of 10.10 per cent. Eleven of RJD's gains came from BJP, three from BJP, two from CPI and one from Samata. Vaghela's RJP too made a gain in distant Bihar to Samata's chagrin.

Adverse swings ranging from 1.86 per cent in West Bengal to 24.53 per cent in Bihar and 25.76 per cent in Orissa cost the UF 29 seats with a combined downswing of 14.39 per cent. As many as 25 of the UF losses were in Bihar besides the four in Orissa. Polling only 3.94 per cent votes, a drop of 11.43 points, JD lost 25 seats, eleven of them to Laloo's rival RJD and six to Samata. It lost four more to BJP, three to Biju Janata Dal and one to Congress. Only former railway minister Ram Vilas Paswan hung on to his Hajipur seat to give JD its lone seat in the entire region.

More than half of the UF vote pie (25.85 per cent) came from CPM, which gained two seats from the Congress in West Bengal, but lost one to BJP in its bastion and another to United Minorities Front in Assam. For its tally of 26 CPM polled 14.09 per cent. Winning four seats with 2.98 per cent, down 0.31 points,

CPI lost two to RJD and one to Congress in Bihar, but wrested one from the latter in Manipur to finish with a net loss of two. Polling 1.21 per cent, Forward Bloc too lost a seat to Trinamul but the RSP retained its four seats even as its vote share fell by a fraction to 1.64 per cent.

In the Northeast, the Congress finished at the top with 13 of the 25 seats won with 39.62 per cent as a good performance in Assam offset its disastrous run in the rest of the region. Gaining six seats in Assam, five from AGP and one from BJP, and dislodging an independent in Meghalaya, Congress lost four elsewhere to finish with a net gain of three. It lost a seat each to BJP (Assam), Manipur State Congress, CPI (Manipur) and an independent in Mizoram.

BJP contested 22 seats in the eight states leaving one each in Manipur, Nagaland and Sikkim, but only one succeeded in Assam even as it polled 19.27 per cent votes about half the Congress share.

Among the UF constituents, AGP remained the top vote getter with 8.5 per cent even as it lost all its five seats to the Congress. CPM followed with 7.53 per cent retaining both the seats in Tripura, but losing one to United Minorities Front in Assam. CPI contributed 1.96 per cent gaining a seat from the Congress in Manipur. The remaining eight seats were shared by Arunachal Congress(2), ASDC, Manipur State Congress, Sikkim Democratic Front and United Minorities Front (one each) besides two independents. The "others", including Janata Dal and SP together polled about a quarter of the total votes in the Northeastern region.

Electorate	: 5,87,66,472
Turnout	: 64.64%
Votes Polled	: 3,79,86,392
Valid Votes	: 3,73,74,415
Invalid Votes	: 5,97,402

BIHAR

Seats: 54	Candidates: 469

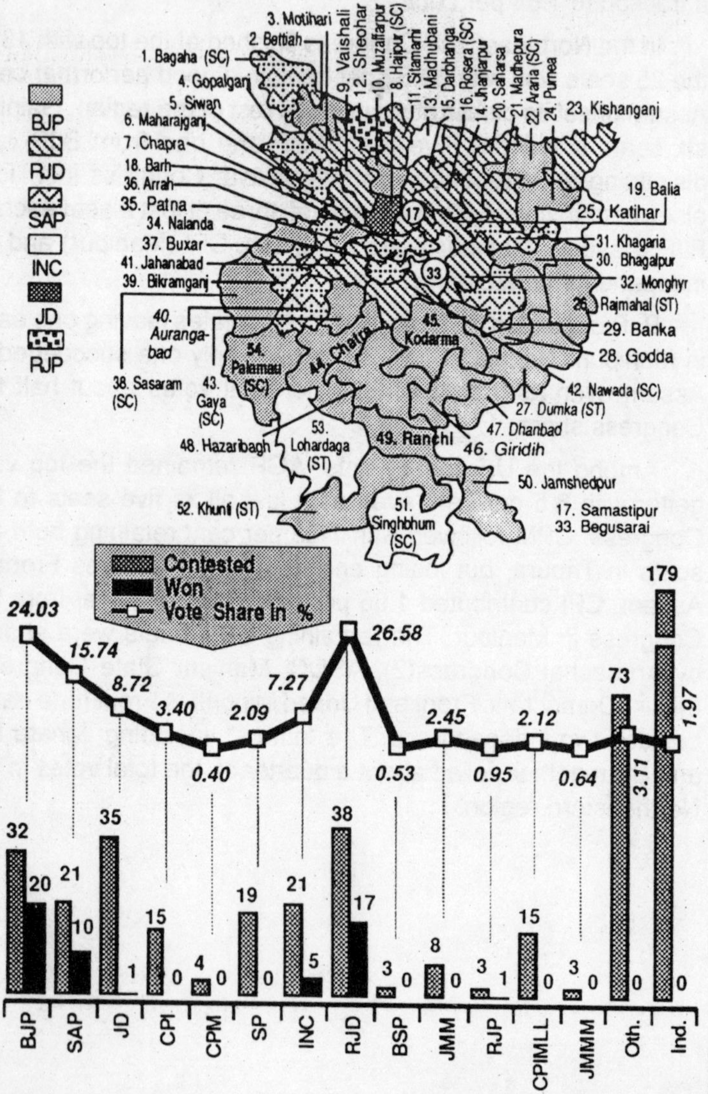

BIHAR: Laloo Proves a Point

The fodder scam notwithstanding, Laloo Prasad Yadav's Rashtriya Janata Dal made hay in Bihar mainly at the cost of the parent Janata Dal even as a 4.78 per cent swing helped the BJP-Samata party combine win 30 of the 54 seats with a modest gain of five seats. While RJD won 17 seats with 26.58 per cent votes, an informal understanding with Laloo's party also helped the Congress to raise its tally from two to five despite an adverse swing of 5.72 per cent. The UF itself was left with only one seat with 25 losses in the face of a massive negative swing of 24.53 per cent.

With a 24.03 per cent vote, up 3.49 points from 20.54 per cent last time, BJP gained seven seats including Patna where a repoll was ordered, four from JD and one each from Congress, SP and JMM. But five losses, three to RJD and two to Congress limited its gains to two. Ally Samata did better to add four more seats to the alliance kitty with 15.74 per cent votes, up 1.29 points over 14.45 per cent it polled in 1996. Samata wrested half a dozen seats from JD, but yielded one each to RJD and Rashtriya Janata Party of Shankersinh Vaghela, who could not win any other Lok Sabha seat even in his home state of Gujarat.

Congress and allies gathered 23 seats, a gain of 21, with the bulk of it coming from RJD. Eleven of RJD seats were wrested from JD, three from BJP, two from CPI and one from Samata. Congress gained four seats, two from BJP, one from CPI and the lone independent in Begusarai. Contesting from jail, alleged don Anand Mohan Singh won the Sheohar seat again, but for RJP instead of Samata to add another 0.94 per cent votes to the alliance share of 34.80 per cent.

In the UF, only Ram Vilas Paswan was able to hang on to his Hajipur (SC) seat to give the JD and the Front its lone seat. In all JD lost 21 seats, including the Madhepura seat where Laloo humbled Sharad Yadav, who had replaced him as JD president after the 1997 party split. Besides the 11 losses to RJD, JD conceded six to Samata and four to BJP. A 23.17 per cent adverse swing reduced the JD vote share to only 8.71 per cent from 31.88 per cent last time. CPI lost three seats, two to

BIHAR

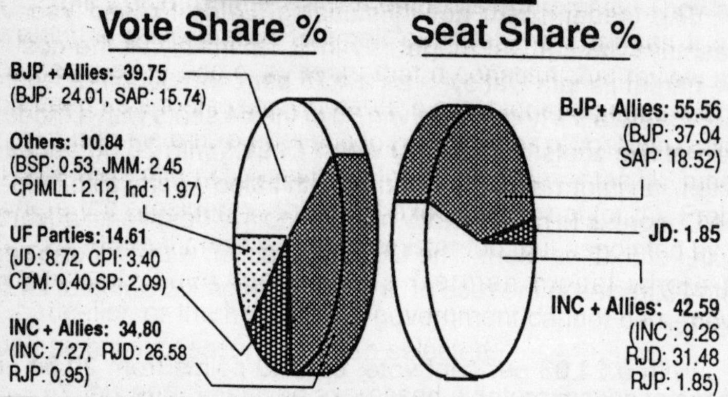

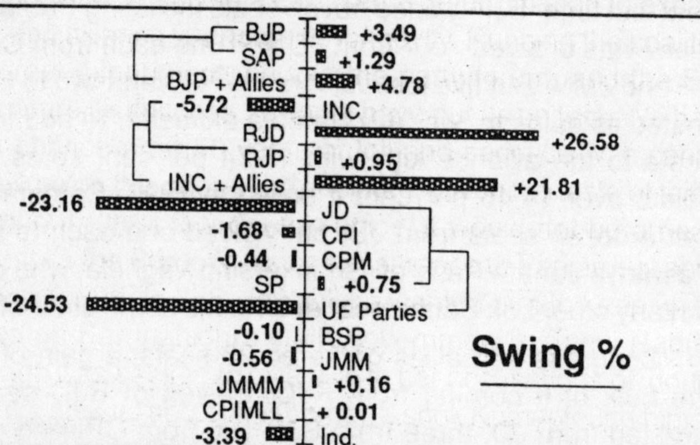

GAINS & LOSSES

Party	Seats Won '96	'98	Retained	Gained	Gained From:	Lost	Lost to:	Net + / -
BJP	18	20	13	7	JD-4, SP-1, INC-1, JMM-1	5	RJD-3, INC-2	+2
SAP	6	10	4	6	JD-6	2	RJD-1, RJP-1	+4
INC	2	5	1	4	BJP-2, CPI-1, Ind.1	1	BJP-1	+3
RJD	-	17	-	17	JD-11, BJP-3, CPI-2, SAP-1	-	-	+17
RJP	-	1	-	1	SAP-1	-	-	+1
JD	22	1	1	0	-	21	RJD-11, SAP6, BJP-4	-21
SP	1	0	0	0	-	1	BJP-1	-1
CPI	3	0	0	0	-	3	RJD-2, INC-1	-3
JMM	1	0	0	0	-	1	BJP-1	-1
Ind.	1	0	0	0	-	1	INC-1	-1
Total	54	54	19	35		35		

RJD and one to Congress, but collected 3.40 per cent for the front, 1.68 points less than last time. SP too lost its lone Purnea seat to BJP as it added another 2.09 per cent to the Front total of 14.60 per cent. Independents and sundry smaller parties collected 10.84 per cent votes.

Of the eight SC seats, half went to BJP for 28.99 per cent and one to its ally Samata for 8.11 per cent. RJD took two for 29.59 per cent and JD one for 19.53 per cent. The five tribal seats were shared by the BJP and Congress with the saffron party taking three for 40.03 per cent. Congress polled 29.21 per cent for its two seats. Among others BSP polled 2.70 per cent votes in the two SC seats it contested, CPI 0.14 per cent and CPM 0.41 per cent in one seat each. CPM polled 0.84 per cent in one ST seat and CPI 0.98 per cent in another.

Of the 21 women candidates only four, two each of RJD and BJP, made it with 12 of them losing their deposits. Losers included former union minister Kanti Singh. At 56.79 per cent women's participation was over eight per cent lower than the state total.

Besides Laloo Yadav, other notables who made it from Bihar included George Fernandes and Nitish Kumar of Samata Party and Yashwant Sinha of BJP. Alleged don M. Shahabuddin retained his Siwan seat. So did Taslimuddin, who briefly served as minister of state for home in the last UF government at the Centre before his past caught up with him. Both won on RJD instead of JD tickets this time.

Electorate	:	2,33,93,600
Turnout	:	58.03%
Votes Polled	:	1,35,74,771
Valid Votes	:	1,33,46,272
Invalid Votes	:	2,27,239

ORISSA

Seats: 21 | **Candidates: 135**

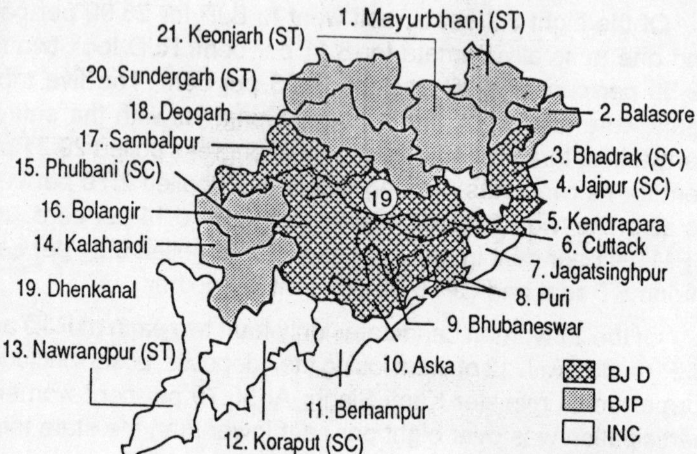

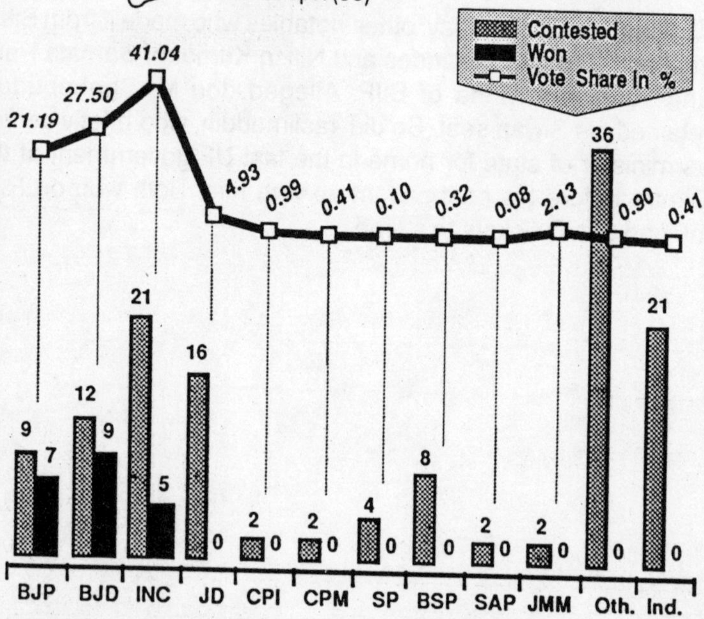

ORISSA: Biju Magic Helps BJP

A tie-up with the Biju Janata Dal floated by the state's popular former chief minister Biju Patnaik's son Naveen, coupled with an anti-incumbency vote against the Congress, helped BJP alliance win 16 of the 21 seats with almost half of the popular vote (48.69 per cent), indicating a massive over 35 per cent swing in its favour. An adverse 3.85 per cent swing cost the Congress, virtually going it alone, eleven seats reducing its tally to five. With the Naveen faction claiming the legacy of Biju, Janata Dal spearheading the UF challenge, was completely wiped out as its vote share plunged from about 30 per cent to less than five per cent (4.93 per cent).

Patnaik's BJD contesting 12 seats won 9 seats for the alliance, six gained from the Congress and three from JD, with a 27.50 per cent vote share. BJP won seven of the nine it contested with 21.20 per cent, 7.78 points more than last time. It snatched six seats from the Congress and one more from Samata Party, its ally in neighbouring Bihar. Samata also contested two seats, but lost deposits in both as its vote share went down by 1.47 per cent to a minuscule 0.08 per cent. Shiv Sena, running a coalition with BJP in Maharashtra, also fielded eleven candidates who all lost their deposits as they collected 0.19 per cent votes.

Congress retained four seats, gained one from JD and lost a dozen, six apiece to BJP and BJD as its vote share dropped from 44.89 per cent to 41.04 per cent. It was the third worst performance for the party which could win only three seats in 1989 with 38.4 per cent votes and four in 1977 with 38.2 per cent. Laloo's RJD too chose to contest ten seats, but lost deposits in all as it collected 0.26 per cent vote.

For the UF, JD contested 16 seats, but lost all the four it held, three to BJD and one to Congress, as it collected 4.93 per cent votes, 25.12 per cent less than last time. SP did battle in four and CPI and CPM in two each, but all the eight candidates failed to save their deposits. But the three parties added 0.99 per cent, 0.41 per cent and 0.10 per cent to the alliance kitty to take its vote share to 6.43 per cent. Two thirds of the 135

ORISSA

Vote Share % / Seat Share %

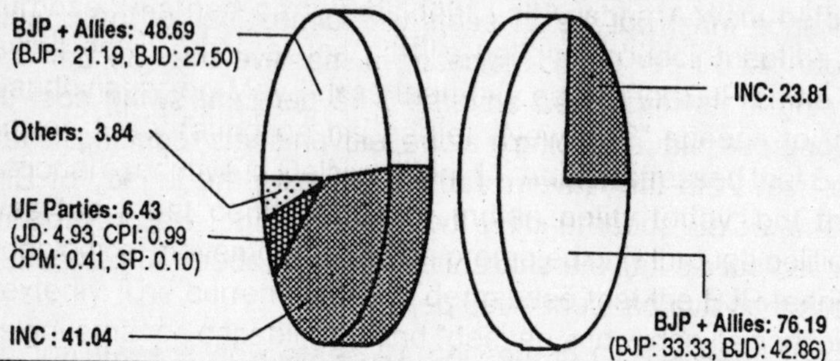

Swing %

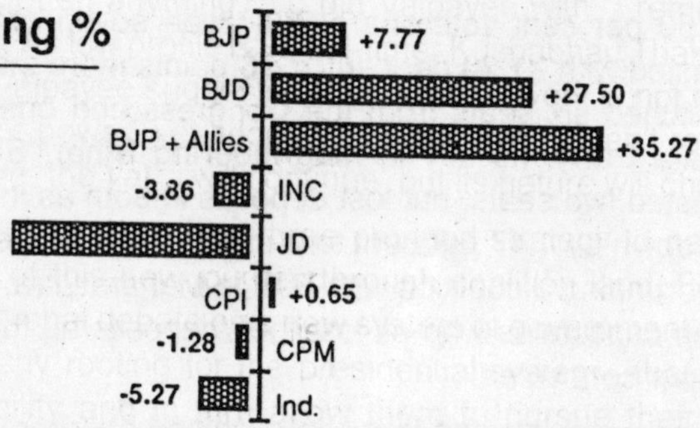

GAINS & LOSSES

Party	Seats Won '96	Seats Won '98	Retained	Gained	Gained From:	Lost	Lost to:	Net +/-
BJP	0	7	-	7	INC-6, SAP-1	-	-	+7
BJD	0	9	-	9	INC-6, JD-3	-	-	+9
INC	16	5	4	1	JD-1	12	BJD-6, BJP-6	-11
JD	4	0	0	0	-	4	BJD-3, INC-1	-4
SAP	1	0	0	0	-	1	BJP-1	-1
Total	21	21	4	17		17		

candidates, including 21 independents, lost their deposits even as all "others" polled 3.30 per cent.

Two of the SC seats were won by BJD with 45.43 per cent votes, while the Congress took the third with 43.70 per cent. But BJP took three of the five ST seats with 37.90 per cent leaving two to Congress for 39.75 per cent. Only two of the ten women candidates won while six lost their deposits. At 53.18 per cent, women's participation was about five per cent lower than the state average.

Congress chief minister J.B. Patnaik's wife Jayanti Patnaik won from Berhampur with former Prime Minister P.V. Narasimha Rao himself denied a ticket for the seat he won in 1996, campaigning for her. A *bahu* of the erstwhile royal family of Bolangir Sangeeta Singh Deo of BJP too made her maiden entry into Lok Sabha beating her Congress rival by 1.58 lakh votes. Another former royal, Bikram Kesari Deo won the Kalahandi seat for BJP. Naveen Patnaik won back his father's Aska seat by 86,211 votes.

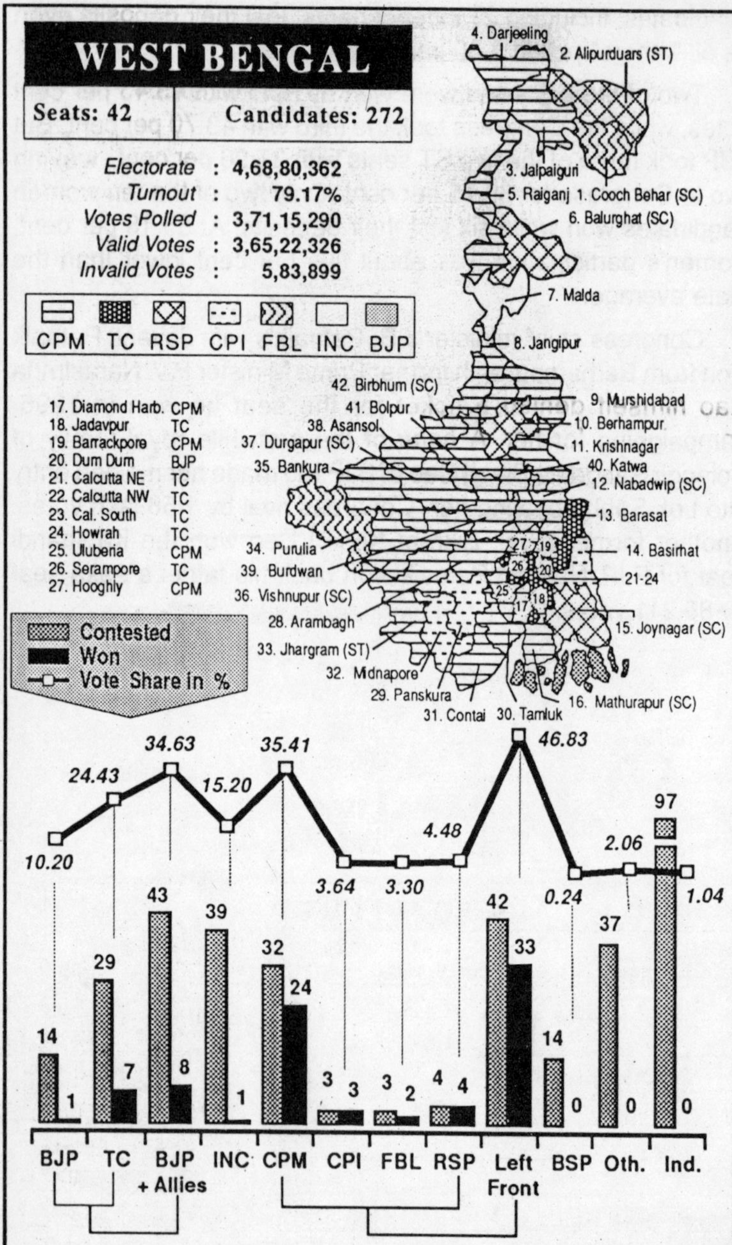
WEST BENGAL
Seats: 42
Candidates: 272
Electorate : 4,68,80,362
Turnout : 79.17%
Votes Polled : 3,71,15,290
Valid Votes : 3,65,22,326
Invalid Votes : 5,83,899
CPM TC RSP CPI FBL INC BJP
17. Diamond Harb. CPM
18. Jadavpur TC
19. Barrackpore CPM
20. Dum Dum BJP
21. Calcutta NE TC
22. Calcutta NW TC
23. Cal. South TC
24. Howrah TC
25. Uluberia CPM
26. Serampore TC
27. Hooghly CPM
4. Darjeeling
2. Alipurduars (ST)
3. Jalpaiguri
5. Raiganj
1. Cooch Behar (SC)
6. Balurghat (SC)
7. Malda
8. Jangipur
42. Birbhum (SC)
41. Bolpur
9. Murshidabad
38. Asansol
10. Berhampur
37. Durgapur (SC)
11. Krishnagar
35. Bankura
40. Katwa
12. Nabadwip (SC)
13. Barasat
34. Purulia
14. Basirhat
39. Burdwan
21-24
36. Vishnupur (SC)
28. Arambagh
15. Joynagar (SC)
33. Jhargram (ST)
32. Midnapore
29. Panskura
16. Mathurapur (SC)
31. Contai
30. Tamluk
Contested
Won
Vote Share in %
BJP: Contested 14, Won 1, Vote share 10.20
TC: Contested 29, Won 7, Vote share 24.43
BJP + Allies: Contested 43, Won 8, Vote share 34.63
INC: Contested 39, Won 1, Vote share 15.20
CPM: Contested 32, Won 24, Vote share 35.41
CPI: Contested 3, Won 3, Vote share 3.64
FBL: Contested 3, Won 2, Vote share 3.30
RSP: Contested 4, Won 4, Vote share 4.48
Left Front: Contested 42, Won 33, Vote share 46.83
BSP: Contested 14, Won 0, Vote share 0.24
Oth.: Contested 37, Won 0, Vote share 2.06
Ind.: Contested 97, Won 0, Vote share 1.04

WEST BENGAL: Still Red, But Not Quite

Two years after leading the Left Front to its fifth successive victory in the assembly polls, chief minister Jyoti Basu, 85, again proved an exception to the anti-incumbency rule as firebrand rebel Mamata Banerjee turned the Congress dream of storming his citadel sour. Instead her newly floated Trinamul Congress helped rival BJP get a foothold in the state. Despite an adverse 1.86 per cent swing, the four Left parties—CPM, CPI, RSP and the Forward Bloc—kept their tally of 33 seats at the top with 46.83 per cent votes instead of 48.69 per cent. BJP and Trinamul Congress picked up eight seats with a combined vote share of 34.63 per cent, leaving the Congress with just one seat for 15.20 per cent, a drop of 24.89 points.

For the Left Front, CPM picked up 24 seats, snatching two from the Congress, but losing one to BJP to finish with a gain of one with 35.41 per cent votes, down 1.29 points from 1996. RSP and CPI retained their four and three seats even as their vote shares came down a fraction of a point to 4.48 per cent and 3.63 per cent respectively. But Forward Bloc lost one of its three seats to Trinamul with its vote falling just a bit to 3.30 per cent.

An alliance with Trinamul Congress coupled with a 3.32 per cent swing brought BJP its first victory in the red bastion. Though its other 13 candidates lost, they raised BJP's vote share just above ten per cent from 6.85 per cent and state leader Tapan Sikdar trounced sitting CPM member Nirmal Kanti Chatterjee by 1.36 lakh votes in Dum Dum. Trinamul, itself polling 24.43 per cent took away almost two-thirds of the Congress vote as it snatched six seats from the parent party and one more from Forward Bloc to record seven wins in 21.

Apart from the six seats lost to Trinamul, the Congress conceded two more to CPM as its vote share dropped from about 40 per cent to 15.20 per cent. Its only success came in Malda where A.B.A. Ghani Khan Chowdhury retained his seat.

The Left Front won all the eight SC seats with CPM taking five for 30.92 per cent, RSP two for 11.79 per cent and the Forward Bloc one for 5.58 per cent. All six Congress candidates lost, so did five of Trinamul and three of BJP, but they won 12.98

WEST BENGAL

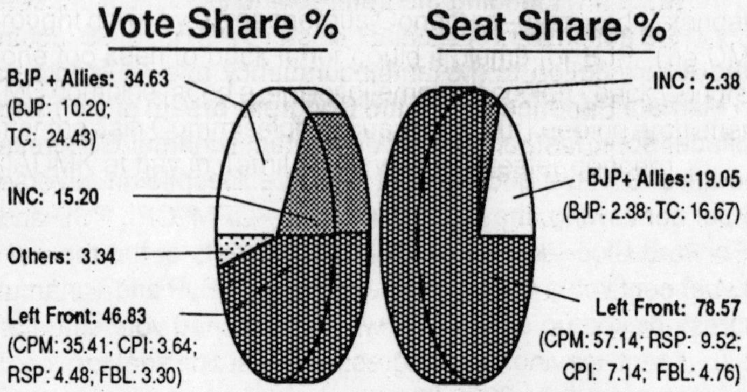

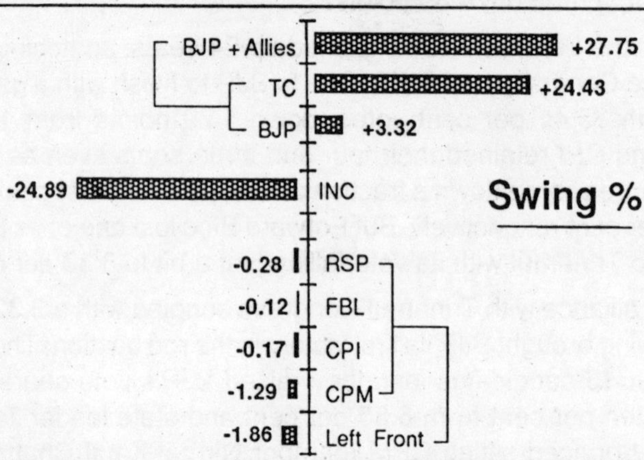

GAINS & LOSSES

Party	Seats Won '96	Seats Won '98	Retained	Gained	Gained From:	Lost	Lost to:	Net + / -
BJP	0	1	-	1	CPM-1	-	-	+1
TC	0	7	-	7	INC-6, FBL-1	0	-	+7
INC	9	1	1	0	-	8	TC-6; CPM-2	-8
CPM	23	24	22	2	INC-2	1	BJP - 1	+1
CPI	3	3	3	0	-	0	-	0
RSP	4	4	4	0	-	0	-	0
FBL	3	2	2	0	-	1	TC-1	-1
Total	42	42	32	10		10		

per cent, 17.26 per cent and 10.44 per cent votes for their respective parties. The two ST seats were shared by CPM and RSP with 28.41 per cent and 25.91 per cent votes. The three losing Congress (10 per cent), Trinamul (10.45 per cent) and BJP (13.64 per cent) nominees, together polled about 34 per cent votes.

Only five of the 21 women candidates made it and nine lost their deposits. Winners included Mamata Banerjee from Calcutta South and Geeta Mukherjee of CPI from Panskura. At 77.99 per cent, women's participation was almost as high as the state average of 79.17 per cent.

India's first communist home minister Indrajit Gupta won his tenth Lok Sabha election, for the fourth time from Midnapore and CPM leader Somnath Chatterjee scored his fourth straight win from Bolpur. Former Congress minister Ajit Kumar Panja won Calcutta North East again but for Trinamul and his elder brother Ranjit Panja snatched the Barasat seat held by Forward Bloc leader Chitta Basu since 1977.

Electorate	:	1,42,77,806
Turnout	:	61.06%
Votes Polled	:	87,17,775
Valid Votes	:	83,75,663
Invalid Votes	:	3,40,654

ASSAM

Seats: 14 | **Candidates: 101**

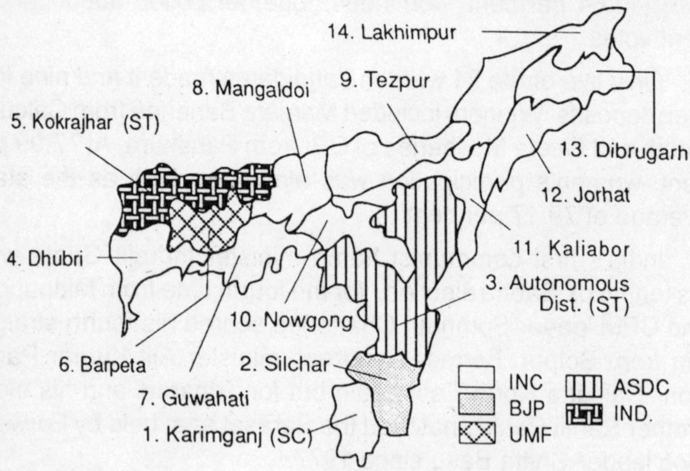

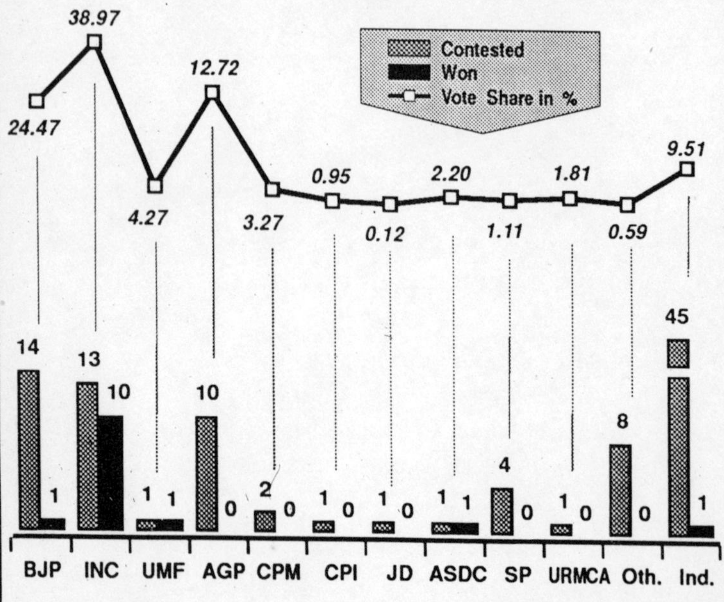

The North East

ASSAM: Congress Stages a Great Comeback

A seven and a half per cent swing, Sonia factor and an anti-establishment vote helped Congress recover lost ground in Assam where it was ousted from power in the simultaneous Assembly poll in 1996. Winning ten of the 14 seats, it doubled its previous tally of five. The anti-incumbency factor hit hard rival Asom Gana Parishad (AGP) led by Chief Minister Prafulla Kumar Mahanta, embroiled in the Letter of Credit scam. Losing all the five seats it held, AGP was completely wiped out as its vote share was reduced to less than half. The third contender, BJP failed to cash in on an 8.63 per cent swing that raised its vote share by about one and half times as it finished again with only one seat.

Contesting 13 seats, Congress won ten seats with 38.97 per cent votes, up 7.49 points from 1996. In doing so two years after it lost power in the state, Congress wrested five seats from AGP and one from BJP, but yielded one to finish with a net gain of five.

While AGP lost all its five seats to Congress as its vote share plunged from 27.04 per cent to 12.72 per cent, a 14.32 point drop, its United Front partner CPM conceded one to the unrecognised United Minorities Front. Only their old ally Autonomous State Demand Committee (ASDC) hung on to its ST seat in the Autonomous District. In all the UF partners, including the SP which fielded four candidates in opposition to the alliance, polled 20.37 per cent, a drop of 13.33 per cent.

In a determined bid to gain a foothold in the northeast, BJP again fielded candidates in all the 14 constituencies, but despite an 8.63 per cent swing that raised its vote share from 15.85 per cent to 24.47 per cent it again finished with only one seat, though a different one. It snatched one from Congress only to trade it for another.

Among the local parties, UMF added 1.69 per cent to its vote share as it won a seat with 4.27 per cent. The lone candidate of United Reservation Movement Council (URMCA) lost but polled 1.81 per cent. United Tribal Nationalists Liberation Front

ASSAM

Vote Share % / Seat Share %

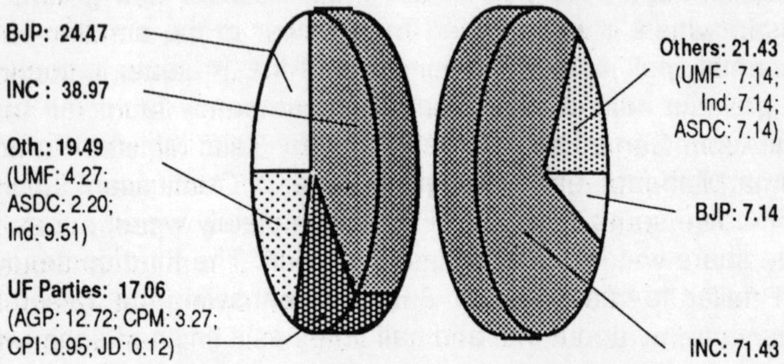

Swing %

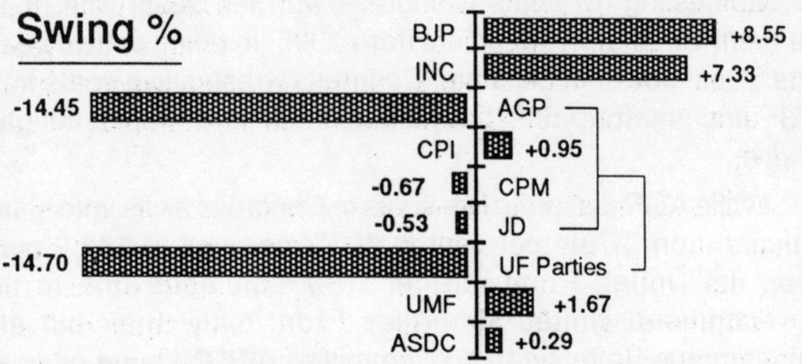

GAINS & LOSSES

Party	Seats Won '96	Seats Won '98	Reta-ined	Gain-ed	Gained From:	Lost	Lost to:	Net + / -
BJP	1	1	0	1	INC-1	1	INC-1	0
INC	5	10	4	6	AGP-5; BJP-1	1	BJP-1	+5
AGP	5	0	0	0	-	5	INC-5	-5
CPM	1	0	0	0	-	1	UMF-1	-1
ASDC	1	1	1	0	-	0	-	0
UMF	0	1	-	1	CPM-1	-	-	+1
IND	1	1	1	0	-	0	-	0
Total	**14**	**14**	**6**	**8**		**8**		

(UTNLF)'s only candidate lost his deposit but collected 0.13 per cent votes, just about a third of last time. Sundry other parties including 45 independents collected about 10 per cent votes but as many as 65 of the 101 candidates in fray could not save their deposits.

The lone SC seat was won by Congress with a 39.88 per cent vote. BJP was only a little behind with 38.24 per cent, while AGP polled 19.7 per cent. The two ST seats were shared by ASDC (16 per cent) and an independent (36.45 per cent). Congress, BJP and AGP polled 14.75 per cent, 14.17 per cent and 4.16 per cent respectively in these reserved seats.

The Congress, BJP and AGP fielded one woman candidate each in three different constituencies. Only Ranee Narah of Congress won in Lakhimpur. Chief Minister Mohanta's wife Joyasree Goswami finished third behind a BJP candidate in Nowgong. The Congress wrested the seat from AGP. At 59.29 per cent, women's participation in the polls was almost as good as the state average of 61.06 per cent despite ULFA threat of violence.

Besides Congress leader Tarun Gogoi in Kaliabar, a notable party winner was alleged don M.K. Subba, said to be convicted for murder in Nepal. He defeated I.P. Hazarika of BJP by 1.3 lakh votes in Tezpur.

ARUNACHAL PRADESH

Electorate	:	5,65,621
Turnout	:	59.17%
Votes Polled	:	3,34,705
Valid Votes	:	3,28,764
Invalid Votes	:	5,827

Seats: 2 | Candidates: 7

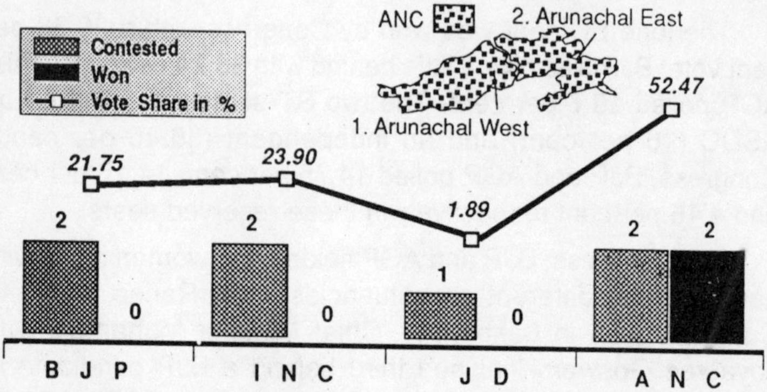

Vote Share %

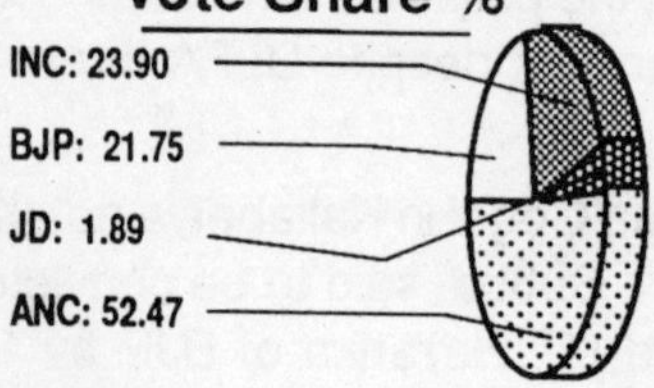

Seat Share %

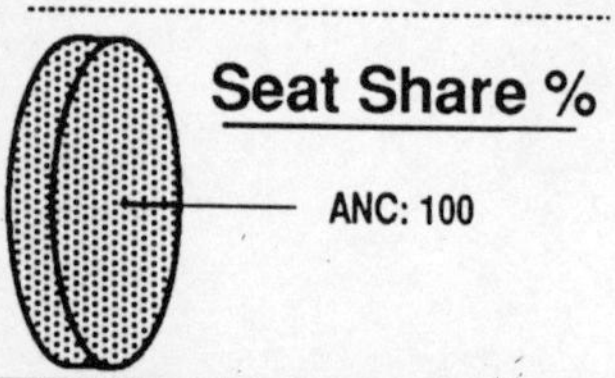

Swing %

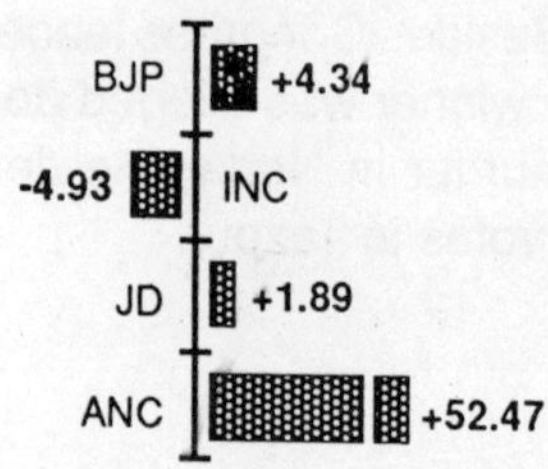

GAINS & LOSSES

Party	Seats Won '96	Seats Won '98	Retained	Gained	Gained From:	Lost	Lost to:	Net +/-
ANC	0	2	-	2	Ind.-2	-	-	+2
Ind.	2	0	0	-	-	2	ANC-2	-2
Total	2	2	0	2		2		

ARUNACHAL PRADESH: Apang Keeps it up

Last time Congress Chief Minister Gegong Apang was accused of engineering the defeat of the party nominees. This time he made it official. His rebel Arunachal Congress won both the seats with 52.47 per cent. Congress which had held the two seats for 16 years since 1980 finished a poor second with 23.90 per cent, a further erosion of 4.94 per cent. BJP, on the other hand, in its third electoral foray added another 4.34 per cent to come a close third with 21.75 per cent.

Apang's son Omak Apang won from Arunachal West and later found a berth in the Vajpayee government. The Arunachal East seat was again won by Wangcha Rajkumar, who did it as an independent last time, but joined the Congress later as an associate member.

Until 1989, the main opposition to Congress had been coming from the People's Party of Arunachal (PPA), which opted out after three unsuccessful runs in 1980, 1984 and 1989 when it polled 40.2 per cent, 34.6 per cent and 35.2 per cent respectively. JD was the main rival in 1991 with 24.7 per cent.

There were no women candidates among the seven in fray, but at 57.85 per cent women's turnout was almost equal to the state average of 59.17 per cent.

Electorate : 13,30,209
Turnout : 56.83%
Votes Polled : 7,55,960
Valid Votes : 7,49,816
Invalid Votes : 6,144

MANIPUR

Seats: 2 | **Candidates: 15**

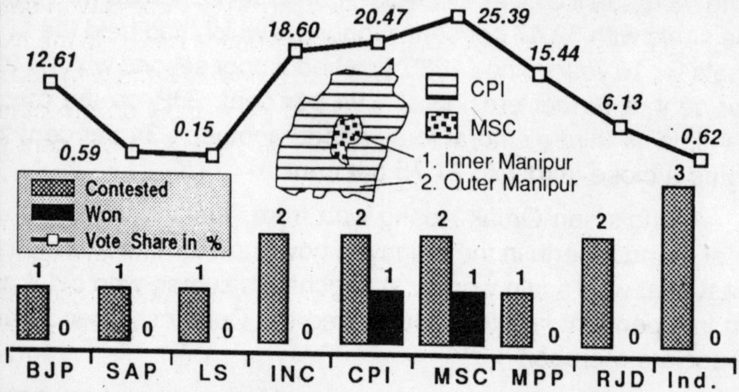

Vote Share %

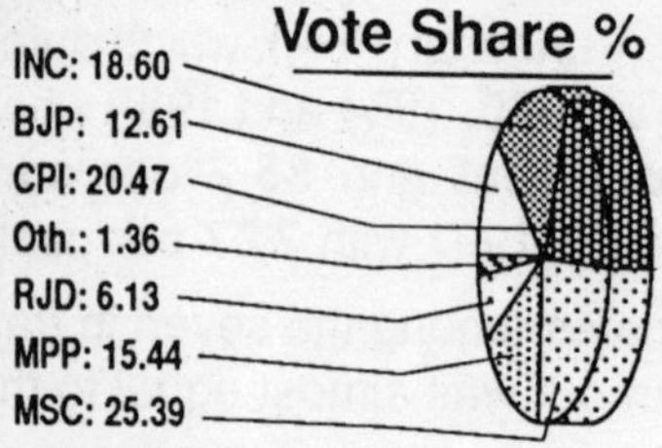

Seat Share %

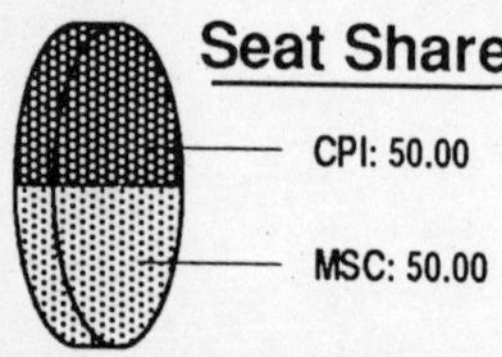

Swing %

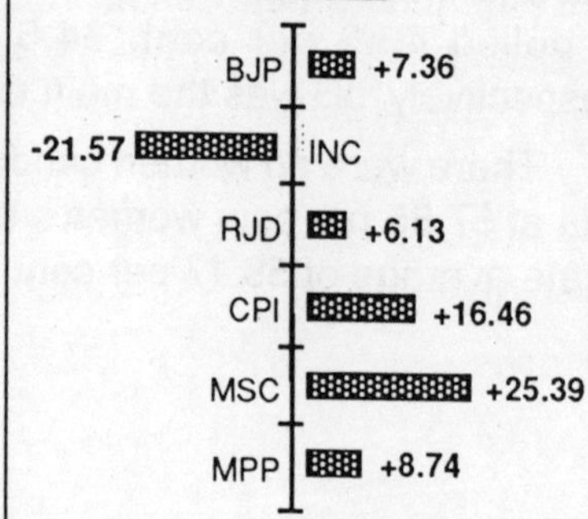

GAINS & LOSSES

Party	Seats Won '96	Seats Won '98	Retained	Gained	Gained From:	Lost	Lost to:	Net + / -
INC	2	0	0	-	-	2	CPI-1, MSC-1	-2
CPI	0	1	-	1	INC-1	-	-	+1
MSC	0	1	-	1	INC-1	-	-	+1
Total	2	2	0	2		2		

MANIPUR: Congress Loses All

A split in the party coupled with a massive 21.57 per cent swing cost the Congress both the seats in the state. Th. Chaoba Singh retained his Inner Manipur seat, but now under the banner of breakaway Manipur State Congress. The Outer Manipur ST seat was snatched away by CPI's Kim Gangte, the lone woman candidate in the fray. BJP more than doubled its vote share, but a victory still eluded it.

MSC topped the popularity chart with 25.39 per cent, while CPI followed with 20.47 per cent, increasing its votes more than five fold from just about four per cent last time. But the CPI candidate in the Inner constituency could not save his deposit. The Congress was relegated to the third position as its votes slipped down from 40.17 per cent to 18.60 per cent, its lowest ever.

One of its candidates also lost his deposit. Manipur People's Party came next with 15.44 per cent, an upswing of 8.74 points. BJP took the fifth position with 12.61 per cent with RJD bringing up the rear with 6.13 per cent. Nine of the 15 candidates, including three independents lost their deposits.

CPI won the Outer ST seat with 30.55 per cent votes with BJP coming a close second with 29.77 per cent. MSC polled 18.39 per cent, while RJD with 10.17per cent finished just ahead of the Congress with 9.75 per cent. At 55.94 per cent, women's turnout was slightly lower than the state average of 56.83 per cent.

Electorate	:	11,57,482
Turnout	:	74.38%
Votes Polled	:	8,60,890
Valid Votes	:	8,39,104
Invalid Votes	:	21,786

MEGHALAYA

Seats: 2 | **Candidates: 13**

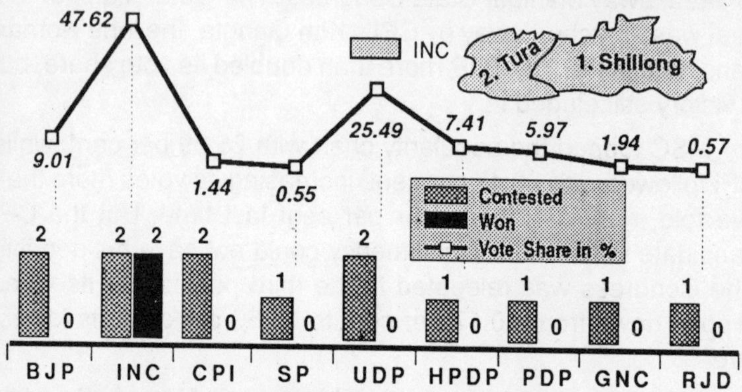

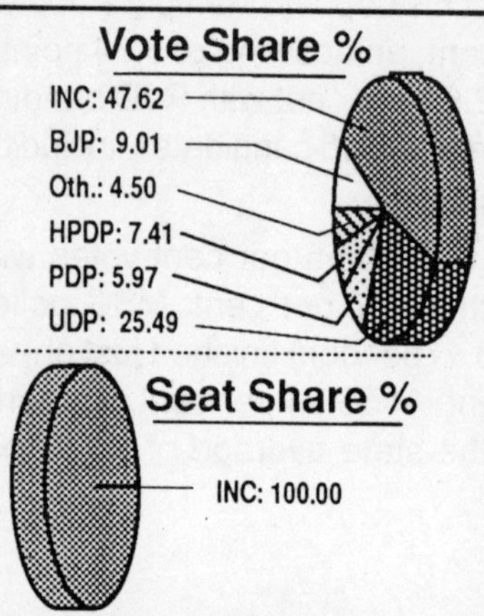

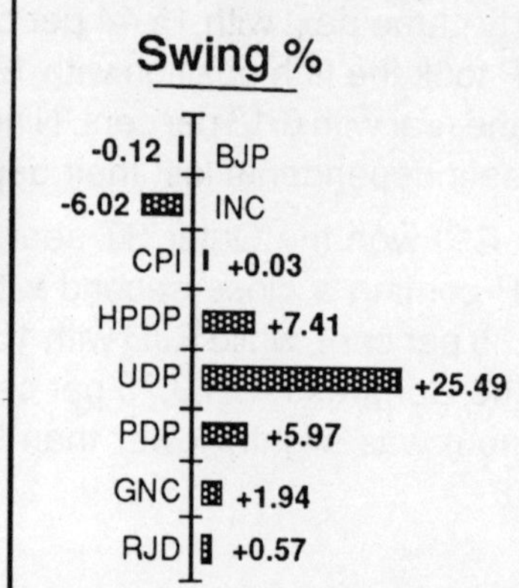

GAINS & LOSSES

Party	Seats Won '96	Seats Won '98	Reta-ined	Gain-ed	Gained From:	Lost	Lost to:	Net + / -
INC	1	2	1	1	Ind -1	-	-	+1
Ind.	1	0	-	-	-	1	INC-1	-1
Total	2	2	1	1		1		

MEGHALAYA: Mixed Fortune for Congress

Congress again pocketed both the seats after a gap of two years even as it narrowly lost power in the state in the simultaneous Assembly poll. While Lok Sabha Speaker Purno A. Sangma recorded his sixth win from Tura, Paty Ripple Kyndiah won back Shillong for the party.

Despite a downswing of 6.63 per cent, Congress finished at the top with 47.62 per cent as against 54.25 per cent last time. The newly formed United Democratic Party failed to win either seat, but polled 25.39 per cent. BJP came third with about nine per cent votes, only a fraction less than last time. Hill State People's Democratic Party came next with 7.41 per cent followed by People's Democratic Party with 5.97 per cent. Another local party Garo National Council with 1.94 per cent finished ahead of CPI which polled 1.44 per cent.

Except two Congress and one UDP candidate, all the remaining ten candidates lost their deposits. They included two women candidates, both put up by BJP. At 74.91 per cent, women's turnout was just a bit higher than the state average of 74.38 per cent.

In the parallel assembly poll, Congress fell a seat short of majority. Backed by 29 in a house of 60, chief minister Salseng C. Marak formed a minority government, but quit on the eve of a confidence vote after losing the speaker's post. Rival B.B. Lyngdoh of United Parliamentary Forum was then invited to form an alternative government.

Electorate : 4,42,457
Turnout : 69.56%
Votes Polled : 3,07,767
Valid Votes : 3,05,576
Invalid Votes : 2,191

MIZORAM

Seats: 1	Candidates: 6

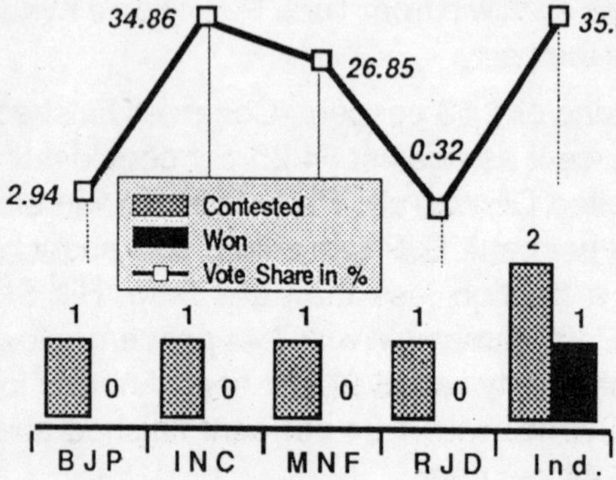

Vote Share %

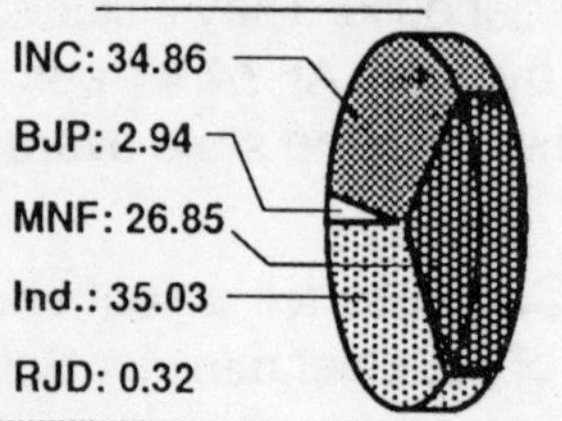

Seat Share %

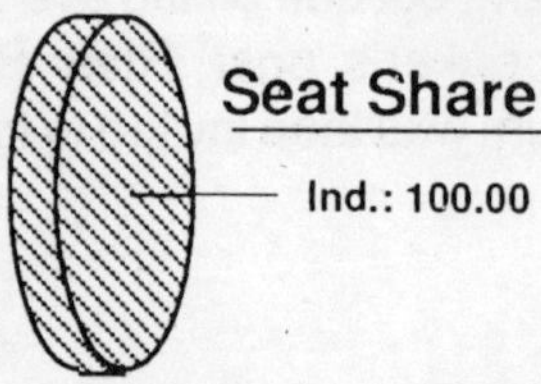

Swing %

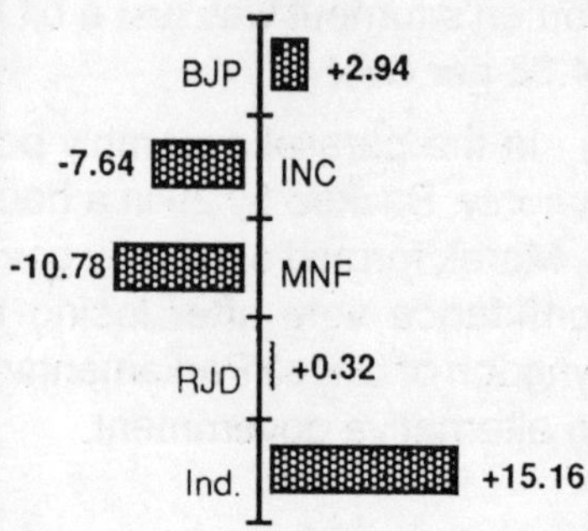

GAINS & LOSSES

Party	Seats Won '96	Seats Won '98	Reta-ined	Gain-ed	Gained From:	Lost	Lost to:	Net +/-
INC	1	0	0	0	-	1	Ind.-1	-1
Ind.	0	1	0	1	INC-1	0	-	+1
Total	**1**	**1**	**0**	**1**		**1**		

MIZORAM: Congress Pipped at the Post

An independent candidate, Dr Lallungmuana, jointly sponsored by Mizo People's Conference (MPC) and the breakaway Mizo National Front (Nationalist) pipped the Congress in a close contest by 535 votes. The Congress which had fielded octogenarian state finance minister J. Lalsangzuala instead of the previous three times winner C. Silvera found its popularity slip down to 34.86 per cent, a 7.65 point drop from the 42.50 per cent last time.

The main opposition MNF candidate, Dr R. Lalthangliana finished a distant third with 26.85 per cent, a 10.85 point downswing since 1996. BJP and RJD too put up candidates who polled 2.94 per cent and 0.32 per cent respectively and both lost their deposits along with an independent. There were no women candidates in fray but at 69.23 per cent, their turnout was as good as the state average of 69.56 per cent.

Before this loss, Congress, which has been in power in the state since 1989, had won the seat four times in a row from 1984. The seat was won by Mizo Union candidate Sangliana in the first parliamentary election in 1972 and by an independent, R Rothuama in 1977 and 1980.

NAGALAND

Electorate	9,26,569
Turnout	45.41%
Votes Polled	4,20,714
Valid Votes	3,97,008
Invalid Votes	23,706

Seats: 1 | Candidates: 2

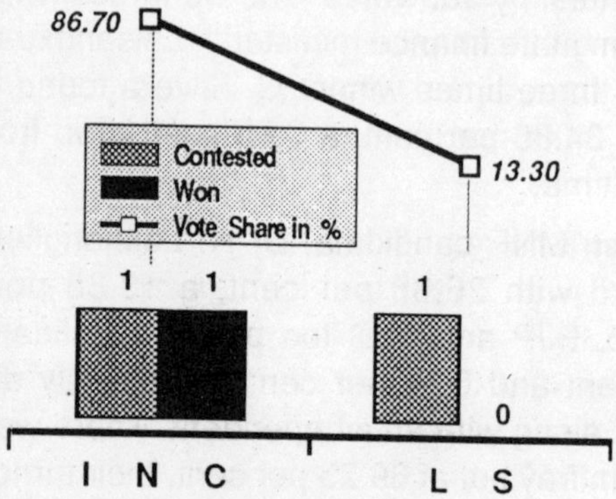

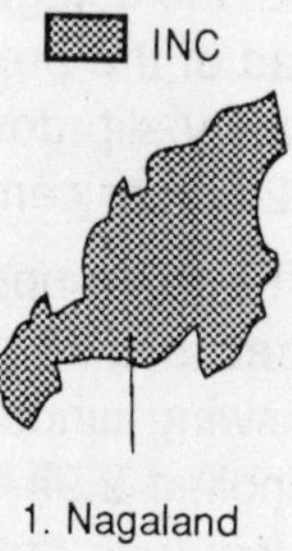

Vote Share %

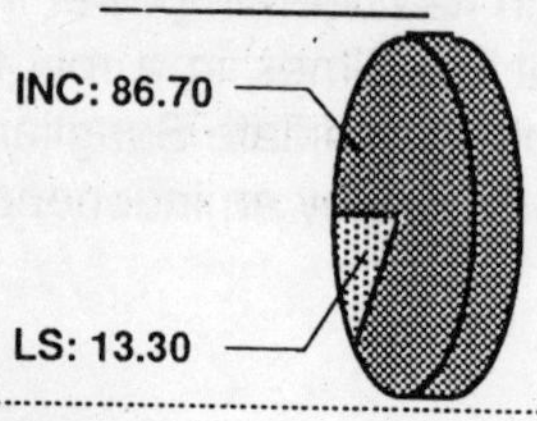

Seat Share %

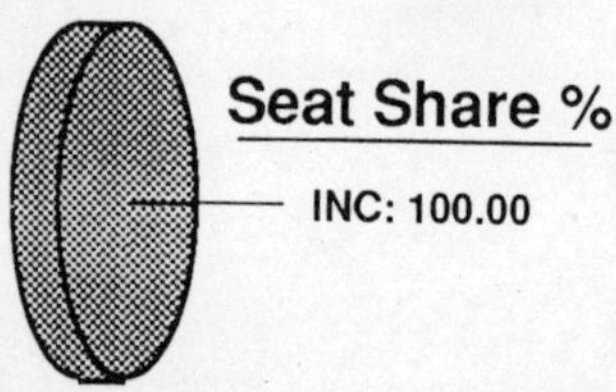

Swing %

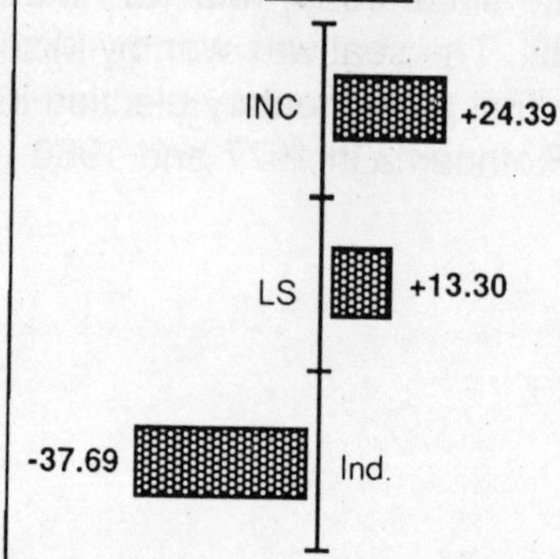

GAINS & LOSSES

Party	Seats Won '96	Seats Won '98	Retained	Gained	Gained From:	Lost	Lost to:	Net +/-
INC	1	1	1	0	-	0	-	0
Total	**1**	**1**	**1**	**0**		**0**		**0**

NAGALAND: Congress Stays Put

Congress not only kept its hold over the lone Nagaland seat it had won back in 1996, but its candidate K. Asungba Sangtam polled a record 86.70 per cent in a poll boycotted by a few militant groups. The rival Lok Shakti candidate gathered 13.30 per cent votes in a straight contest as the Congress share went up by 24.17 per cent from 62.31 per cent last time. It was the fourth victory for the Congress since 1984. It had lost the seat to the Nagaland People's Council in 1991, but recovered it in 1996.

In spite of a call by the underground Naga Hoho (Parliament), 45.41 per cent of the electorate, including 43.07 per cent women, came out to vote in the eighth Lok Sabha poll since 1971. The Naga National Organisation won the seat without contest in 1967 with present Congress chief minister S.C. Jamir as its nominee. There have been six straight contests in the state since 1971 with triangular fights in 1984, 1991 and 1996.

In the parallel state assembly election, Congress came back to power with 43 uncontested returns in favour of the party in the 60-member assembly. Jamir, the first Lok Sabha member from the state, again headed the government.

SIKKIM

Seats: 1 | Candidates: 3

Electorate : **2,36,494**
Turnout : **67.14%**
Votes Polled : **1,58,787**
Valid Votes : **1,55,871**
Invalid Votes : **2,916**

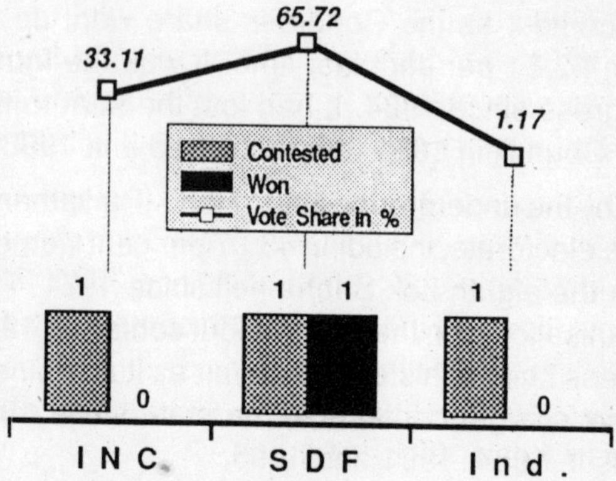

Vote Share %

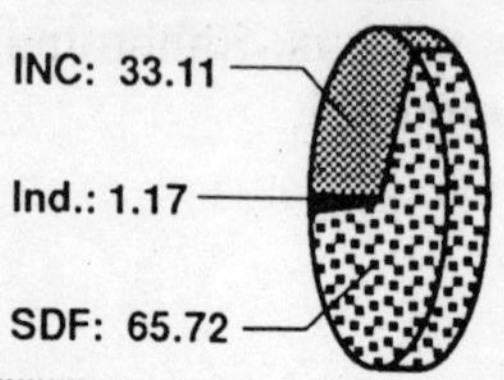

Seat Share %

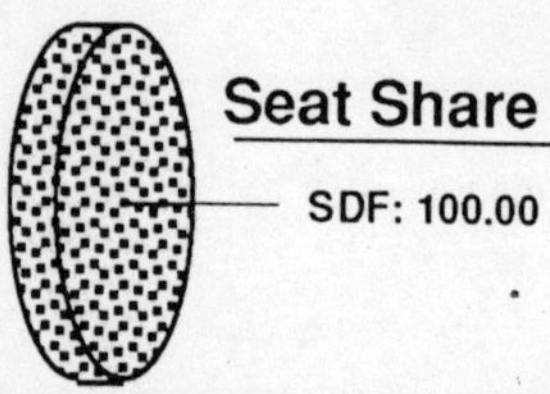

Swing %

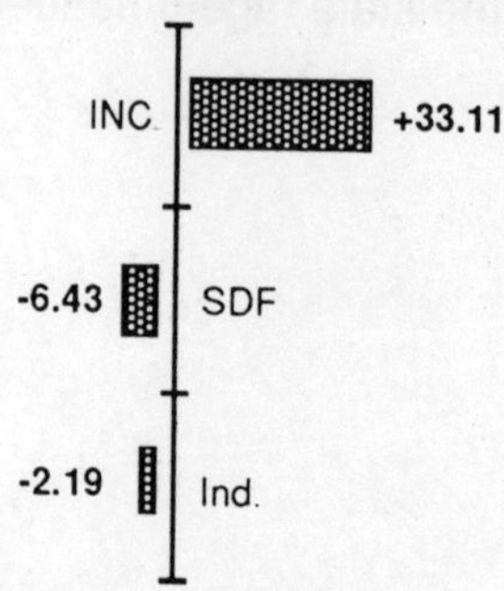

GAINS & LOSSES

Party	Seats Won '96	Seats Won '98	Retained	Gained	Gained From:	Lost	Lost to:	Net +/-
SDF	1	1	1	0	-	0	-	0
Total	**1**	**1**	**1**	**0**		**0**		**0**

SIKKIM: SDF Hangs On

The ruling Sikkim Democratic Front (SDF) of chief minister Pawan Kumar Chamling hung on to the state's lone seat despite a 6.37 per cent swing against it. Bhim Prasad Dahal, who had scored the party's first Lok Sabha victory in 1996 with 72.15 per cent votes retained it with 65.78 per cent. In a triangular contest, Congress polled 33.11 per cent, while an independent polling 1.17 per cent votes lost his deposit. No women stood for election, but at 62.50 per cent women's turnout was about five per cent lower than the state average.

The Sikkim Sangram Parishad of Chamling's predecessor Nar Bahadur Bhandari, ousted from power in 1994, did not field a candidate this time. Bhandari himself polling 24.50 per cent had been drubbed by Dahal in the 1996 Lok Sabha poll.

Congress won the first election in 1977. Sikkim Janata Parishad took the seat in 1980. Bhandari won it as an independent in 1984 with his party keeping it in 1989 and 1991.

TRIPURA

Seats: 2 | Candidates: 11

Electorate : 17,27,463
Turnout : 80.86%
Votes Polled : 13,96,760
Valid Votes : 13,70,465
Invalid Votes : 26,295

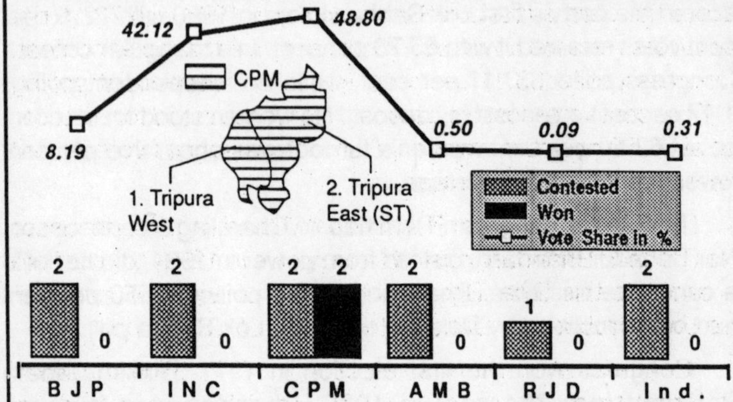

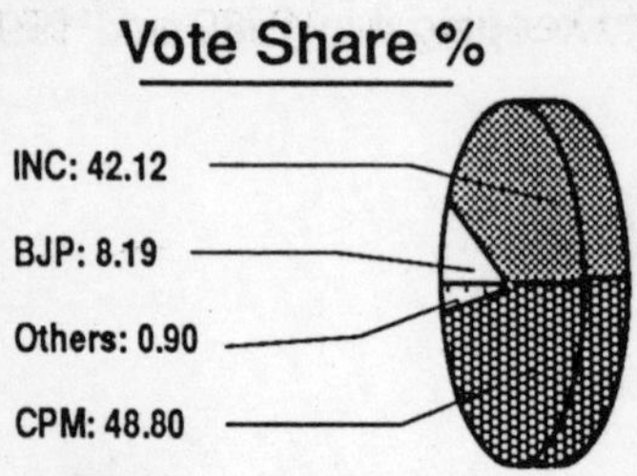

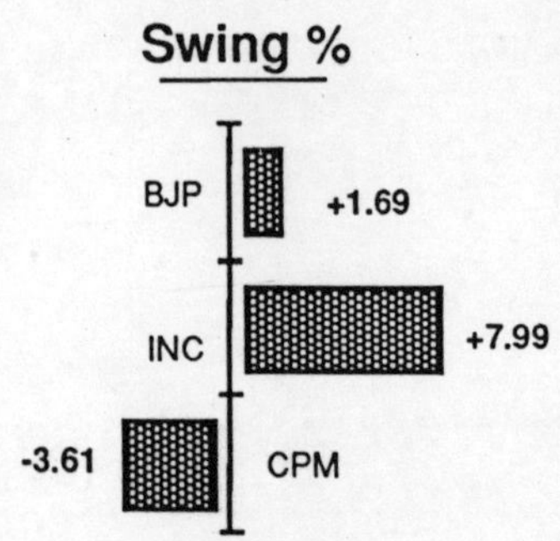

GAINS & LOSSES

Party	Seats Won '96	Seats Won '98	Retained	Gained	Gained From:	Lost	Lost to:	Net + / -
CPM	2	2	2	0	-	0	-	0
Total	2	2	2	0		0		

TRIPURA: Marxists Romp Home Again

Two years after wresting the two state seats from the Congress, CPM kept its hold over them even as its vote share slipped by 3.61 per cent. But polling 48.80 per cent instead of 52.41 per cent last time it was still far ahead of the Congress with 42.12 per cent. The Congress which had held the two seats for 12 years between 1984 and 1996 raised its votes by about eight per cent, but still a far cry from the peak of 82.83 per cent polled in 1991, when the CPM had withdrawn from the contest at the last minute alleging rigging.

BJP finished third with 8.19 per cent, up 1.69 points, but both its candidates still lost their deposits. So did five others who together polled less than one per cent. The loser included the lone woman candidate Madhuri Kalai of Amra Bangalee party.

Samar Chouhury won the Tripura West seat for CPM instead of Badal Choudhury. The East (ST) seat was retained by Baju Ban Riyan with 50.31 per cent votes as against 54.36 per cent last time. The Congress raised its share in the ST seat by more than ten points polling 38.90 per cent votes with BJP taking 9.69 per cent. At 80.47 per cent, women's turnout was almost as high as the state average of 80.86 per cent. In the parallel Assembly poll the Left Front returned to power winning 36 of the 54 Assembly seats.

9

The West: Mixed Fortunes

Western India with 118 seats in the Lok Sabha brought mixed luck for the two major players, BJP and the Congress, both of whom made strategic alliances at the local level. While BJP continued its tie up with coalition partner Shiv Sena in Maharashtra, the Congress forged a new front with the Republican Party of India and Samajwadi Party in the state. And if Gujarat came back into BJP hands in the parallel Assembly poll with modest gains in Lok Sabha, Maharashtra brought good cheer to the Congress as it held on to its position in Madhya Pradesh. The United Front again drew a blank in the region as whatever little support it had, slipped down further.

Together polling 44.76 per cent, BJP and Shiv Sena still finished ahead with 61 seats—a loss of 15 across the board despite a 3.63 per cent swing in its favour. The rival Congress-RPI-SP alliance finished five behind even as they gained 19 seats thanks to a 6.30 per cent swing in its favour that raised their combined vote share to 43.65 per cent. One seat went to the Peasants and Workers Party, but 2.44 per cent votes, excluding the 1.44 per cent polled by SP, could not win anything for the UF. BSP raised its regional vote share marginally to 3.42 per cent but lost its two seats to BJP.

BJP itself polling 36.46 per cent, about three per cent more than last time, gained 13 seats, but lost 19 to finish with a net deficit of six in a regional tally of 55. Nine of its gains came from the Congress in Gujarat (3), Madhya Pradesh (4) and Dadra and Nagar Haveli and Daman and Diu (one each). It made four other gains in Madhya Pradesh, wresting two from BSP and one each from the breakaway Tiwari Congress and an independent backed by Madhavrao Scindia. BJP lost as many

W E S T	
Seats: 118	Candidates: 937

Electorate : **13,06,31,436**
Turnout : **59.22%**
Votes Polled : **7,73,64,979**
Valid Votes : **7,53,70,347**
Invalid Votes : **19,71,728**

Party	Contested	Won	Lost Deposit	1998 Vote %	1996 Vote %	Vote Swing %
BJP + Allies	**138**	**61**	**20**	**44.91**	**41.19**	**+ 3.72**
BJP	95	55	0	36.46	33.33	+ 3.13
SHS	33	6	10	8.30	7.80	+ 0.50
SAP	10	0	10	0.15	0.06	+ 0.09
INC + Allies	**125**	**56**	**13**	**42.21**	**36.34**	**+ 5.87**
INC	110	52	2	40.43	34.05	+ 6.38
RPI	15	4	11	1.78	2.29	- 0.51
UF Parties	**92**	**0**	**86**	**3.88**	**4.30**	**- 0.42**
J D	52	0	51	1.77	1.97	- 0.20
CPI	9	0	9	0.29	0.58	- 0.29
CPM	5	0	4	0.29	0.53	- 0.24
SP	24	0	21	1.44	1.01	+ 0.43
MGP	2	0	1	0.09	0.21	- 0.12
BSP	**62**	**0**	**55**	**3.42**	**3.22**	**+ 0.20**
Others	**520**	**1**	**508**	**5.58**	**14.95**	**- 9.37**

as 17 seats to the Congress, five in Madhya Pradesh and a dozen in Maharashtra, where RPI snatched two more. Swings for BJP ranged from a negative 0.24 per cent in Gujarat to 4.41 per cent in Madhya Pradesh, not counting Goa where it gained 16.29 per cent but without success.

Ally Shiv Sena, polling 8.30 per cent—up 0.50 points—lost ten seats, eight to Congress and two to RPI, but gained one from the Congress, all in Maharashtra to finish with a net loss of nine in a tally of six.

Thanks to the alliance with RPI and SP, the Congress gained about 6.5 per cent votes to win 52 seats on its own. In all it gained 28 seats, 17 of them from BJP alone, a dozen in Maharashtra and five in Madhya Pradesh. It won eight more from the Shiv Sena in Maharashtra, two in Goa from MGP and UGDP and the Gwalior seat with Madhavrao Scindia's return to the party fold. In turn, it yielded nine to BJP, four in Madhya Pradesh, three in Gujarat and the two Dadra-Nagar Haveli and Daman-Diu seats. It also lost a seat each to PWP and the Sena to finish with a net gain of 17. Ally RPI too wrested two seats each from BJP and Shiv Sena in Maharashtra with a regional vote of 1.78 per cent. Swings for the Congress ranged from a negative 2.20 per cent in Gujarat to 8.38 per cent in Madhya Pradesh and 8.86 per cent in Maharashtra. In Goa it won two seats despite an adverse swing of 2.77 per cent , but lost Dadra-Nagar Haveli and Daman-Diu in the face of massive swings of 51.49 per cent and 48.64 per cent respectively.

In the UF, JD polling 1.76 per cent and CPI and CPM with 0.29 per cent each all lost about 0.25 apiece. Only SP in a separate alliance with Congress in Maharashtra gained 0.43 points togather 1.44 per cent to give the UF a regional vote share of 3.88 per cent.

GOA

Seats: 2 | Candidates: 12

Electorate : 8,80,746
Turnout : 61.16%
Votes Polled : 5,38,664
Valid Votes : 5,32,766
Invalid Votes : 5,898

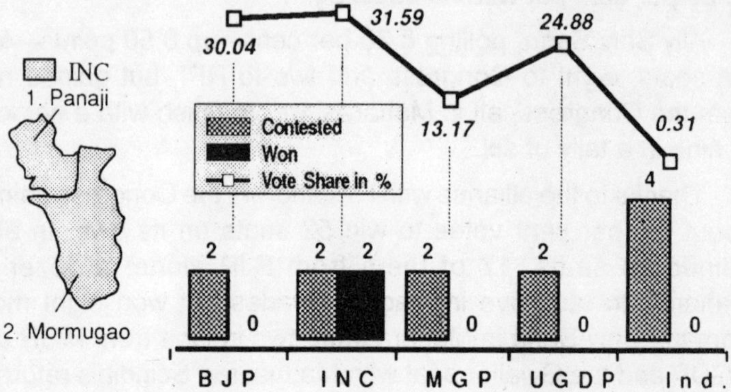

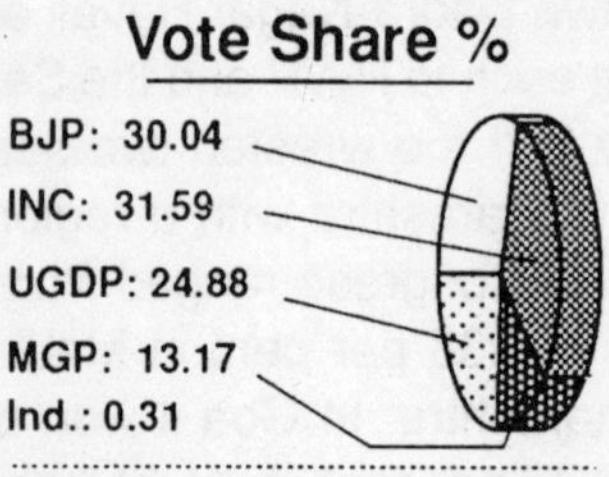

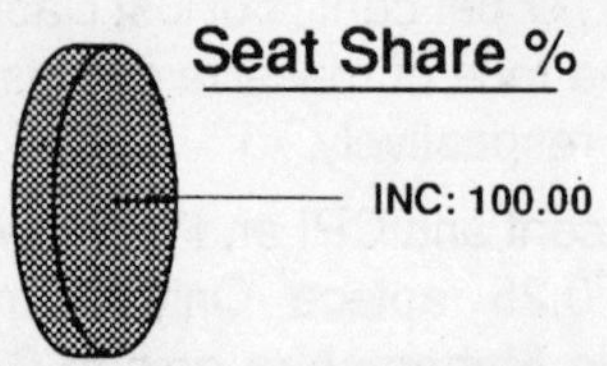

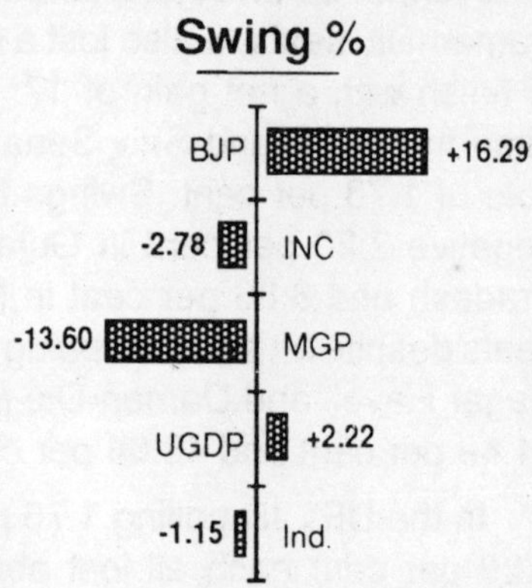

GAINS & LOSSES

Party	Seats Won '96	Seats Won '98	Retained	Gained	Gained From:	Lost	Lost to:	Net +/-
INC	0	2	-	2	MGP-1, UGDP-1	-	-	+2
MGP	1	0	0	0	-	1	INC-1	-1
UGDP	1	0	0	0	-	1	INC-1	-1
Total	2	2	0	2		2		

GOA: Return of the Congress

Two years after two local parties snatched the two seats from it in Goa, the Congress regained them despite a further erosion in its vote bank thanks ironically to BJP which came within striking distance due to a massive 16.29 per cent swing in its favour. Polling 31.50 per cent votes, 2.77 per cent less than last time, Congress wrested the Panaji seat from Maharashtrawadi Gomantak Party (MGP) and took back the Mormugao seat from the United Goan Democratic Party (UGDP).

But the victories of Ravi Sitaram Naik in the first and Sardinha Francisco Caetano in the second were essentially due to BJP slicing away more of the MGP-UGDP vote rather than that of the Congress as it raised its share from 13.75 per cent to 30.04 per cent—just about one and a half per cent less than the Congress share.

The two state parties together polled 38.05 per cent, down over 11 points since 1996 when they cornered nearly half the votes. While two UGDP candidates polled 24.88 per cent, the MGP nominees could tot up only 13.17 per cent. One of its nominees even lost his deposit.

Four independents, including one woman in Mormugao, together polling 1656 votes also lost their deposits. At 58.79 per cent, women's participation was about two points lower than the state average.

Electorate	:	2,87,70,306
Turnout	:	59.31%
Votes Polled	:	1,70,62,837
Valid Votes	:	1,62,91,157
Invalid Votes	:	7,58,884

GUJARAT

Seats: 26 | **Candidates: 139**

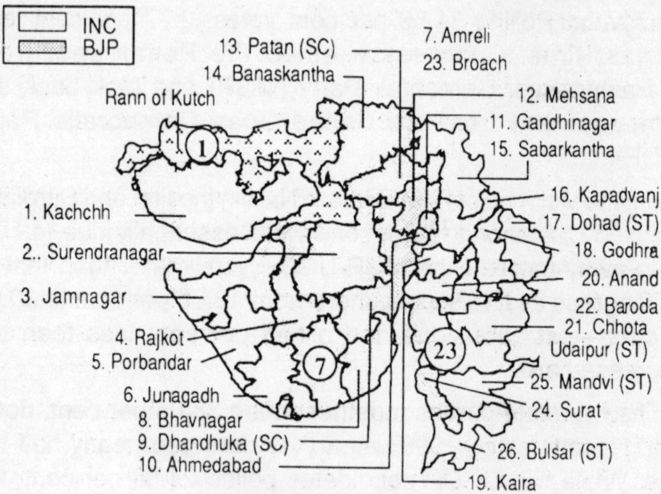

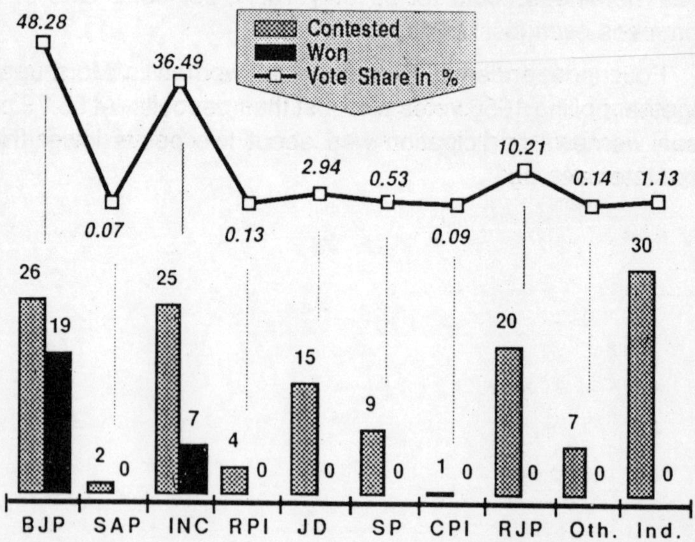

GUJARAT: BJP Blazes Back

Less than two years after its government was brought down by rebel leader Shankersinh Vaghela, BJP stormed back into power in the parallel Assembly poll even as it won 19 of the 26 Lok Sabha seats with 48.28 per cent votes. The Congress too paid the price for backing the Vaghela government with an adverse 2.20 per cent swing bringing down its tally to seven won with 36.49 per cent votes. Vaghela's own Rashtriya Janata Party was completely wiped out with 13 of its 20 candidates losing deposit even as they polled 10.21 per cent votes.

BJP which had lost four seats last time recovered three from the Congress in the face of a slight adverse swing of 0.24 points to finish one less than its 1991 tally of 20. It won all but four of the 20 general seats with the support of nearly half the voters (49.66 per cent). Taking both the SC seats with 45.44 per cent, it also won one of the four ST seats with 40.72 per cent.

BJP president Lal Krishna Advani took back his old Gandhinagar seat won by Atal Bihari Vajpayee in 1996 when Advani chose not to contest because of his alleged involvement in the Hawala scam. But it was party colleague Vallabh Kathiriya, a cancer surgeon who made news with a 3.54 lakh vote—the largest margin—victory over his RJP rival, Vithal Radadiya in Rajkot.

Losing three seats to BJP, Congress could win only four general seats with 34.49 per cent votes, but it won three of the four ST seats with 48.30 per cent. Its lone SC seat was won with 33.24 per cent votes.

Among UF constituents, all but one of the 15 JD candidates lost their deposits, while polling 2.94 per cent, up 2.52 points. So did all the nine candidates of SP and one of CPI in scraping up 0.53 per cent and 0.09 per cent respectively. In all 80 candidates including 30 independents, together polling 1.13 per cent votes lost their deposits.

JD contested all the six SC/ST seats polling a little over one per cent in the first and 3.75 per cent in the second category of reserved seats. CPI, SP and Samata all put up a candidate each in the tribal belt but together polled no more than one per cent.

GUJARAT

Vote Share % / Seat Share %

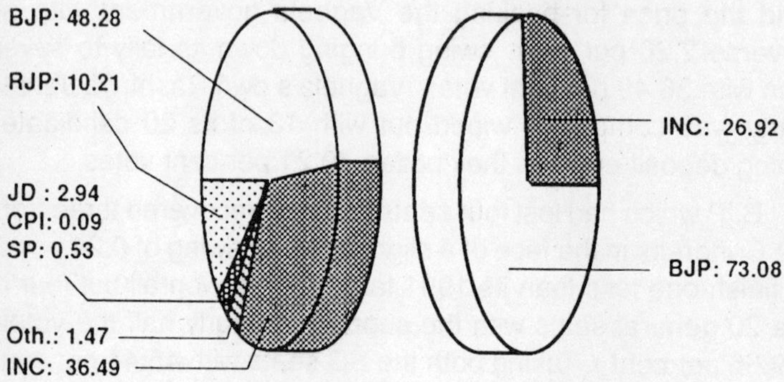

Swing %

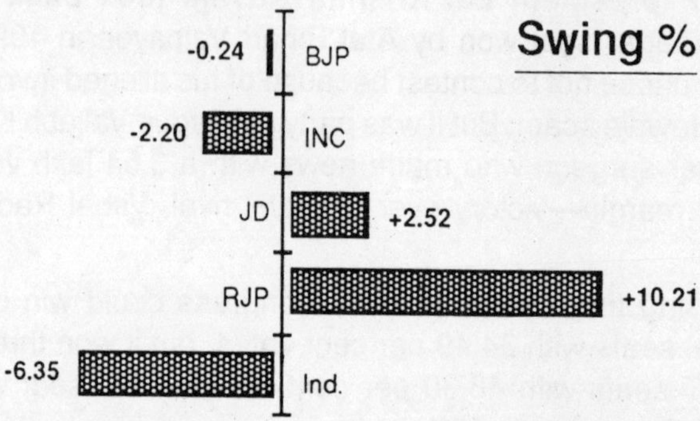

GAINS & LOSSES

Party	Seats Won '96	'98	Ret-ained	Gain-ed	Gained from	Lost	Lost to	Net +/-
BJP	16	19	16	3	INC-3	0	-	+ 3
INC	10	7	7	0	-	3	BJP-3	- 3
Total	**26**	**26**	**23**	**3**		**3**		

Of the seven women candidates, four won, three from BJP and one from Congress, while the other three lost their deposits. At 55.10 per cent women's turnout was four points lower than the state average of 59.31 per cent.

In the parallel Assembly poll, BJP bounced back into power winning 117 seats in the 182-member Assembly against Congress' 53 and the RJP's four. Vaghela protege Dilip Parikh became the first chief minister in power to lose his seat. Keshubhai Patel, considered the architect of BJP sweep, formed the new government.

Electorate : 4,46,07,368
Turnout : 61.74%
Votes Polled : 2,75,40,576
Valid Votes : 2,69,30,007
Invalid Votes : 6,05,216

MADHYA PRADESH

Seats: 40 | **Candidates: 400**

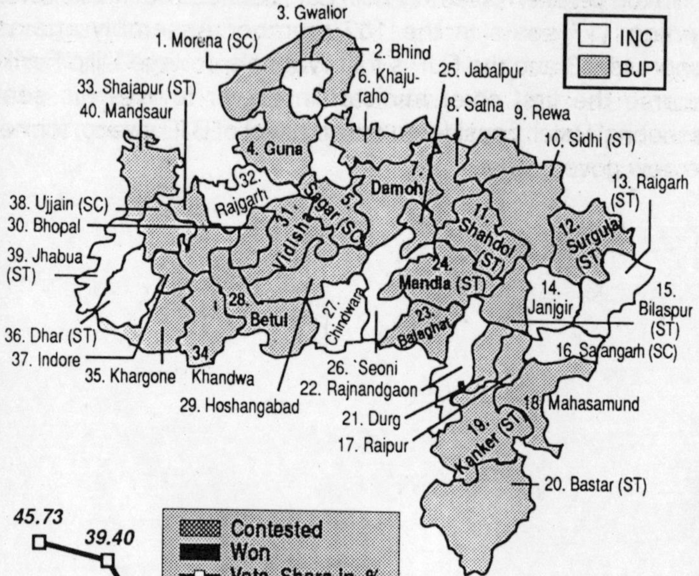

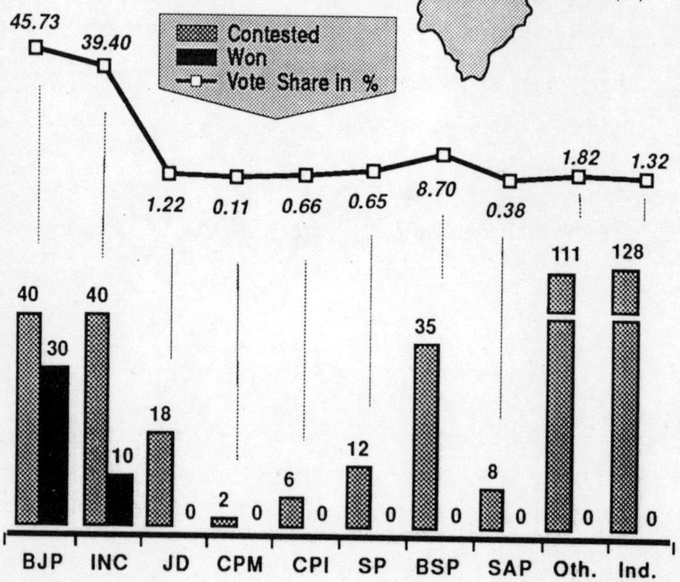

MADHYA PRADESH: BJP Marches Forward

In a virtual straight contest, BJP walked away with three-fourths of the spoils leaving rival Congress with only ten seats in spite of an over eight per cent swing in its favour. If the Sonia factor helped it get more votes, an anti-incumbency mood and greater polarisation prevented them from being translated into more seats. Between them, BJP and Congress cornered more than 85 per cent of the votes. And with BSP taking about nine per cent, 26 other parties and 128 independents were left to share the remaining six per cent.

Polling 45.73 per cent, BJP gained three seats with 4.41 per cent more votes. Wresting four from the Congress, two from BSP and one each from Tiwari Congress and an independent, the saffron party made eight fresh gains, but then lost five of its seats to the Congress. It won 19 of the 25 general seats with 45.76 per cent votes and polled almost two points more to win all but one of the six SC seats with 47.74 per cent. BJP took six of the nine ST seats with a slightly lower share of 44.28 per cent.

Two former BJP chief ministers Kailash Joshi and Sunder Lal Patwa suffered defeats in Rajgarh and Chhindwara and the state BJP chief Nand Kumar Sai lost by 4382 votes to Ajit Jogi of Congress in Raigarh. But Sushil Chandra Verma defeated former party colleague Arif Baig, now in rival Congress by 1.94 lakh votes, the highest margin in the state.

The Congress polling 39.40 per cent votes gained two seats, but considering that breakaway Madhya Pradesh Vikas Congress of Madhavrao Scindia and the Tiwari Congress, now back in its fold, had won one seat each last time, it had really finished even. Besides Scindia's Gwalior seat, Congress gained five seats from the BJP, but conceded four others to it. Its six general seats were won with 39.07 per cent votes, while its three ST victories came with 42.75 per cent. But only one of its six SC candidates won with the party polling 36.16 per cent.

Two senior Congress leaders Arjun Singh and V.C. Shukla lost in Hoshangabad and Raipur respectively. While Singh lost to timber merchant Sartaj Singh, a three-time MP, who also

MADHYA PRADESH

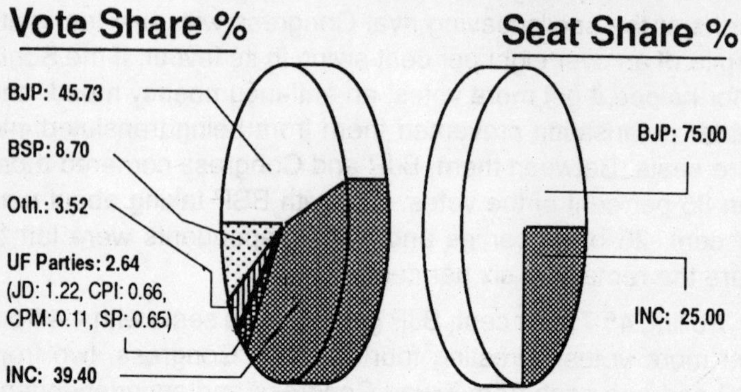

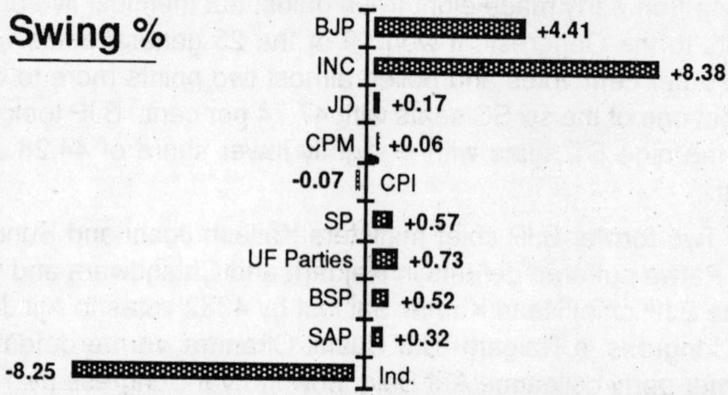

GAINS & LOSSES

Party	Seats Won '96	Seats Won '98	Reta-ined	Gain-ed	Gained From:	Lost	Lost to:	Net + / -
BJP	27	30	22	8	INC-4, AIICT-1 BSP-2, Ind.-1	5	INC-5	+3
INC	8	10	4	6	BJP-5, MPVC-1	4	BJP-4	+2
BSP	2	0	-	-	-	2	BJP-2	-2
AIICT	1	0	-	-	-	1	BJP-1	-1
MPVC	1	0	-	-	-	1	INC-1	-1
Ind.	1	0	-	-	-	1	BJP-1	-1
Total	**40**	**40**	**26**	**14**		**14**		

served in Vajpayee's previous 13-day government, Shukla fell to little known Ramesh Bais. But former ministers Scindia and Kamal Nath (Chhindwara) and former UP Governor Motilal Vora won.

BSP came third in the popularity stakes with 35 of its candidates polling 8.70 per cent votes, yet only seven of them could save their deposits. While in general seats it polled 8.79 per cent, its share was 5.50 per cent in the ST and 13.06 per cent in the SC seat.

Former Congress Central minister Arvind Netam contested from two constituencies, Janjgir and Kanker, on BSP ticket, but finished third in both. Another tribal leader, Dilip Singh Bhuria, who had won the Jhabua (ST) seat five times in a row since 1980 for the Congress, lost by over 82,000 votes as a BJP nominee this time. The Congress retained the seat. Four UF constituents together polled just 2.64 per cent with JD taking 1.22 per cent, CPI 0.66 per cent, SP 0.65 per cent and CPM a mere 0.11 per cent. All their 38 candidates lost their deposits.

Barring the BJP, Congress and seven candidates of BSP, all others totalling 313 lost their deposits. They included 128 independents who together polled 1.30 per cent. Of the 28 women candidates, only four, three of BJP and one Congress, won, while 21 others lost their deposits. Winning BJP women included Rajmata Vijaya Raje Scindia in Guna and Uma Bharati in the temple town of Khajuraho.

At 55.95 per cent, women's partcipation was about six points lower than the state average.

Electorate : 5,62,05,250
Turnout : 57.11%
Votes Polled : 3,20,96,308
Valid Votes : 3,14,92,290
Invalid Votes : 5,99,283

MAHARASHTRA

Seats: 48 | **Candidates: 377**

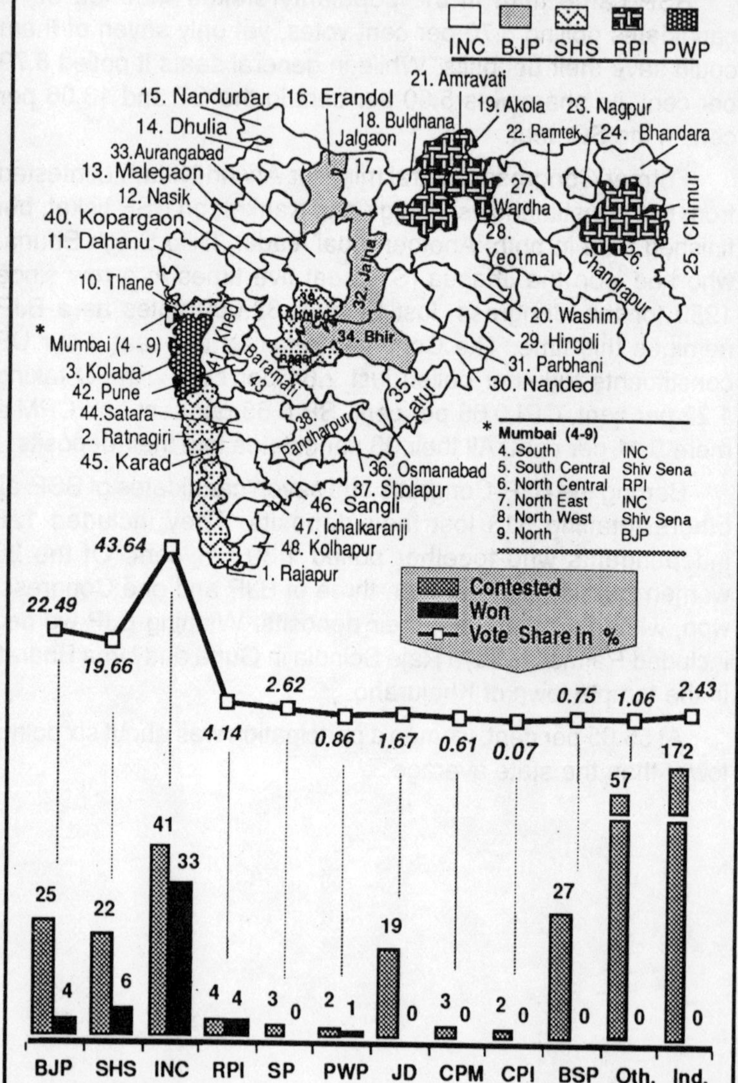

MAHARASHTRA: Pawar Upsets Sena-BJP Applecart

An alliance between the Congress, Republican Party of India and the Samajwadi Party of Mulayam Singh Yadav coupled with disenchantment with the three-year rule of Shiv Sena-BJP helped Maratha leader Sharad Pawer to forge a magnificent win in the state that even tilted the balance of power within the Congress at the Centre. A 8.64 per cent swing in favour of the Congress-RPI-SP alliance boosted its seat share from 15 to 37 won with the support of more than half the voters (50.40 per cent). The rival Sena-BJP combine was left with only ten seats despite a relatively minor 3.51 per cent swing in its favour that raised its vote share to 42.15 per cent. One seat went to the Peasants and Workers Party (PWP) for 0.86 per cent.

Polling 43.64 per cent, nearly nine points more than last time, Congress gained 20 seats, a dozen from the BJP and eight from Shiv Sena, but lost two, to more than double its tally from 15 to 33. The losers were A.R. Antulay, who went down to PWP's Ramsheth Thakur in Kolaba and Dada Patil Shelke, who lost Ahmednagar to Sena's Balasaheb Vikhe Patil. Ally RPI, which has a support base in the Vidarbha region, won all the four seats it contested even as its vote share went down by 0.78 points from 4.92 per cent to 4.14 per cent. Wresting a couple of seats from both BJP and the Sena, RPI also helped gain the backing of Dalits. But SP could not win any of the three seats where it put up candidates though it brought in 2.62 per cent votes to the alliance and probably the support of Muslims.

Former chief minister Sharad Pawar won again from Baramati, as did former Lok Sabha Speaker Shivraj Patil from Latur, while RPI leader Ramdas Athavale defeated another Dalit N. Athavale in the Sena bastion of Mumbai North Central.

In the rival Sena-BJP combine, BJP dropped 14 seats, conceding a dozen to the Congress and two to RPI. Even as its vote share went up marginally (0.68 points) from 21.81 per cent to 22.49 per cent, BJP managed to keep only four of its 18 seats. The Sena polling 19.66 per cent votes, 2.83 points more than last time, lost ten of its 16 seats, eight to Congress and two to

MAHARASHTRA

Vote Share % **Seat Share %**

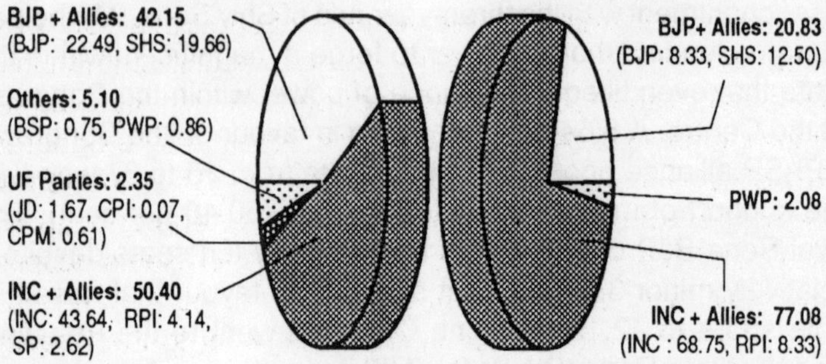

Swing %

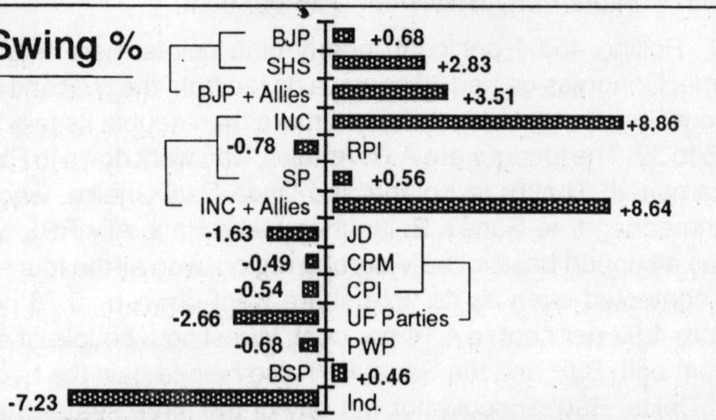

GAINS & LOSSES

Party	Seats Won '96	Seats Won '98	Reta-ined	Gain-ed	Gained From:	Lost	Lost to:	Net +/-
BJP	18	4	4	-	-	14	INC-12, RPI-2	-14
SHS	15	6	5	1	INC-1	10	INC-8, RPI-2	-9
INC	15	33	13	20	BJP-12, SHS-8	2	SHS-1, PWP-1	+18
RPI	0	4	-	4	BJP-2, SHS-2	-	-	+4
PWP	0	1	-	1	INC-1	-	-	+1
Total	**48**	**48**	**22**	**26**		**26**		

RPI. But it hung on to five seats and wrested one from the Congress to finish with a tally of six.

BJP spokesman Pramod Mahajan lost by over 47,000 votes in Mumbai North-East to Gurudas Kamat of Congress, but nevertheless became political adviser to the Prime Minister. Former Central minister, Suresh Kalmadi, a last minute deserter from the Congress, also lost from Pune as an independent backed by BJP.

Three United Front partners together polled 2.35 per cent, less than half of a little over five per cent they collected last time, as all but one CPM nominee among their 34 candidates lost deposits. At 1.67per cent, JD share was reduced to just half, while CPI and CPM scraped together less than one per cent.

The Congress won all the seven reserved seats, three SC and four ST polling 48.89 per cent and 42.48 per cent respectively. But at 53.02 per cent Congress got more support in general seats. The rival combine's support base was more evenly spread out, polling as it did 42.65 per cent in general and about 41.81 per cent in SC seats. In the four ST seats, where BJP alone did battle, it polled slightly less at 38.62 per cent. Within the alliance, while both BJP (21.84 per cent) and Sena (20.81 per cent) had an almost equal share in general seats, Sena polled more in two SC seats (29.71 per cent). The BJP share in one SC seat was 12.10 per cent. In the UF, JD, CPI and CPM fielding one candidate each in three ST seats together polled about 11 per cent, but three JD candidates could win no more than 2.67 per cent votes in the SC seats. And in the general seats their share was still lower at 1.65 per cent. Two BSP candidates collected less than five thousand votes in the reserved seats with the party itself getting only 0.75 per cent all over the state.

All but 98 of of the 377 candidates, including 172 independents, lost their deposits. Of the 20 women, only two belonging to Congress won, while 15 others lost their deposits. At 53.34 per cent women's participation was about four points lower than the state average of 57.11 per cent.

Electorate	:	95,832
Turnout	:	77.43%
Votes Polled	:	74,205
Valid Votes	:	72,531
Invalid Votes	:	1,658

DADRA & NAGAR HAVELI

Seats: 1	Candidates: 4

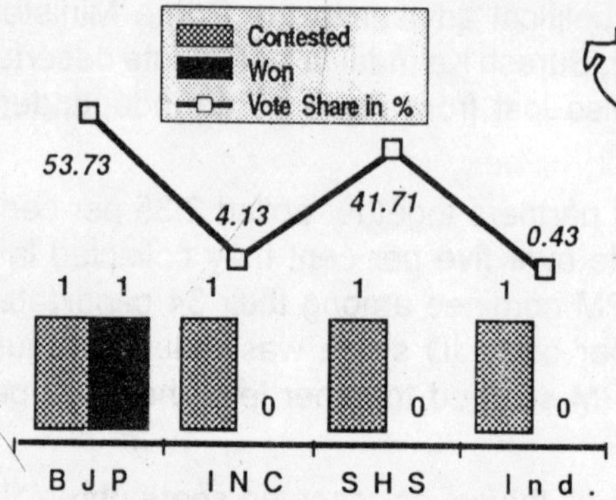

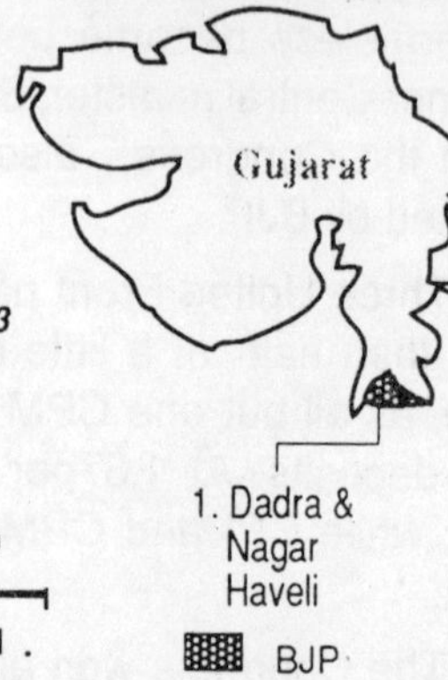

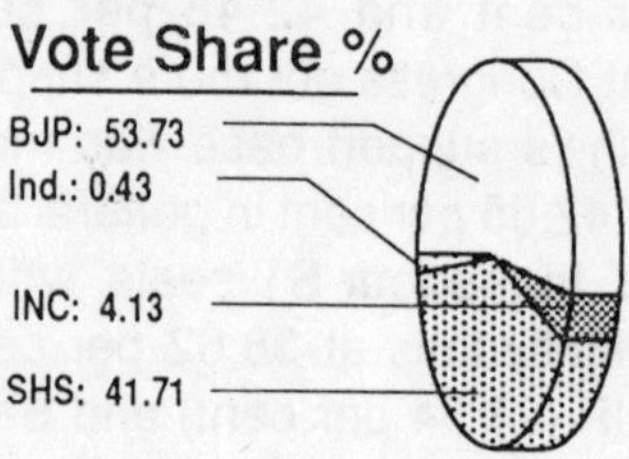

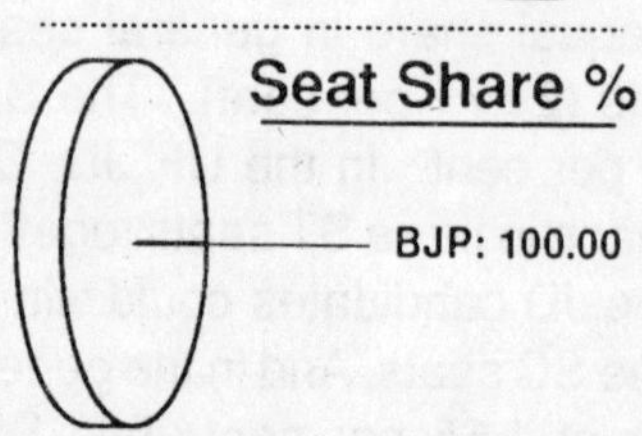

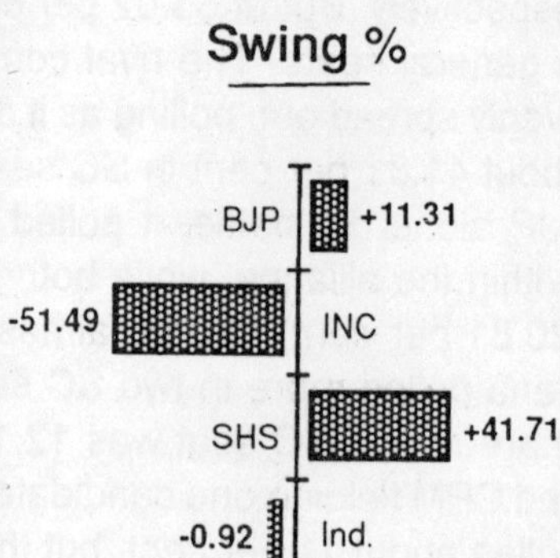

GAINS & LOSSES

Party	Seats Won '96	Seats Won '98	Retained	Gained	Gained From:	Lost	Lost to:	Net + / -
BJP	0	1	0	1	INC-1	0	-	+1
INC	1	0	0	0	-	1	BJP-1	-1
Total	1	1	0	1		1		

DADRA & NAGAR HAVELI: Switch Ends Congress Run

Mohanbhai Delkar won again, but this time on the BJP ticket to end the Congress victory run as it tasted defeat only for the third time in nine elections. Delkar first won as an independent in 1989 defeating Congress' S.J. Gavali. Gavali, in turn, had given Congress its first defeat five years earlier as an independent. Joining the Congress in 1991, Delkar again beat Gavali, now fighting as a BJP nominee. He repeated the feat in 1996, but switched over to BJP to record his fourth straight victory from this tiny former Portuguese enclave.

As a BJP nominee this time, Delkar polled 53.73 per cent votes, about two per cent less than he did as the Congress nominee last time, but quite a climbdown from 61.74 per cent he polled in 1991, again for the Congress. His victory raised the BJP share by over 11 points from 42.42 per cent. The second place was taken by a Shiv Sena nominee with 41.71 per cent votes. Consequently, the Congress share plunged to 4.13 per cent, it lowest ever and its nominee could not even save his deposit. Its previous worst was in 1989 when it first lost to Delkar polling 28.6 per cent. Its best came in 1980 when it won 61.9 per cent of the popular vote. Getting just 313 votes, an independent too lost his deposit in the four-cornered contest.

There were no women candidates, but they came out in large numbers to vote. At 79.50 per cent their turnout was about two points higher than the territory average of 77.43 per cent.

DAMAN & DIU

Seats: 1	Candidates: 5

Electorate : 71,934
Turnout : 72.83%
Votes Polled : 52,389
Valid Votes : 51,596
Invalid Votes : 789

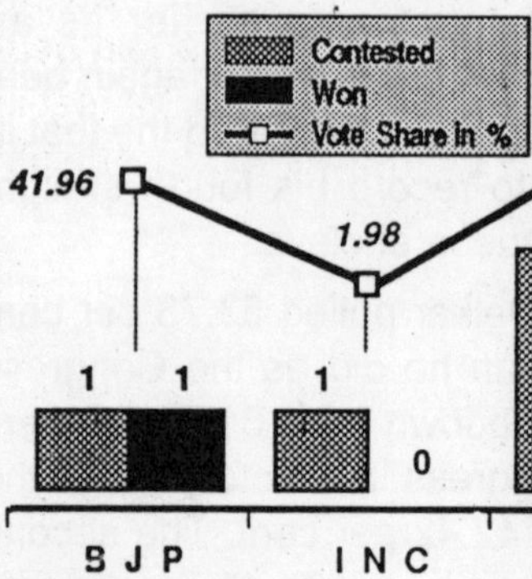

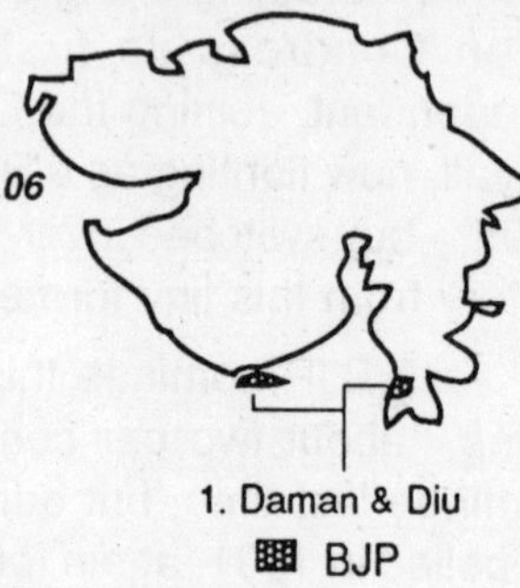

Vote Share %

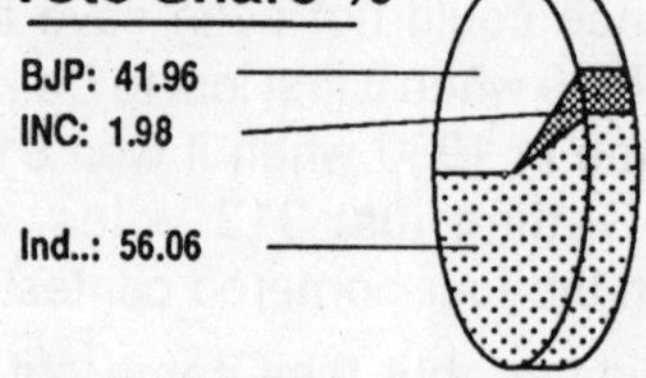

Seat Share %

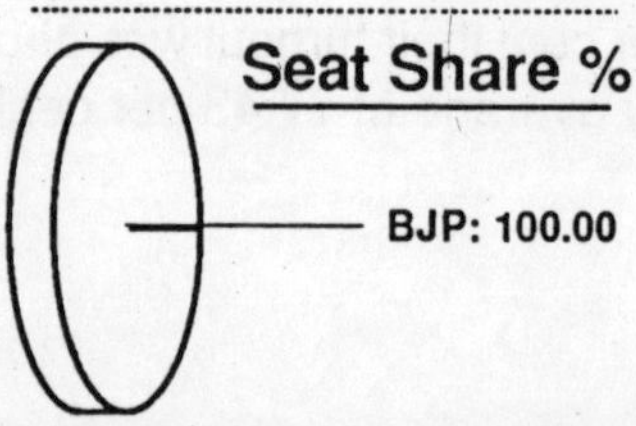

Swing %

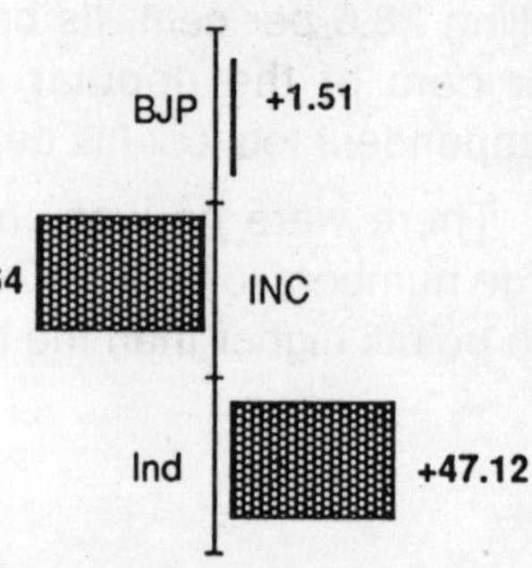

GAINS & LOSSES

Party	Seats Won '96	Seats Won '98	Retained	Gained	Gained From:	Lost	Lost to:	Net +/-
BJP	0	1	0	1	INC-1	0	-	+1
INC	1	0	0	0	-	1	BJP-1	-1
Total	**1**	**1**	**0**	**1**		**1**		

DAMAN & DIU: BJP Gets Even

Devjibhai J. Tandel avenged his 1996 defeat to win back the lone seat from the former Portuguese enclave for the BJP. DJ, who won the seat for the third time in four elections since 1989, had lost to G.K. Tandel of the Congress last time. DJ first beat GK as an independent candidate in 1989. Two years later he won the seat for BJP with GK turning independent. Back in Congress, GK wrested it from him in 1996 only to lose it two years later.

Devjibhai's victory this time raised the BJP vote share to 41.96 per cent, up by just 1.51 points, but with GK again becoming independent, the Congress share went plunging to 1.98 per cent, its lowest ever from an all time high of 50.62 per cent in 1996. Its previous worst was 22.7 per cent in 1991 when BJP won with just 31.9 per cent.

While seven independents had polled 8.94 per cent last time, three of them polled 56.06 per cent now, but with GK getting the bulk of it, two of them lost their deposits as did the Congress nominee. The deposit losers included the lone woman candidate Hemlata Baria who polled only 97 votes. At 75.34 per cent, women's participation in the polls was even better than the Territory average of 72.83 per cent.

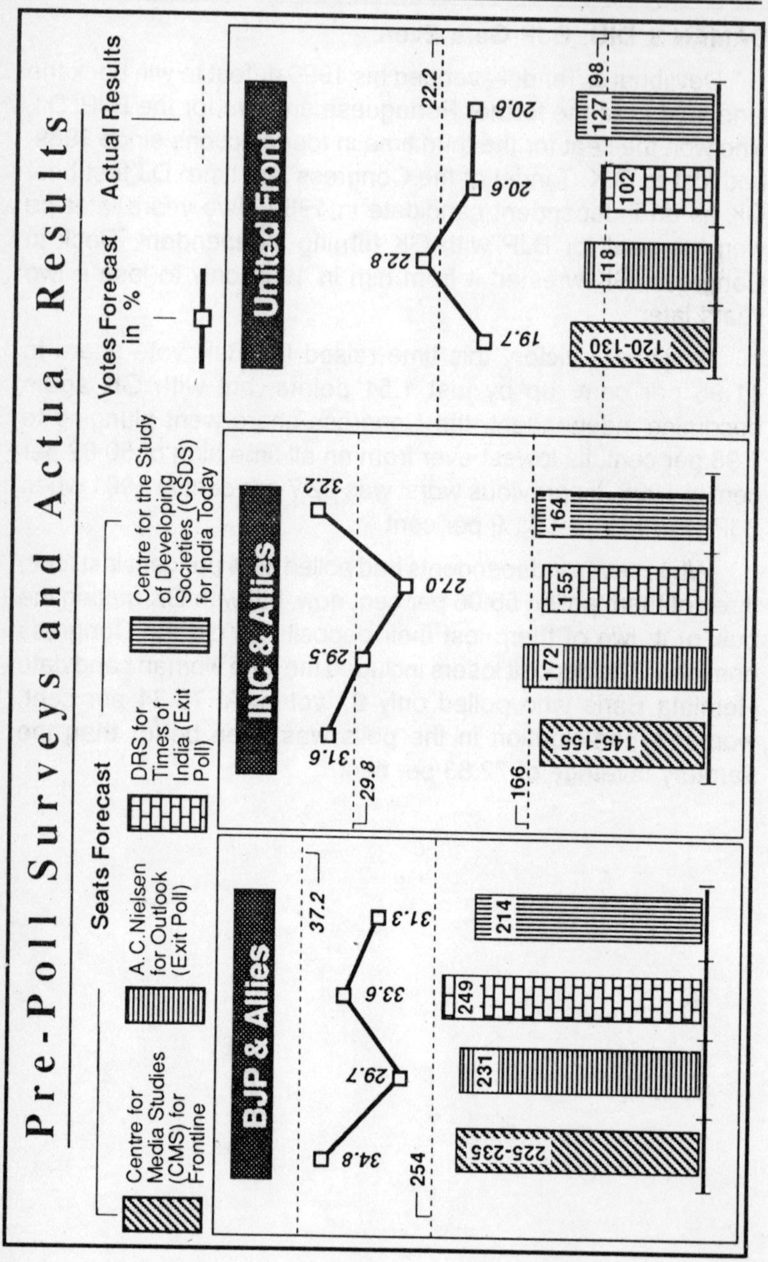
Pre-Poll Surveys and Actual Results
Seats Forecast
Centre for Media Studies (CMS) for Frontline
A.C.Nielsen for Outlook (Exit Poll)
DRS for Times of India (Exit Poll)
Centre for the Study of Developing Societies (CSDS) for India Today
Votes Forecast in %
Actual Results
BJP & Allies
34.8
29.7
33.6
31.3
37.2
254
225-235
231
249
214
INC & Allies
31.6
29.5
27.0
32.2
29.8
166
145-155
172
155
164
United Front
19.7
22.8
20.6
20.6
22.2
98
120-130
118
102
127

10
The Crystal Gazers

Astrologers, palmists and sundry other fortune tellers were back in business along with the pollster with his computers and swing charts to tell the voter what the morrow would bring—another hung House—before the Press Council and the Election Commission played spoilsport. At least 17 opinion polls were conducted by different agencies at a cost of over Rs. 25 million. Unlike the previous few polls, when pollsters had made fairly good guesses, few could get the full picture right this time. In particular, most pollsters and analysts failed to gauge the latent mood swing in Tamil Nadu that brought about the dramatic comeback of Jayalalitha and her AIADMK.

Four major pollsters—Centre for Media Studies (CMS) for *Frontline*, A.C. Nielsen for *Outlook*, Development and Research Services (DRS) for the *Times of India* and the Centre for Study of Developing Societies (CSDS) for *India Today*—picked up varying samples and models to come up with the same conclusion — it would be hung again— but with different guesses about who would get how many seats and votes and which way would the pendulum swing for whom.

The DRS exit poll based on the largest sample of 25,537 voters spread over 96 constituencies in 15 states gave BJP and allies 249, five less than the actual, underestimating its vote share (37.18 per cent) by 3.6 points. For the Congress, it was even more off the mark in predicting 155 seats with 27 per cent instead of 166 with 29.77 per cent. In the case of UF, it gave them four more seats (102 instead of 98) but fewer votes— 20.6 per cent instead of 22.18 per cent. But Tamil Nadu, Maharashtra and Rajasthan completely floored them. It gave BJP alliance much less in Tamil Nadu—four instead of 30- and far more in

Maharashtra (24) and Rajasthan (15) instead of ten and five that it actually got in the two states.

The *Outlook* exit poll based on a sample of 16,312 voters spread over 89 constituencies in 16 states estimated the BJP share too low at 231 with 29.7 per cent and that of the Congress too high at 172 with 29.5 per cent votes. To the UF also it gave too many seats—118—with 22.8 per cent votes

The CSDS poll for *India Today* used a much smaller sample with a much wider spread covering 114 seats in 21 states with 8938 voters. To gauge mood shifts, its post poll survey covered the same 452 polling stations which were done after the 1996 poll and before this poll in early February. Its interviewers, in fact, CSDS claimed succeeded in tracking down 6,806 of the original respondents. Even so it came closest in predicting 164 seats with 32.2 per cent votes for the Congress, but it was the widest off the mark in the case of BJP whom it gave only 214 with 31.3 per cent. Again its prediction for UF also was way too high at 127 with 20.6 per cent vogtes.

The CMS poll covering the smallest sample of 8,900 voters in only 61 constituencies in 16 states chose to indicate ranges for the three formations rather than actual seats. It put BJP and allies ahead with 225-235 seats for 34.5 per cent votes. Congress followed with 145-155 seats for 31.6 per cent votes, while the UF trailed with 120-130 seats for 19.7 per cent votes. CMS, however, claimed that it had given an early indication that Jayalalitha was on the comeback trail.

Another exit poll telecast by TVI too was almost right for Congress with 165 seats, but gave only 211 to the BJP and an astonishingly high 146 to UF. Tamil Nadu again was where it went completely wrong in predicting all but three seats for the UF. But it gave BJP six more in Maharashtra and four extra in Rajasthan.

Analysts suggested that besides history, anti-incumbency factor and the right alliance, what tilted the scales in favour of the the AIADMK-BJP alliance in Tamil Nadu was the Coimbatore blasts days before the state went to the polls. A.C. Nielsen, which in its opinion poll for the *Outlook* weekly had given the alliance

25 fewer seats than it actually got, for one suggested that their fieldwork was done at a time when BJP's new alliances in West Bengal, Orissa, Karnataka and Tamil Nadu were still taking shape. In fact, in all these states Nielsen polls carried out nearly three weeks before the elections, failed to pick up accurately the impact these alliances would make in the voting pattern. Their end-January poll did indicate a seven per cent swing towards the alliance in Tamil Nadu, but they considered it insufficient to carry it over the hump in view of the poor performance of both BJP and AIADMK in 1996. "Obviously the swing gathered momentum over the following three weeks," Partha Rakshit, Managing Director of the agency said.

"We got the 'big picture' right", said G.V.L. Narasimha Rao of the Development and Research Services (DRS) which conducted the exit poll telecast over state-owned Doordarshan. It not only projected the seats accurately but also got the underlying voting per centages for the three political formations right. Besides votes and seats, the polls also captured accurately the mood of the voters and issues of concern to the electorate, claimed the DRS psephologist. But he admitted that their estimates of seats turned out to be wide of the mark in three important states— Rajasthan, Maharashtra and Tamil Nadu. Rao considered the case of Tamil Nadu really intriguing. He blamed an unusually high turnout in Rajasthan and an equally unusual low turnout in Tamil Nadu for their wrong estimates besides voters' "refusal to cooperate". The DRS exit poll interviewers were asked to interview every fourth voter coming out of a selected booth, without any replacements. Those who refused to fill out dummy ballots for the exit poll were ignored. But it appears there was a significantly large number of 'refusals' by voters in Tamil Nadu, Rao said. But the fact that despite inaccuracies at the state level, they did get their national tally right was not by accident but by design. The margin of error at the constituency level is much higher than at the state level. At the national level it's even lower. For as the sample size increases, the errors tend to cancel each other out, Rao explained.

The late swing explanation is generally seen—and rightly so— as the last refuge of the failed psephologist or the defeated candidate, said *India Today* which had projected only 214 seats for BJP and allies. The shift it claimed took place during the campaign citing an analysis of the swings in the three phases of polling. The tide started turning against the Congress and in favour of the BJP after the first phase, it claimed. That's why the backlash against the BJP in Rajasthan and the success of Jayalalitha came as surprises. The weekly, however, admitted the explanation was inadequate for it did not tell why the late swing took place.

Apart from last minute swings, undecided voters, turnout and lying factor can all upset a forecast even if it's based on a carefully planned survey, pollsters say. Exit polls tend to be more accurate than opinion polls because there are no undecided voters and people tend to be less cagey after they have cast their votes.

Another pitfall in a multi-party situation is conversion of votes polled by a party into seats as splits and alliances and the spread of votes can make all the difference. A device used by pollsters to convert a multi-party scenario into a two party situation is the Index of Opposition Unity (IOU). Higher the IOU, lesser the split in opposition votes. Well, it used to work at one time when one was looking at Congress and non-Congress situations. IOU is dead now that the Congress has lost power in all but four states. But some still swear by it saying it would work if computed for the dominant party in a state. For instance, it could be calculated for the CPM in West Bengal and BJP in UP or Gujarat. Determined by dividing the highest opposition party vote by the total opposition vote, an IOU of one would indicate total opposition unity as in a straight contest between two major parties. An IOU of 0.5 would indicate a two way split of opposition votes.

But more than the IOU, the most important factor is how a typical constituency is picked up and how data is collected. Pollsters suggest that there are certain 'bell weather' constituencies which reflect the national or the regional mood. Picked up on the basis of past voting patterns, these constituencies are used to gauge swings for or against a political party.The swings in turn are superimposed on other seats to see who may win. Pollsters also resort to the "cube law" as a rough and ready reckoner of seats. Evolved by western psephologists essentially for two party systems, it suggests that the seats won by a party are usually "in proportion to the cube of the per centage of votes polled by that party". Thus a two per cent swing should translate into eight per cent more seats. Indian psephologists have modified the cube law too. Here the total votes of opposition parties are multiplied by the IOU and assigned to an 'ideal' second party to calculate the seats that might be won by all the 'opposition' parties together. The 'swing' and 'split' factors are also taken into account. Sometimes the swings and splits cancel each other out and at other times they work in the same direction to give a new complexion to an electoral battle. A study of all elections since 1952, however, suggests that the swings play a more decisive role. Fine tuning for the 'lying factor' —voters may not be telling the truth—and late mood swings can help pollsters make fairly accurate predicions. Pollsters claim that a carefully planned exercise should not have more than two per cent margin of error for votes. But this could result in a ten per cent error in seats, enough to turn victory into defeat—and make or mar reputations. If the last three general elections suggested that psephology has arrived in India, 1998 suggested that there are as yet many imponderables and methodolgies need to be further improved in tune with the emerging political situation.

Even before the results stretched the credibility of the opinion polls, they came in for criticism with the Press Council suggesting a ban on them and some legal experts questioning the validity of such a move. Examples were cited of some western countries which have put a ban on publication of opinion polls during the last week of an election or over the entire election period lest they influence the outcome of the real thing. Critics suggested that apart from the 'bandwagon'—backing the winning horse— or the 'counter-bandwagon'—rooting for the underdog—effect, opinion polls tended to focus on the eventual outcome and thus diverted attention from the issues. Others doubted the extent to which opinion polls could affect the outcome of an election, but suggested they could nevertheless still play a positive role by focusing on issues instead of turning it into a betting game. Responsibly conducted by professionals with clear indication of how, when, where and who did it to arrive at what conclusion, they were any day better than the informed guesswork that the media tended to indulge in otherwise, they said. Informed readers don't take newspaper reports as seriously as the supposedly scientific opinion polls, countered Press Council chairman Justice P.B. Sawant. In support of its contention, the Press Council conducted an opinion poll of its own of 2,500 voters in Mumbai, Delhi and Chennai. It was "alarmed" to find that half the voters had read and remembered a particular opinion poll and of them 70 per cent said they believed it. The Election Comission agreed and imposed a ban on their publication from end of campaign in the first phase until the close of poll in the final phase. Exit polls could be conducted, but again could not be published until the end of polling. Some newspapers went to the Supreme Court, but it declined to stay the Election Commission order, yet left it to the editors to publish or not to publish. With the exception of a newspaper or two, the media generally preferred to wait. In defence of the polls, psephologist K. Balakrishnan associated with the Times-Doordarshan said opinion polls had become very important as a feedback channel with the decline in public confidence in politicians in the democratic world. Conduct of reliable opinion polls in a vast, diverse and underdeveloped country like India was a difficult and complex exercise. And if for this reason some don't turn out to be accurate that should not be a reason for scrapping them, but only for having more of them, more frequently to make them better. Banning them, he suggested, would be akin to the kneejerk reaction of a medieval warlord: If you don't like the message, shoot the messenger!

Index